Limits of Law, Prerogatives of Power

Interventionism after Kosovo

Michael J. Glennon

palgrave

First published 2001 by   045799544

PALGRAVE™
175 Fifth Avenue, New York, N.Y. 10010 and
Houndmills, Basingstoke, Hampshire, England RG21 6XS.
Companies and representatives throughout the world.

PALGRAVE™ is the new global publishing imprint of
St. Martin's Press LLC Scholarly and Reference Division and
Palgrave Publishers Ltd (formerly Macmillan Press Ltd).

ISBN 0-312-23901-7

Library of Congress Cataloging-in-Publication Data

Glennon, Michael J., 1947–
    Limits of law, prerogatives of power : interventionism after Kosovo/
    Michael J. Glennon.
        p. cm.
    Includes bibliographical references and index.
    ISBN 0-312-23901-7 (cloth)
1. Intervention (International law) 2. Kosovo (Serbia)—History—Civil
    War, 1998- I. Title.

KZ6368 .G59 2001
341.5'84—dc21
2001021862

A catalogue record for this book is available from the British Library.

Design by Newgen Imaging Systems (P) Ltd

First edition: August 2001
10 9 8 7 6 5 4 3 2 1

Printed in the United States of America.

To Joanna

You cannot have power for good without having power for evil too. Even mother's milk nourishes murderers as well as heroes.

—George Bernard Shaw

Major Barbara, act 3.

CONTENTS

ACKNOWLEDGMENTS

Portions of this book are drawn from previous writings, most notably "The New Interventionism: The Search for a Just International Law," 78 *Foreign Affairs* 2 (May/June, 1999); "The Charter: Does It Fit?" 36 *The United Nations Chronicle* 32 (No. 2, July 1999); "Sovereignty and Community After Haiti: Rethinking Collective Use of Force," 89 *American Journal of International Law* 70 (January 1995); and "The Constitution and Chapter VII of the UN Charter," 85 *American Journal of International Law* 74 (1991).

I have also drawn from several presentations, including "Law and the Practice of Humanitarian Intervention," given at the United States Department of State, Washington, D.C., June 5, 2000; "A Neo-Interventionism in a New International Order?" given at the Western European Union, Institute for Security Studies, Paris, June 29, 1999; "The New Interventionism: What's Next?" given to Lawyers Alliance for World Security, Washington, D.C., June 21, 1999; "Military Intervention in the Post–Cold War Era," given at the United States Air Force Academy, Colorado Springs, Colorado, February 15, 1995; and testimony before the United States Commission on Improving the Effectiveness of the United Nations, San Francisco, February 2, 1993.

I benefited from the thinking of fellow participants in a number of projects and symposia over the years. Of particular influence were discussions regarding "International Law, NATO, and Kosovo," at the World Affairs Council with Abraham Sofaer in San Francisco on July 27, 1999; "Authority of the President to Use Force against Iraq," a panel discussion at the American Society of International Law, Washington, D.C., April 3, 1998; "U.S. Intervention Policy for the Post–Cold War World: New Challenges and New Responses," at the Eighty-Fifth meeting of the Atlantic Assembly (under the auspices of Columbia University), April 7–10,

1994 at Arden House, Harriman, New York; deliberations of the International Law Association's Committee on the Use of Force in Relations among States, on which I served; and "Contradictions and Conflicts between Sovereignty and International Stability: Problems of Intervention and Management in a Fragmented World," a conference sponsored by the Ditchley Foundations, Ditchley Park, England, February 1987.

This book would not have been possible without the generosity of many people. Tom Farer and David W. Kesselman made invaluable comments on an earlier version of the manuscript. (A reader should not hold them responsible for my views, however, which are not necessarily theirs.) Fen Hampson and Ramesh Thakur provided useful documents and materials. Glenda McGlashan's typing and computer skills turned cyberwords into physical pages. The able research assistance of John Brottem, Gabriel Chao, Kate Hansford, Kristina Launey, Blake Nordahl, Chris Scheuring, and Matthew Seeger brought to my attention much that I would otherwise have missed. Useful insights and research were provided by various students, including Connie Schwindt and Daniel Abbott. Librarians Susan Llano and Peg Durkin devoted significant time and energy to this project. And Dean Rex Perschbacher of the University of California, Davis Law School provided support and encouragement.

Thanks are due mostly to my wife, Joanna, from whom this work has benefited in so many ways that no expression of gratitude can be adequate.

Introduction

Of humanity's great civic and economic experiments of the twentieth century, none was more majestic in design or tragic in consequence than the effort to subject the use of force to the rule of law. The rules and institutions established to govern the use of force in the Covenant of the League of Nations, and, later, the United Nations Charter, traced directly to the two bloodiest wars ever fought. By one estimate, 175 million people died war-related deaths in the twentieth century[1]—more than in all previous wars combined. Yet by the century's close, so thorough had been the failure of those rules and institutions that, in reality if not in form, the international community had largely returned to a nonlegalist, geopolitical system that had dominated international organization since the emergence of the nation-state 350 years earlier.

In this book, I attempt to explain the failure of the legalist system—specifically, its use-of-force rules* and the institutions that oversee them—principally as that system took shape in the UN Charter.† I try to do so in a way accessible not only to specialists in international law or international relations, but to all who are

---

*The book thus deals with *jus ad bellum* rather than *jus in bello,* with the rules governing when armed force can be used as opposed to the manner in which it can be employed.

†I hasten to note that this is not yet another lament for a failed United Nations. Whether the United Nations has succeeded or failed is not at issue here; the United Nations consists of many organizations, some of which have done well, such as the International Atomic Energy Agency, and others not so well, such as the UN Economic and Social Council. The UN's institutions that manage the use of force, however, have failed in that mission, as have the Charter's norms governing the use of force.

broadly informed about international control of the use of force and concerned about its breakdown. Kosovo represented as momentous an event for the legal order as the fall of the Soviet Union did for the geopolitical order. The question now is where we are today. To answer that question, we need to know where things stood before Kosovo and to identify what led to the system's collapse. Then, perhaps, we may get a glimpse of what lies ahead and some insight into whether and how a successful legalist system might some day be reconstructed.

I argue that no rule—neither the prohibition against nondefensive force prescribed by the UN Charter, nor an alleged customary rule prohibiting or permitting humanitarian intervention or some other use of force—has succeeded in obliging states to refrain from intervention. I suggest that there is, today, no coherent international law concerning intervention by states. States disagree profoundly on fundamental issues—issues on which consensus is necessary for a treaty or customary rule to work. The majority of states are today unwilling to place their trust in any system of centralized coercion to make or enforce rules concerning intervention; the risk of abuse, they believe, is too great. This fear explains the abiding authority of one rule that remains very much in effect: the ban against intervention by the United Nations Security Council. Apart from this prohibition, while vestiges of legalist rhetoric survive, interventionism has come to be governed more by the geopolitical context in which it occurs than by disembodied, acontextual rules of law. Basic principles of the legalist regime, such as those concerning sovereignty and customary international law formation, have largely faded from policy makers' screens when decisions are made to intervene or not to intervene. The received rules of international law neither describe accurately what nations do, nor predict reliably what they will do, nor prescribe intelligently what they should do when considering intervention. With respect to interventionism by individual states, legal restraint is illusory; it is (to recall Castlereagh's description of the Holy Alliance) "a piece of sublime mysticism and nonsense."[2] In a world where geopolitical considerations have eclipsed legalist constraints on the use of force, the propriety of intervention is now judged more by wisdom than by law.

The term that might leap to a reader's mind is "realism." But this description of my thesis would be only half right. Most realists believe that power rather than law does *and should* control. I argue that power does control the use of force today, but that control by law ultimately would be preferable. The conditions that would permit effective legalist restraints on force simply do not now exist.

My perspective is, therefore, different from that of traditional realists *and* idealists. Louis Henkin, for example, has written: "It is probably the case that *almost all nations observe almost all principles of international law and almost all of their obligations almost all of the time.*"[3] It is not the purpose of this book to assess whether that claim is true. As the reader will soon surmise, I find it unverifiable. It *is* the purpose of this book to take a fresh look at the international rules and institutions that govern intervention of the sort undertaken by NATO in Yugoslavia. It is widely agreed that the most important rules are rules governing use of force;* the most important obligation is the obligation not to use force unless in self-defense or pursuant to approval by the United Nations Security Council. These rules and obligations go to the core element of nationhood—the right of survival as a sovereign entity. If sovereignty does not protect a state against military intervention, it is hard to see how sovereignty can protect a state against lesser intrusions. Thus new and troubling questions have emerged. How should we think about the rules governing use of force by states when 19 Western democracies, representing 780 million people, act in breach of that most paramount of obligations? What was the law? Why did it fail? *Is* there law? What *should* it be? *How* should it be made? Where are we left if *a substantial number of nations violate the most important principles of international law and their most important obligations when it matters?*

In examining these questions, one is struck by the insistence of international lawyers to fit facts and ideas into modes of analysis that have only the most tenuous relationship to the way states actually behave. Paralyzed by the most severe cognitive dissonance, international law scholars continue to think about state behavior in much the same way that it was imagined by the scholastics of the Middle Ages. The most breathtaking of assumptions are made on basic issues, such as "causes" of state behavior and the "motive" of states, the "reaction" of the international community, and the rules to which it "consents." Based on these assumptions, elaborate theories

---

*Article 2(4) of the UN Charter, Henkin has written, is the "principal norm of contemporary international law." Louis Henkin, *How Nations Behave* 129 (1968). For the text of Article 2(4) see page 17.

are constructed to justify, say, the idea that the UN rules on use of force are not merely customary international law, but a kind of superlaw, *jus cogens,* that is all but unchangeable.

It is time for a critical, top-down reassessment of the whole use-of-force edifice. If, as Henry Kissinger has written, the year 1812 "marked the moment when it became evident that Europe was not to be organized by force,"[4] the year 1999 marked the moment when it became evident that force was not governed by law. With Kosovo, it became clear that we need to think anew about where we have been, where we are, where we are going—and where we *want* to go. We need to do that, to the extent possible, without preconceptions and without blinders, questioning first principles and reexamining cherished dogmas.* The world today, it need hardly be said, is a vastly different place than the world of Westphalia where, following the Thirty Years' War, the idea of state sovereignty emerged in 1648. It is, indeed, a wholly different place from the world in which the United Nations emerged in 1945. Yet the UN Charter continues to impose use-of-force rules from an earlier era, to the point of prohibiting intervention in the internal affairs of states—even for the purpose of stopping intrastate genocide.

The American people seem eager to debate these issues. A year before the general election of 2000, pollsters asked them what questions they considered the most important for candidates. Ranked second—right behind "how to provide health insurance for the uninsured"—was "whether U.S. troops should get involved in internal conflicts."[5] Yet the question was all but ignored in the presidential campaign.

Why? The scholasticism and rigidity of international law, with its inexorably state-centric approach to world order and justice, has been one of the principal impediments to fresh thought and public

---

*I am, of course, not the first to urge such a reassessment. Twenty-five years ago, Richard Lillich—ahead of his time, as usual—wrote the following: "Surely the abject inability of the United Nations to take effective action to terminate the genocidal conduct and alleviate the mass suffering in Bangladesh necessitates a fundamental reassessment... of the role of self-help, and especially of humanitarian intervention, in international affairs today." (Richard Lillich, "A Reply to Ian Brownlie and a Plea for Constructive Alternatives," in *Law and Civil War in the Modern World* 229, 230 [John Norton Moore ed., 1974].)

discussion. It should come as no surprise that, as Professor Phillip Trimble has noted, "governments love international law."[6] They should love it—it is tilted heavily towards them, often at the expense of their populations.* International law became the captive instrument of governments even as they oppressed their people. Like domestic governmental agencies coopted by the businesses they were created to regulate, international law and its institutions came to protect governments that traduce the values of their people. The belief is now widespread in the West that the focus must shift from states to individuals. As Václav Havel put it, the "enlightened efforts of generations of democrats, the terrible experience of two world wars … and the evolution of civilization have finally brought humanity to the recognition that human beings are more important than the state."[7]

Revisiting these issues may imply an ahistorical criticism of choices made in the past, by states or scholars, in acting or thinking about hard questions that arose in contexts very different from that of today. This is not my intent. All know that the world was very different in 1945 when those choices were made. In 1945, the founders of the United Nations valued stability over justice for a reason: the world had just gone through a hitherto unimaginable holocaust, the consequence, it seemed, of unbridled state discretion to use force. The felt need was to curb interstate violence. And the norms then devised may well have been right for the times. Who is to say that humanity could have survived the Cold War had the UN's founders in 1945 permitted intervention of the sort carried out by NATO in Yugoslavia? Today, however, while humanity's needs have not changed, new ways exist to meet those needs without posing risks of global annihilation.

As I argue in this book, the "evolution of civilization" to which Havel referred necessitates a wholesale reevaluation of rules supposedly governing interventionism. I argue that the decaying legalist regime has produced a catechism that is overly schematized and scholastic, disconnected from the real world of state behavior, and unrealistic in its aspirations for state conduct. That catechism inverts the appropriate weight to be accorded to actual practice in

---

*As Hans Morgenthau famously put it, international law is an "ideology of the status quo." Hans J. Morgenthau, *Politics Among Nations* 86–7 (4th ed. 1966).

shaping the law, causing international lawyers to get it precisely backwards: They dismiss practice where they should not—where states use force in a manner at odds with the UN Charter—and do not dismiss it where they should—where the United Nations itself does so. Furthermore, the legalist catechism is grounded on the myth that the "international community" is a unitary actor, which of course is not true. Nor are its permeating assumptions of state *purposes* that produce identifiable *acts* and *effects,* and an international *reaction*—all capable of categorization. The legalist regime governing the use of force is, on analysis, grounded upon premises that are unproved and often unprovable.*

I argue in this book that current international law dogma is out of sync with emerging humanitarian values. I suggest that in thinking about interventionism, we drop legalist mythology. States easily see through this mythology, and they have adopted a more realistic cost-benefit analysis in judging the merits of intervention. But this should not be seen as a refinement of the legal model, let alone as a substitute for it. While the law may sometimes incorporate cost-benefit analysis in various "balancing tests," cost-benefit analysis

---

*What Hinsley has written of international relations applies doubly to international law: "Neither the conviction that we might not be wholly successful nor the sheer mass of the facts should deter us any longer from attempting to raise the study of international relations—that field in which assumptions and hypotheses have always abounded but in which the effort to test assumptions has rarely been made—to a more scientific level." F. H. Hinsley, *Power and the Pursuit of Peace: Theory and Practice in the History of Relations Between States* 6 (1963). He continues: "It is not to be expected that modern men would remember that their own political divisions had themselves arisen out of a medieval structure which had been at least as homogeneous—or suspect that a single administrative and technological framework for political action would not necessarily produce a single political system: A successful international organization or a world state…. But these considerations do nothing to excuse our subsequent failure to subject the failure of our experiments in international organization to the test of our own experiences. Rousseau and Kant could judge what the results might be only in light of their political theory. We have not only misinterpreted their conclusions and failed to use the history of international relations to test our own. We have also ignored or misinterpreted the practical results of international experiments which we have accumulated in the past fifty years." (*Id.* at 7.)

is, at a fundamental level, not law. Indeed, one can question whether a legal system does not admit to failure when it adopts case-bound balancing tests, which in their subjectivity and nonuniversality rob law of its predictability.* The case-by-case approach of a balancing test is, *juridically*, a cop-out, an acknowledgment that no reasonable rule can be fashioned to govern all circumstances that can foreseeably arise. In the long term, the legalist model still holds more promise for reconciling justice with peace. The rule of law has been humanity's most effective means of establishing civil *domestic* societies; there is no reason to believe that, some day, the rule of law cannot be equally effective in shaping a civil *international* society, as it is today in a politically and economically integrated Europe. A legalist system can only work, however, to the extent that it reflects underlying geopolitical realities. The central geopolitical reality today is an unbridgeable attitudinal chasm among peoples of the world. That gulf precludes the establishment of an effective rule of law to govern use of force. How that roadblock can and should be confronted is the great issue of our era, and the central inquiry of this book.

The book can be summarized as follows:[†]

Chapter 1 traces the development of the legalist model from the Concert of Europe through the League of Nations, and the United

---

*While Judge Sofaer's "common law," multifactor analysis focuses on the same elements that I would consider probative for decision makers, for this reason I do not share his view that our approach should be considered law. See Abraham D. Sofaer, "International Law and Kosovo," 36 *Stan. J. Int'l L.* 1, 2 n. 2 (2000).

[†]At this point, a word is in order as to where the book fits into the landscape of international law and relations.

The international legal system consists of a root regime and various subregimes. (A regime is simply the sum total of all principles, norms, rules, and decision-making procedures that give rise to actors' expectations on a given subject.) The root regime comprises meta-rules. These are rules about rules, precepts that govern the operation of the system. Rules governing the making and interpretation of treaties, for example, and rules about what counts as a customary norm are the sorts of rules found in the root regime.

The subregimes comprise the ordinary, substantive rules that govern the day-to-day conduct of states. These rules regulate everything from international postal delivery to agricultural subsidies. The subregimes thus divide by subject matter; they relate to different kinds of activities. Examples are civil aviation, law of the seas, human rights, and international trade. Rules

Nations. It examines the law of the Charter, showing that intervention of the sort undertaken by NATO was flatly prohibited by Article 2(4). Official and scholarly justifications are reviewed and rejected, including arguments that NATO's acts were implicitly authorized by the Security Council.

Chapter 2 begins a consideration of the practice of intervention. What should we make of incidents in which force was used in violation of the Charter's prohibition? This necessitates a broader look at weaknesses in the rules that undergird the prohibition against intervention. The first is international law's convoluted treatment of the notion of state custom. I point out that issues about custom arise in two different contexts—when the custom of the parties is used to determine the meaning of a treaty, and when it is used as a separate, stand-alone source of authority to legitimate the conduct of a state. International law, I suggest, fails to keep these two uses straight. The result is that if a state in effect turns its back on its obligations under a treaty, such as the UN Charter, international

---

continued

of the root regime are by definition common to each of the subregimes. As a book about the use-of-force subregime, this book is thus necessarily about rules of the root system that apply to use of force.

Indeed, much of the book is directed at assessing the soundness of international law's meta-rules that shape substantive rules regulating intervention. (I critique these rules of international law on their own terms. For an assessment of those rules using game theory, see Jack L. Goldsmith and Eric A. Posner, "A Theory of Customary International Law," 66 *U. Chi. L. Rev.* 1113 [1999].) The reason is obvious: Weakness in the normative structure of international law's root system may have profound implications not simply for the use of force, but for international relations generally. Rules governing sovereignty and norm creation are examples. Sovereignty is *the* ordering principle in the root regime and, thus, of every subregime. An erosion of sovereignty within the use-of-force subregime could portend the erosion of sovereignty within other subregimes as well—perhaps even within the root regime. Rules about how norms are created also reside in the root regime. Illogic in the way customary norms are made concerning use of force could signal weakness in other subregimes that also rest on the shaky scaffolding of custom. A full consideration of the potential "contagion" of other subregimes from the breakdown of law in the use-of-force subregime is for another book. For now, it will suffice to note that the efficacy of international meta-rules related to the use of force is itself monumentally important—whatever the wider ramifications.

law still sees that state as merely "construing" its obligations under the treaty—however antiquated the treaty may have become. Second, international law assumes that the building blocks of custom—state acts—can be objectively identified. In fact, the identification process is not at all objective and varies from one culture to the next—with the result that customary rules lack true universality. International law is illogical in considering "nonacts" as acts. International law is inaccurate in its assumptions about state motive and intent. And international law is presumptuous and self-justifying in assuming that state conduct is evidence of state acceptance of the legalist model. In fact, as I point out, numerous potential factors may be causative—if the concept of causation is apt at all. Even if one does accept the legalist system's shaky methodology, the most sensible view is that a treaty breached often and for a sustained period is subject to "desuetude," that is, to supersession by subsequent, inconsistent custom. This view is reinforced by rules of international law that presume a state free to act unless a firm limitation or prohibition is established.

Chapter 3 continues to look at custom, moving from structural rules to rules pertaining specifically to use of force. The point here is to consider whether customary international law concerning interstate use of force may have come to permit what NATO did in Kosovo. It reviews the actual record, outlining bloodletting far beyond what could reasonably be called compliance with the Charter's ban on interstate force. The chapter suggests the futility of trying to classify specific uses of force by purpose, effect, or by the reaction of the international community. The chapter suggests that the Charter's framers, like the framers of the League Covenant, contemplated a "hard" version of collective security, one in which member states could be obliged to use force in the event one state attacked another. In practice, though, the system devolved into a "soft" version in which no such obligation attaches—and in which, contrary again to the expectations of the Charter's framers, no constabulary force was created that the Security Council might have used to counter such attacks. It suggests that the Charter failed for the same reason that the League Covenant failed: Member states declined to accept an automatic commitment to use force in response to an armed attack, leaving victim states to fend for themselves. I conclude that international law is able to provide no satisfactory answer concerning the validity of humanitarian intervention, in Kosovo or elsewhere.

Chapter 4 moves from interstate to intrastate violence, pointing out that the Charter fails completely to deal with violence occurring wholly within a state. The chapter examines the Charter's restraints on Security Council power to intervene in internal strife and the Council's tortured efforts to do so notwithstanding those limitations. It suggests that legal overreaching by the Security Council undermined the very regime that the Council sought to enforce. Under Article 39 of the Charter, the Council cannot use force absent at least a threat of cross-border violence; however, its repeated breach of that limit undercut its standing to criticize states for breaching the limit of Article 2(4). I suggest that there are persuasive reasons for distinguishing the practice of the Council from that of individual state actors when it comes to giving legal effect to that practice—reasons that go to the heart of the idea of the rule of law, and that preclude a governmental organ from acting *ultra vires* and defining the scope of its own power. *Creators* of a treaty—states—define the contours of that treaty; *creatures* of a treaty—such as the UN Security Council—do not.

Chapter 5 considers the feasibility of a legalist use-of-force system. The chapter reconsiders, in light of the Kosovo conflict, the age-old question whether international law is really law, examining how the Security Council veto undercuts the Charter's premise of the "sovereign equality" of states. It then explores the enormous gap that divides states on values fundamental to the establishment of an authentic legalist system to govern the use of force. While the gap between Western and non-Western values will gradually close over time, at present the division has opened the door to other systems of validation, namely, appeals to systems such as justice and legitimacy. Because such alternatives are—unlike law—not grounded upon explicit, formally given consent, none can lay claim to universality, illusions of "objectivity" notwithstanding. All that remains for judging interventionism is the relativity of consequentialism.

Chapter 6 examines whether a legalist use-of-force regime is desirable. It begins by noting the strange parallel universe in which a *de jure* international law that is largely ignored coexists with a *de facto* geopolitical regime that is largely controlling. It then moves to evaluate different ways of thinking about NATO's intervention in Kosovo. I suggest that civil disobedience is as legitimate in international law as it is in domestic law—even though underlying judgments about whether international law is "just" will inevitably be subjective. The most sensible approach is to acknowledge that the Charter was violated by NATO's intervention in Kosovo; to acknowledge that the entirety of the law is not represented by the Charter alone; and to acknowledge that the law governing intervention is at best hopelessly confused and at worst illusory. The transitional alternative of case-by-case decisions on intervention leaves too much room for abuse, but no legalist remedy (such as amendment of the Charter) can now be had because the requisite international consensus is lacking. An interim solution of regionalization seems to be emerging—intervention by preexisting coalitions of neighboring democracies that weigh the costs against the benefits of each putative intervention, an inexact and nonlegalist approach that can nonetheless lay the groundwork for the eventual establishment of a true legalist system to govern use of force.

ONE

Kosovo and the United Nations Charter

Before law came geopolitics.

Before the twentieth century's great legalist experiments in international governance, the affairs of states were ordered by geopolitics—by geography and economics, by diplomacy and trade, and, not least, by military might.

For the better part of human history, the interplay of such forces produced anarchy and massive brutality. War was fought frequently and pitilessly. Cities were burnt, farmlands laid waste, populations exterminated, and survivors enslaved. But war was not abated by law. It was abated, in the end, by politics. It was abated when states came at long last to conclude that their interests were served better by order than by disorder. That conclusion was reached, in Europe, after the greatest bloodshed that the continent had theretofore experienced, the Napoleonic Wars.

The year was 1814. The place was Vienna. There, with Napoleon locked safely away on the island of St. Helena, the leading statesmen of Europe gathered to fashion a new order. It was a political order, not a legalist order. Its object was to keep the peace. It had no binding rules. Its methods were the methods of diplomacy—discussion, negotiation, and compromise.

It was called the Concert of Europe, and it worked. Battlefield casualties in nineteenth-century Europe dropped to one-seventh the level of the previous century. Peace and prosperity reigned throughout the Continent to an extent never before seen. In fostering communication, openness, and respect—among the Great Powers—the Concert created a culture of civility and laid the groundwork for legalist institutions to come.

The actual establishment of legalist constraints to control violence did not occur until the twentieth century. But the idea was not
new. The dream had been born many centuries before.[1] "[T]he
ancients were not unacquainted with it," Rousseau wrote, outlining
a plan that built upon the earlier work of the Duc de Sully, whose
own organizational scheme drew heavily upon that of the Greek
city-states.[2] The century before, an elaborate design of William Penn,
published in 1693, envisioned international collaboration to enforce
order. If one member state attacked another member state, Penn
suggested, "a small force in every other sovereignty … will certainly
prevent that danger."[3] The Abbé de St. Pierre proposed an early,
albeit inward-looking, version of collective security in 1712. "In
return for joining the Union," he wrote, "each Prince will be assisted
against rebels with the forces of his confederates."[4] A European
army would be created, with contributions of troops to be assessed
monthly, based upon a state's revenues.[5] In 1735, the Spanish
statesman Cardinal Giulio Alberoni outlined "a scheme of perpetual dyet for establishing the public tranquility" of Europe.[6] William
Ladd, writing a century later, proposed an international executive
with organizational support and a standing army.[7]

Until the horrors of twentieth-century warfare, however, rulers
remained unimpressed by such pipe dreams. In a letter to Voltaire,
Frederick the Great wrote that St. Pierre's plan "is most practicable;
for its success all that is lacking is the consent of Europe and a few
similar trifles."[8] Cardinal Fleury, chief minister of Louis XV,
reportedly told Alberoni: "You have forgotten, Sir, a preliminary condition on which your five articles depend. You must begin by sending out a troop of missionaries to prepare the hearts and minds of
the contracting sovereigns."[9]

This early gap between theoreticians and decision makers was
occasionally bridged by thinkers who were skeptical of the possibility
of a workable international peace-keeping organization. Immanuel
Kant wrote in *Perpetual Peace* in 1795 that the concept of a world
republic was unrealistic, suggesting instead an ever-expanding union
of nations aimed at preventing war.[10] One influential critique of earlier organizational schemes was that of James Lorimer, the Scottish
political philosopher sometimes hailed as the "father of European federalism."[11] Lorimer, writing in the mid-nineteenth century, argued for
only the loosest of bodies, integrated less rigorously than even a con-
federation, which would have no power to intervene in states' internal
affairs.[12] When tragedy struck at Verdun and Flanders, world leaders

turned to these earlier schemes as inevitably better than the alternative that had just been endured.*

A. The League of Nations

The institutional and normative architecture of the United Nations emerged not in 1945 from San Francisco or Dumbarton Oaks, but from Versailles, with the drafting in 1919 of the Covenant of the League of Nations.[13] With the League of Nations, the world community turned its back on the geopolitical, balance-of-power system that had reigned hitherto—a system, it was thought, that had brought about the deaths of 47 million people in World War I—and substituted a new, legalist system to control the exercise of state power. "The tents have been struck," said South African Prime Minister Jan Christiaan Smuts, "and the great caravan of humanity is once again on the march."[14] "What we seek," President Woodrow Wilson declared, "is the rule of law, based upon the consent of the governed and sustained by the organized opinion of mankind."[15]

The structure of the League foreshadowed that of the United Nations.[16] Its assembly met three times a year in Geneva. Each member state (at its peak it had 60) had one vote. The League's Council consisted of permanent members (France, Great Britain, Italy, Japan, and later Germany and the Soviet Union) and nonpermanent members elected by the assembly. Under Article V of the Covenant, decisions of the Council required the unanimous agreement of all members. A secretary general was responsible for administrative matters.

The League's normative structure, like that of the United Nations, was built on two pillars: a limitation on self-help by states, and the placement of enforcement power (of sorts) in a central, supranational authority. The "acceptance of obligations not to

---

*"Every scheme for the elimination of war that men have advocated since 1917," Hinsley observed, "has been nothing but a copy or an elaboration of some seventeenth-century programme—as the seventeenth-century programmes were copies of still earlier schemes. What is worse, these programmes are far more widely accepted as wisdom now than they were when they were first propagated." F. H. Hinsley, *Power and the Pursuit of Peace: Theory and Practice in the History of Relations Between States* 3 (1963).

resort to war" was central to the Covenant's scheme. The key requirement was set forth in Article X:

> The Members of the League undertake to respect and preserve as
> against external aggression the territorial integrity and existing
> political independence of all Members of the League. In case of
> any such aggression or in case of any threat or danger of such
> aggression the Council shall advise upon the means by which this
> obligation shall be fulfilled.

The Council was granted broad power under Article XI to deal
with war and threats of war:

> Any war or threat of war, whether immediately affecting any of
> the Members of the League or not, is hereby declared a matter of
> concern to the whole League, and the League shall take any
> action that may be deemed wise and effectual to safeguard the
> peace of nations.

The parties agreed in Article XII not to resort to war until three
months after submitting a dispute for peaceful settlement:

> The Members of the League agree that, if there should arise
> between them any dispute likely to lead to a rupture they will
> submit the matter either to arbitration or judicial settlement or
> to enquiry by the Council, and they agree in no case to resort to
> war until three months after the award by the arbitrators or the
> judicial decision, or the report by the Council.

The Covenant's limits on use of force by states were therefore
ambiguous. Article X implied disapproval of aggression, but the
prohibition was not absolute, in that Article XII established only a
"cooling off period," at the end of which use of force apparently
would not constitute aggression.[17] It is fair to say, as Hinsley does,
that whereas the UN Charter would later prohibit all war, the
Covenant prohibited only *illegal* war, that is, war in violation of
law and covenants.[18] Nonetheless, the impropriety of war as a
means of self-help was presumed,[19] and in its framers this presump-
tion engendered boundless optimism. "It's not too much to hope
that this is the last Balkan war," Woodrow Wilson said, "and maybe
the last European war for a long, long, long time."[20]

B. *The United Nations Charter*

The United Nations was sold to the public, "for psychological reasons, as a decidedly new organization rather than as a revived and remodeled League of Nations."[21] But reconstruction merely rearranged the burnt timbers of the League. "[T]he similarities between the League and the United Nations," Brierly observed, "are many and fundamental."[22]

Delegates of the 51 states participating in the San Francisco conference attempted to build on both elements of the League Covenant model.[23] They sought to make the limitation on states' use of force more comprehensive and to equip its central authority (the Security Council) with power to use force to preserve the peace. The text of the Charter spells out the means by which those twin goals were to be achieved.

The centerpiece of the Charter regime is a flat prohibition against the use of force by individual states in Article 2(4):

> All Members shall refrain in their international relations from the threat or use of force against the territorial integrity or political independence of any state, or in any other manner inconsistent with the Purposes of the United Nations.

The prohibition is reinforced by a ban against UN intervention in the domestic jurisdiction of any state, set out in Article 2(7):

> Nothing contained in the present Charter shall authorize the United Nations to intervene in matters which are essentially within the domestic jurisdiction of any state or shall require the Members to submit such matters to settlement under the present Charter; but this principle shall not prejudice the application of enforcement measures under Chapter VII.

One exception is permitted (by Article 51)—self-defense:

> Nothing in the present Charter shall impair the inherent right of individual or collective self-defence if an armed attack occurs against a Member of the United Nations, until the Security Council has taken measures necessary to maintain international peace and security. Measures taken by Members in the exercise of this right of self-defence shall be immediately reported to the

Security Council and shall not in any way affect the authority and responsibility of the Security Council under the present Charter to take at any time such action as it deems necessary in order to maintain or restore international peace and security.

Broader leeway to use force is afforded the UN Security Council in Chapter VII, but not much. Under Article 39, the Council is itself permitted to use or authorize use of force, but only upon a finding of a "threat to the peace, breach of the peace, or act of aggression":

> The Security Council shall determine the existence of any threat to the peace, breach of the peace, or act of aggression and shall make recommendations, or decide what measures shall be taken in accordance with Articles 41 and 42, to maintain or restore international peace and security.

Once it has made such a finding, the Council may authorize the use of air, sea, or land forces under Article 42:

> Should the Security Council consider that measures provided for in Article 41 would be inadequate or have proved to be inadequate, it may take such action by air, sea, or land forces as may be necessary to maintain or restore international peace and security. Such action may include demonstrations, blockade, and other operations by air, sea, or land forces of Members of the United Nations.

These forces may be under the direction of individual states or of the Council itself, in standing or stand-by forces that they supplied to it under Article 43:

1. All Members of the United Nations, in order to contribute to the maintenance of international peace and security, undertake to make available to the Security Council, on its call and in accordance with a special agreement or agreements, armed forces, assistance, and facilities, including rights of passage, necessary for the purpose of maintaining international peace and security.
2. Such agreement or agreements shall govern the numbers and types of forces, their degree of readiness and general location, and the nature of the facilities and assistance to be provided.

3. The agreement or agreements shall be negotiated as soon as possible on the initiative of the Security Council. They shall be concluded between the Security Council and Members or between the Security Council and groups of Members and shall be subject to ratification by the signatory states in accordance with their respective constitutional processes.

Use of force in the form of an enforcement action taken by a regional agency also is required to be approved beforehand by the Security Council under Article 53:

The Security Council shall, where appropriate, utilize such regional arrangements or agencies for enforcement action under its authority. But no enforcement action shall be taken under regional arrangements or by regional agencies without the authorization of the Security Council, with the exception of measures against any enemy state, as defined in paragraph 2 of this Article, provided for pursuant to Article 107 or in regional arrangements directed against renewal of aggressive policy on the part of any such state, until such time as the Organization may, on request of the Governments concerned, be charged with the responsibility for preventing further aggression by such a state.

C. Legality of NATO Action in Kosovo under the Charter

With these rules in mind, let us consider the legality under the United Nations Charter of NATO's action in Kosovo, beginning with the Charter's text and moving to relevant Security Council resolutions. In the next chapter, I will examine whether the actual practice of states may have allowed such action without Security Council approval.

1. Application of the Text of the Charter

The principle underpinning Article 2(4) of the Charter was stated succinctly 400 years before its framing by the Spanish theologian and scholar Francisco de Vitoria. "There is a single and only just cause for commencing a war," he wrote, "namely, a wrong received."[24]

There can be little question that NATO's action in Kosovo, if not
authorized by the Security Council, would have violated Article 2(4)
of the Charter. Brierly's formulation is clearly correct: "The broad
effect of Article 2(4) ... is that it entirely prohibits the use or threat of
armed force against another state except in self-defence or in execution of collected measures authorized by the Council or Assembly."[25]
The import of the Charter has repeatedly been stated by the UN
General Assembly. In its 1965 Declaration on the Inadmissibility of
Intervention, the General Assembly said the following:

> No state or group of states has the right to intervene, directly or
> indirectly, for any reason whatever, in the internal or external
> affairs of any state. Consequently, armed intervention and all
> other forms of interference or attempted threats against the per-
> sonality of the State or against its political, economic and cul-
> tural elements, are condemned.[26]

In its 1970 Declaration on the Strengthening of International
Security, the General Assembly "[s]olemnly reaffirm[ed] that States
must fully respect the sovereignty of other States and the right of
peoples to determine their own destinies, free of external intervention, coercion or constraint, especially involving the threat or use of
force, overt or covert ... ."[27]

In its 1970 Declaration on Principles of International Law concerning Friendly Relations and Co-operation among States, the
General Assembly again interpreted the Charter (unanimously) as
meaning that "[n]o State or group of States has the right to intervene in any form or for any reason whatsoever in the internal or
external affairs of any state." It added this sentence:

> Consequently, armed intervention and all other forms of interfer-
> ence or attempted threats against the personality of the State or
> against its political, economic and cultural elements, are in viola-
> tion of international law.[28]

In its 1981 Declaration on the Inadmissibility of Intervention and
Interference in the Internal Affairs of States, the General Assembly
again reaffirmed that "[n]o State or group of States has the right to
intervene, in any form or for any reason whatever, directly or indi-
rectly, in the internal or external affairs of any state." It added that
the "principle of non-intervention and non-interference" comprehends

"[t]he duty of a State to refrain from armed intervention, subversion, military occupation or any other form of intervention and interference, covert or overt, directed at another State or group of States, or any act of military, political or economic interference in the internal affairs of another State" and also "[t]he duty of a State to refrain from the promotion, encouragement or support, direct or indirect, of rebellious or secessionist activities with other States, under any pretext whatsoever ... ."[29] In its 1993 review of the implementation of the Declaration on the Strengthening of International Security, the General Assembly again called upon all States to "refrain from the use or threat of use of force, aggression, intervention, [and] interference," urging further that "all States ... take further immediate steps aimed at promoting and using effectively the system of collective security as envisaged in the Charter ... ."[30]

The Assembly has thus construed the Charter as imposing a rule of *per se* invalidity with respect to intervention.[31] The rule admits of no exception: Intervention is always unlawful, regardless of the identity of the state undertaking the intervention, and regardless of motive or effects. The Charter's prohibition applies to individual states as well as to states acting in coalitions, including military alliances such as NATO and even the Security Council and General Assembly. Indeed, to the extent that provisions of the NATO Treaty permit such intervention, Article 103 of the Charter provides that obligations under the Charter prevail. (In fact, the use-of-force restraints of the Charter are incorporated by reference in Article 1 of the North Atlantic Treaty, which provides that the "Parties undertake ... to refrain in their international relations from any threat or use of force in any manner inconsistent with the purposes of the United Nations."[32] Violation of the Charter by a NATO member state would thus constitute a violation of the NATO Treaty as well.*)

While it may be true that Article 2(4) is ambiguous at the margins, it is "unwarranted," as Oscar Schachter has written, "to suggest that Article 2(4) lacks the determinate content to enable it to function as a legal rule of restraint."[33] At an irreducible minimum, the provision bans any threat or use of force against the territorial

---

* House of Commons, Select Committee on Foreign Affairs, Fourth Report ¶ 135 (May 23, 2000), http://www.publications.parliament.uk/pa/cm199900/cmselect/cmfaff/28/2813.htm (last visited Feb. 23, 2001).

integrity or political independence of any state. Some have suggested that the scope of the prohibition is narrowed by the provision's qualifying words, "in any other manner inconsistent with the purposes of the United Nations." The argument is, in effect, that force may be used when consistent with the purposes of the United Nations.[34] But plainly the words do not mean that: The qualification is in fact a broadening of the prohibition to include not only uses of force against the territorial integrity or political independence of any state but, in addition, *other* uses of force against a state that are inconsistent with the purposes of the United Nations. (Some commentators, such as Henkin, thus dismiss the qualification altogether.*) But in assessing action such as NATO's against Yugoslavia, it is not necessary to delve into the purposes of the United Nations. If "force" was not threatened and used by NATO against the "territorial integrity" of Yugoslavia, it is difficult to imagine circumstances in which that standard would ever be met.

Some claim that intervention that "does not result in territorial conquest or political subjugation"[35] is not subject to the prohibition of the Charter, but this view is mistaken. Nor is there any possibility of fitting NATO's acts under Article 51, which permits defensive use of force. The claim of the State Department spokesman that Article 51 supported NATO's attack is preposterous. No "armed attack" occurred against any of the NATO states, nor was any anticipated. And, in any event, Security Council approval is required under Article 53 for use of force by a "regional agency" (which is a label that does not apply to NATO). No Security Council approval was given. Each of these contentions is discussed in turn.

The preparatory work, or *travaux préparatoires*, of the UN Charter's use-of-force provisions have been combed at length by respected commentators looking for any indication that the framers of the Charter intended some exception to the blanket prohibition against nondefensive force.[36] They have found none. Michael Akehurst, for example, wrote that "the *travaux préparatoires* indicate that the reference to territorial integrity, political independence, and purposes of the United Nations was added to Article 2(4), not

---

*"To me," Henkin wrote, "the Charter, in both language and intent, outlaws any use of force against the territorial integrity or political independence of other states for *any* purpose, such use being *ipso facto* contrary to the purposes of the United Nations." Louis Henkin, *How Nations Behave* 291–92 (2nd ed. 1979).

in order to limit the prohibition on the use of force, but in a clumsy attempt to strengthen it."[37] Ian Brownlie extensively reviewed the *travaux préparatoires* and concluded that Article 2(4) prohibits virtually any use of force by a state.[38] Louis Henkin accurately described the intent of the original 55 parties to the United Nations Charter:

> They determined that even sincere concern for national "security" or "vital interests" should no longer warrant any nation to initiate war. They agreed, in effect, to forego the use of external force to change the political status quo. Nations would be assured their fundamental independence, the enjoyment of their territory, their freedom—a kind of right to be let alone.[39]

Oscar Schachter's interpretation of the *travaux* distills the weight of authority.

He wrote:

> [I]nternational law does not, and should not, legitimize use of force across national lines except for self-defense (including collective defense) and enforcement measures ordered by the Security Council. Neither human rights, democracy nor self-determination are acceptable legal grounds for waging war, nor for that matter, are traditional just war causes or righting of wrongs. This conclusion is not only in accord with the U.N. Charter as it was originally understood; it is also in keeping with the interpretation adopted by the great majority of States at the present time. When governments have resorted to force, they have almost invariably relied on self-defense as their legal justification.[40]

Tom Farer put it succinctly: "*The nub of the matter,*" he wrote, "*is that if one deems the original intention of the founding members to be controlling with respect to the legitimate occasions for the use of force, humanitarian intervention is illegal.*"[41] This conclusion was reiterated by the International Court of Justice in the Nicaragua case: "The use of force," said the Court, "could not be the appropriate method to monitor or ensure ... respect [for human rights]."[42] This language, Nigel Rodley concludes, "unmistakably places the Court in the camp of those who claim that the doctrine of humanitarian intervention is without validity."[43] In 1986, the British Foreign Office summed up its view that humanitarian intervention was unlawful:

> [T]he overwhelming majority of contemporary legal opinion comes down against the existence of a right of humanitarian intervention, for three main reasons: First, the UN Charter and the corpus of modern international law do not seem specifically to incorporate such a right; secondly, state practice in the past two centuries, and especially since 1945, at best provides only a handful of genuine cases of humanitarian intervention, and, on most assessments, none at all; and finally, on prudential grounds, that the scope for abusing such a right argues strongly against its creation....In essence, therefore, the case against making humanitarian intervention an exception to the principle of non-intervention is that its doubtful benefits would be heavily out-weighed by its costs in terms of respect for international law.[44]

It is difficult to find a statement made before or during the bombing on behalf of any NATO government justifying NATO's action under a doctrine of humanitarian intervention. After the campaign ended, however, the Foreign Affairs Committee of the British House of Commons undertook a comprehensive inquiry into the Kosovo operation and issued a lengthy report, the most extensive released thus far by any NATO governmental body. In it, the Committee reported that both the Foreign Secretary and the Minister of State told the Committee that states had the right to use force in the case of "overwhelming humanitarian necessity where, in the light of all the circumstances, a limited use of force is justifiable as the only way to avert a humanitarian catastrophe."[45]

NATO's Secretary General also offered legal justifications after the campaign had ended. He cited the Security Council's "successive resolutions" on Kosovo which were "ignored" by Yugoslavia. "[T]he UN Charter itself," he said, "calls for action to be taken by the international community to respond to threats to peace and security, and in response to grave humanitarian emergencies...and... there is an ever-growing body of international law, including of course the Universal Declaration of Human Rights, that require the international community to respond when massive violations of human rights are being committed."[46]

In the United States, no argument was made that the law permitted humanitarian intervention, and official legal justifications of any sort were hard to come by. Such legal defenses of NATO's actions as were presented constantly shifted from one ground to the next, with no press notice whatsoever. The official U.S. position came out in dribs and drabs; so far as can be determined, no formal legal justification has been released to this day.

The State Department began, for example, by claiming without explanation that no Security Council authorization was needed. The claim was later refined by indicating that it pertained only to a "permissive" environment in Kosovo—but the claim that no authority was needed was repeated even after it had become clear that the environment would not be permissive. On June 15, 1998, the Department spokesman was asked "what legal authorization the United States thinks it has to threaten, without any UN Security Council resolution, military action in a sovereign nation—call it Serbia, call it FRY?" He responded: "We believe that, as a result of and stemming from and relying upon the existence of Article 51 of the UN Charter, as well as the Washington Treaty that created NATO, that there is a position that such a Security Council resolution would be desirable, but not imperative."[47] No one present asked for clarification of the new reliance upon Article 51 or the implicit claim that NATO would be acting defensively. On October 1, 1999, the Department spokesman said: "We have taken a position of principle that even in the absence of Security Council resolution, NATO would have the authority to act."[48] No one present asked where NATO could get such authority. By March of 1999, the Administration had begun to settle on the idea that NATO's attack had actually been approved by the Security Council. Secretary of State Madeleine Albright said:

> Acting under Chapter 7, the Security Council adopted three reso-lutions—1160, 1199 and 1203—imposing mandatory obliga-tions on the FRY; and these obligations the FRY has flagrantly ignored. So NATO actions are being taken within this frame-work, and we continue to believe that NATO's actions are justi-fied and necessary to stop the violence.[49]

No reporter asked how any of the three resolutions could be con-strued as authorizing use of force. The same day, Albright was asked in an interview whether the United States had not "gone beyond" Security Council authorization in Resolution 1199 "as you have done with Iraq?" "No," the Secretary responded, "I do not think that we have. I think that there is a humanitarian crisis going on—1199 speaks specifically about the importance of a humanitarian crisis creating a security problem."[50] A week later, Col. P. J. Crowley, a spokesman for the National Security Council, said, "We believe there is legitimate and sufficient legal grounds for the United States and NATO for the use of force in this situation." He cited two recent United Nations resolutions calling on Yugoslavia to take measures to end the suffering in Kosovo.[51] In the action against the United States brought by Yugoslavia in the International Court of Justice, the United States argued that NATO's actions were justified by the following factors, among others. These include:

- The humanitarian catastrophe that has engulfed the people of Kosovo as a brutal and unlawful campaign of ethnic cleansing has forced many hundreds of thousands to flee their homes and has severely endangered their lives and well-being;
- The acute threat of the actions of the Federal Republic of Yugoslavia to the security of neighbouring States, including threat posed by extremely heavy flows of refugees and armed incursions into their territories;
- The serious violation of international humanitarian law and human rights obligations by forces under the control of the Federal Republic of Yugoslavia, including widespread murder, disappearances, rape, theft and destruction of property;
- The resolutions of the Security Council, which have determined that the actions of the Federal Republic of Yugoslavia constitute a threat to peace and security in the region and, pursuant to Chapter VII of the Charter, demanded a halt to such actions.

Under these circumstances, a failure by NATO to act immediately would have been to the irreparable prejudice of the people of Kosovo. The Members of NATO refused to stand idly by to watch yet another campaign of ethnic cleansing unfold in the heart of Europe.[52]

This apparently is as close as the United States has come to offering a legal justification. These and other statements in defense of NATO's actions demonstrate a point elaborated later: that however manifest the violation, states invariably seek to avoid confrontation by claiming that their actions comport with preexisting international norms.

States also eschew specific explanation of controversial action, which would particularize the precedent in a manner that could come back to haunt them. The argument that "humanitarian intervention" is now broadly permissible, for example, was probably seen by NATO leaders as a rationale that could lead to unforeseeable consequences, which may be why NATO did not forthrightly advance the argument. A statement issued on March 25, 1999, by the European Council provided the following explanation:

> It cannot be permitted that, in the middle of Europe, the predominant population of Kosovo is collectively deprived of its rights and subjected to grave human rights abuses. We, the countries of the European Union, are under a moral obligation to ensure that indiscriminate behaviour and violence, which became tangible in the massacre at Racak in January 1999, are not repeated. We have a duty to ensure the return to their homes of the hundreds of thousands of refugees and displaced persons. Aggression must not be rewarded. An aggressor must know that he will have to pay a high price. That is a lesson to be learned from the twentieth century.[53]

Similarly, on March 27, 1999, NATO Secretary General Javier Solana said the following:

> NATO military actions are intended to support the political aims of the international community. All Allies stand united in this action and in our determination to bring a halt to violence in Kosovo and to prevent further humanitarian catastrophe.[54]

In an earlier letter dated October 9, 1998, which was addressed to permanent representatives of the North Atlantic Council, NATO's governing body, Solana said:

> The relevant main points that have been raised in our discussion yesterday and today are as follows:
>
> • The FRY has not yet complied with the urgent demands of the International Community, despite UNSC Resolution 1160 of 31 March 1998 followed by UNSC Resolution 1199 of

23 September 1998, both acting under Chapter VII of the UN Charter.

- The very stringent report of the Secretary General of the United Nations pursuant to both resolutions warned *inter alia* of the danger of an humanitarian disaster in Kosovo.
- The continuation of a humanitarian catastrophe, because no concrete measures towards a peaceful solution of the crisis have been taken by the FRY.
- The fact that another UNSC Resolution containing a clear enforcement action with regard to Kosovo cannot be expected in the foreseeable future.
- The deterioration of the situation in Kosovo and its magnitude constitute a serious threat to peace and security in the region as explicitly referred to in the UNSC Resolution 1199.

On the basis of this discussion, I conclude that the Allies believe that in the particular circumstances with respect to the present crisis in Kosovo as described in UNSC Resolution 1199, there are legitimate grounds for the Alliance to threaten, and if necessary, to use force.[55]

Of course, Russia and China took vigorous issue with the assertion that NATO's action was permitted by international law. On March 25, 1999, the Commonwealth of Independent States issued the following joint statement:

The decision by the North Atlantic Treaty Organization (NATO) to use force against a sovereign State—the Federal Republic of Yugoslavia—which was taken without the participation of the United Nations Security Council, is contrary to the norms of international law, establishes a precedent for disregarding the Security Council as the supreme body bearing primary responsibility for the maintenance of peace and international security, and also undermines all efforts to achieve a peaceful settlement of the conflict in the region.[56]

Russian Foreign Minister Igor Ivanov warned that "[o]ne cannot judge who is right and who is wrong and punish the guilty single-handedly without any mandate from the international community. This is a straight way to anarchy and chaos in the world."[57] During the Kosovo crisis, Viktor Chernomyrdin, a former prime minister of

Russia who served as President Boris Yeltsin's special envoy for Kosovo, wrote in a *Washington Post* op-ed that the reason that the Russian people were increasingly "hostile" towards the United States was that "a sovereign country is being bombed—with bombing seen as a way to resolve a domestic conflict. This approach clashes with international law, the Helsinki agreements and the entire world order that took shape after World War II."[58]

In China, on March 24, 1999, the Vice Foreign Minister said that "[t]he Chinese Government opposes the use of force or the threat of the use of force in international affairs, and opposes interference in other nations' internal affairs no matter what the excuse or by what means, and opposes any random action that circumvents the UN Security Council … ."[59] China frequently reiterated both its opposition and the charge that NATO's action violated international law. At a news briefing in April 1999, for example, the foreign ministry spokesman said that "NATO's action circumvented the UN Security Council when it conducted military interference in Yugoslavia. This entirely violates the UN Charter and norms of the international law."[60]

Both Russia and China repeated their objections in the United Nations Security Council. On March 26, 1999, on the occasion of the vote on the Russian resolution disapproving NATO's action, the Russian representative said that "[w]hat's in balance is between the law and the lawless … . Today's vote is not only about the problem of Kosovo, it goes directly to the authority of the Security Council in the eyes of the world community."[61] The Chinese representative said that the "Chinese government strongly opposes such an act blatantly violating the principles of the United Nations Charter as well as international law, and challenging the authority of the Security Council."[62]

There is no question that Russia and China were correct in arguing that NATO's bombing violated the Charter. To label as "aggression" a government's treatment of its own people is inaccurate. The term applies to unlawful use of force by one state against another. There was no second state against which force was used. Similarly, "indiscriminate behaviour and violence," even rising to the point of "grave human rights abuses," do not provide a right to use force against a state under the Charter. Nor is there any "duty" in international law to repatriate refugees. As to Mr. Solana's argument, obviously "the international community" had no common "political aims"—unless that community is defined as excluding Russia and China, among others. If it had had such aims, the institution in which it had agreed to formulate and execute them was the UN Security Council. And there simply is no support for the contention that the UN Charter imposes a *duty* to intervene in response to a threat to international peace and security—let alone to human rights violations. It is the scope of the *right* to so respond that is at issue, a question considered at length in the pages of this book.

It is therefore hard to escape Oscar Schachter's blunt conclusion: "The idea that wars waged in a good cause such as democracy and human rights would not involve a violation of territorial integrity or political independence demands an Orwellian construction of those terms."[63]

2. Possible Authorization by the Security Council

While use of force against Yugoslavia would thus have been unlawful without Security Council approval, that defect would have been cured if the Security Council had authorized NATO's action; clearly a "threat to the peace" existed. To what extent can the Council reasonably be seen as having done so?

a) Prior resolutions of the Security Council. Before the war in Kosovo broke out, the Security Council adopted three resolutions that bore on the issue of Kosovo. As noted earlier, various U.S. and NATO officials suggested that these resolutions provided sufficient legal authority for NATO to use force against Yugoslavia.

The first was Resolution 1160, adopted in March 1998. In it, the Council decided "that all States shall, for the purposes of fostering peace and stability in Kosovo, prevent the sale or supply to the Federal Republic of Yugoslavia, including Kosovo, by their nationals or from their territories or using their flag vessels and aircraft, of arms and related matériel of all types, such as weapons and ammunition, military vehicles and equipment and spare parts for the aforementioned, and shall prevent arming and training for terrorist activities there ... ." The Council further emphasized "that the failure to make constructive progress towards the peaceful resolution of the situation in Kosovo will lead to the consideration of the additional measures."[64]

The second measure adopted by the Security Council was resolution 1199, adopted in September 1998. In it, the Council endorsed "steps taken to establish effective international monitoring of the situation in Kosovo, and in this connection welcome[d] the establishment of the Kosovo Diplomatic Observer Mission ... ." It further urged "States and international organizations represented in the Federal Republic of Yugoslavia to make available personnel to fulfil the responsibility of carrying out effective and continuous international monitoring in Kosovo until the objectives of this resolution and those of resolution 1160 (1998) are achieved."[65]

The third and final resolution, 1203, was adopted in October 1998. In it, the Council said that it "endorses and supports" agreements Yugoslavia entered into with NATO and the OSCE concerning the verification of compliance by Yugoslavia with resolution 1199, and said further that it "*demands* the full and prompt implementation of these agreements by the Federal Republic of Yugoslavia." The Council further affirmed that, "in the event of an emergency" involving the "safety and security" of the Verification Missions of NATO and the OSCE, "action may be needed to ensure their safety and freedom of movement as envisaged in the agreements" with NATO and the OSCE.[66]

Did these resolutions authorize the use of force? In the past, the Security Council has left no doubt concerning its intent whether use of force was authorized. In Korea, the Gulf War, and Bosnia, it adopted resolutions that made clear that states were allowed to use force. The Korea resolution recommended "that the Members of the United Nations furnish such assistance to the Republic of Korea as may be necessary to repel the armed attack and to restore international peace and security in the area."[67] The Gulf War Resolution authorized member states "co-operating with the Government of Kuwait ... to use all necessary means to uphold and implement resolution 660 (1990) and all subsequent relevant resolutions and to restore international peace and security in the area."[68] Addressing the issue of Bosnia in 1995, the Council in Resolution 1031 authorized member states "to take all necessary measures to effect the implementation of and to ensure compliance with Annex 1-A of the Peace Agreement" and to "take all necessary measures, at the request of IFOR, either in defense of IFOR or to assist the force in carrying out its mission ... ."[69]

In contrast, the Kosovo resolutions excerpted above contain no wording remotely like the Korea, Gulf War, or Bosnia resolutions that authorized the use of force. Resolution 1160 merely puts in place an embargo against the shipment of implements of war; it does not authorize use of force to enforce the embargo against noncomplying states. Resolution 1199 authorizes only monitoring of the situation, hardly an authorization to use force. "Because of Russian objections," the *New York Times* reported, "[Resolution 1199] never mentions a use of force ... ."[70] And while resolution 1203 "demands" compliance with certain agreements, nothing in it suggests that if the demand is not met, use of force is authorized; the resolution leaves open crucial questions that would need to be resolved before force could be used, including whether it could be used by NATO, the OSCE, or only by the Security Council. Even then, force could be used only for the narrow purpose of protecting the Verification Mission—which was neither the real nor the stated justification for NATO's ultimate use of force against Yugoslavia.

The language of prior Security Council resolutions thus provides scant support for the contention that the Council authorized NATO to use force against Yugoslavia. If the Yugoslavia resolutions had contained such language, they would no doubt have been vetoed by either China or Russia. For NATO, law observance was not the primary goal.* Those searching for Security Council approval of NATO's actions must therefore look elsewhere.

b) Implied authorization. Russia proposed that the Security Council condemn NATO's action, but on March 26, 1999, the proposal was defeated twelve to three. It might be argued that the Council's refusal to disapprove NATO's action constituted implicit approval.† Such an inference is not unknown in domestic jurisprudence. Perhaps the most famous example is the *Steel Seizure Case*,[71] in which Justices Black, Jackson, and Frankfurter inferred congressional disapproval of President Truman's seizure of the steel mills from

---

*"The Alliance has become the fireman for an enlarged Europe, a stabilizer for all seasons," said Dominique Moisi, the deputy director of the French Institute for International Relations. "That is a critical role, one that should be carried out within the context of the law. If possible, that is." Roger Cohen, "NATO Shatters Old Limits in the Name of Preventing Evil," *N.Y. Times*, Oct. 18, 1999. "We realize we are pushing the envelope and making up history as we go along," said U.S. special envoy Richard C. Holbrooke. William Drozdiak, "U.S., European Allies Divided Over NATO's Authority to Act," *Wash. Post*, Nov. 8, 1998, at A33.

†In fact, such an argument was made by Christopher Greenwood of the London School of Economics. See "Law and Right: When They Don't Fit Together," *The Economist*, Apr. 3, 1999.

Congress's rejection of proposals that would effectively have autho-rized that seizure. The problem with such an inference, however, is that it mistakenly assumes either positive or negative intent where there in fact might have been only an intent to remain *neutral*. The United States Congress in *Steel Seizure* and the Security Council in Kosovo might, in other words, have intended that *no* intent be inferred from their rejection of prohibitory or authorizing measures. With respect to the Security Council, a further difficulty is encoun-tered because of the existence of the veto. To get around a potentially blocking veto on the Council, a member state might simply propose a measure sure to go down to defeat, and then claim that the Council intended an effect opposite that of the defeated measure. Intent ought not be so easily manipulated.*

c) Subsequent ratification. During the Cuban Missile Crisis the State Department justified U.S. use of force on a theory that the Security Council had approved through acquiescence. The Organi-zation of American States (OAS), its lawyers argued, is a regional organization within the meaning of Article 53 of the UN Charter. The OAS had (on October 23, 1962) recommended the action later taken by the United States. The UN Security Council was placed on notice of both the OAS resolution and the proposed U.S. action pursuant to it. The Soviet Union brought before the Council a reso-lution condemning the U.S. action, but the Council declined to adopt it.[72] The "failure of the Security Council to disapprove regional action," the Department argued, "amounts to authorization within the meaning of Article 53 ... ."[73]

A similar argument has been made that Resolution 1244, adopted by the Security Council on June 10, 1999, had the effect of legally "endorsing" NATO's action.† The argument is not persuasive.

---

*For the argument that explicit and not implicit Security Council autho-rization is necessary before a nation may use force that does not derive from the right to self-defense under Article 51 of the Charter. See Jules Lobel and Michael Ratner, "Bypassing the Security Council: Ambiguous Authorizations To Use Force, Cease-Fires and the Iraqi Inspection Regime," 93 *Am J. Int'l L.* 124 (1999).
† See, for example, International Institute for Strategic Studies, *Strategic Survey, 1999/2000*, at 26 (2000) ("It is difficult to reconcile that decision with the view that NATO had committed an illegal act of aggression.").

First, the terms of that Resolution do not indicate Security Council approval of NATO's action; the Resolution simply deals with the situation as the Council found it. If the Council had wished to maintain its previous posture of silence with respect to NATO's action, the Resolution would not have read any differently, and rejection of the Resolution would not have been carried out any differently. Second, even if Resolution 1244 had indeed "endorsed" NATO's action, a retroactive endorsement in no way substitutes for prior authorization. The historical precedent is now what it always will be: NATO acted without Security Council approval. If the Resolution had had that effect, it no doubt would have been vetoed by Russia or China.

A final argument in this regard is that regional organizations may use force provided they receive subsequent Security Council ratification, as the Economic Community of West African States (ECOWAS) arguably did[74] following its 1990 uninvited[75] intervention in Liberia. But this argument, too, is unpersuasive. There is no more reason to permit subsequent ratification to substitute for prior authorization in connection with intervention by regional organizations than there is in connection with individual states or coalitions of states. "Without Security Council authorization," one commentator noted, "ECOWAS essentially undertook an unauthorized enforcement action."[76] Intervenors who act without the Security Council's prior authorization cannot be certain that the Security Council actually backs them, or that the Security Council will eventually give its approval. If there were genuine grounds for such certainty, an actual prior authorization could not fail to be forthcoming. In any event, NATO, like ECOWAS,* is not a regional organization for Chapter VIII purposes—and even if it had been, as noted above, Resolution 1244 did not constitute ratification.

D. Conclusion

The text of the Charter prohibited NATO's intervention absent Security Council approval, and the Security Council did not approve. There seems little question that the conclusion of the Foreign Affairs Committee of the British House of Commons was correct: "Our

---

* "[T]here is no record of ECOWAS reports to the Security Council pursuant to Article 54 of the Charter." Sean D. Murphy, *Humanitarian Intervention: The United Nations in an Evolving World Order* 345 (1996).

conclusion is that *Operation Allied Force* was contrary to the specific terms of what might be termed the basic law of the international community—the UN Charter … ."[77]

One further possibility remains: that states in effect had changed the meaning of the Charter *before* the Kosovo conflict by intervening so often in similar circumstances as to expunge or narrow the limitation. It is to this possibility that we now turn.

TWO

The Effect of State Practice on the Charter

In classic international law doctrine, custom is an independent source of authority. A state seeking legal justification for its act may rely not only upon a treaty such as the UN Charter but also upon what states actually do and have done. Article 38 of the Statute of the International Court of Justice lists the sources of authority that the Court is to apply in deciding disputes under international law. Listed second, after treaties, is "international custom, as evidence of general practice accepted as law." Under traditional doctrine, a practice need not be universally followed to qualify as custom; it need merely be generally and consistently practiced by a representative group of states capable of participating in the practice. And, in classic doctrine, to qualify as custom, practice must be backed by *opinio juris sive necessitatis*—the belief of states that the practice is pursued as a matter of legal right or obligation, not mere comity or convenience.

A. When Words Collide with Deeds

Thus, at least in principle, there is no reason why a customary norm cannot provide the controlling norm for a dispute, even though it conflicts with an earlier treaty norm. According to the American Law Institute, "A new rule of customary [international] law will supersede inconsistent obligations created by an earlier agreement if the parties so intend and the intention is clearly manifested."[1] We saw this, for example, when the 1958 Law of the Sea Conventions were superseded as states adopted 200-mile exclusive resource zones in the sea. Such supersession apparently can occur quickly. In the *North Sea Continental Shelf Cases,* the I.C.J. propounded what has been called the doctrine of "instant customary law."[2] The

Court said: "[T]he passage of only a short period of time is not necessarily, or of itself, a bar to the formation of a new rule of customary international law." Existing custom thus can be changed only by subsequent practice that is at the outset manifestly illegal—"a challenging theoretical problem," Josef Kunz famously wrote in 1953, which "has not as yet found a satisfactory solution."[3]

Nonetheless, the received wisdom is that subsequent, inconsistent custom has not supplanted pertinent provisions of the UN Charter. Some commentators have relied in part upon the Charter's status as a constitutive treaty in asserting its immunity from supersession by subsequent custom. Some have even argued that those portions of the Charter governing use of force represent a kind of supernorm, *jus cogens,* which can be modified only by a subsequent international law norm of the same character.[4] Some have suggested further that the state behavior in question is properly viewed not as custom but rather as a practice relevant to interpretation of a treaty. Some have pointed out that acts inconsistent with the Charter lack the required element of *opinio juris,* in that states have not claimed to act under the authority of a new rule, different from that prescribed by the Charter; rather, they invariably have claimed to act in accordance with the Charter. Finally, some have suggested that the argument that subsequent custom has superseded the Charter's use of force rules is no more persuasive than the contention that frequent crime has supplanted certain criminal laws.

These commentators are wrong. None of these arguments is persuasive.

First, the Charter is *not* a world constitution. If it were, many states, including the United States, probably would not have ratified it. The United States, for one, already has a Constitution. In some respects the Charter is indeed *sui generis:* It sets up institutions that, through the parties' consent, exercise authority over them. But there is no reason to view that characteristic, or the fact that the Charter creates a unitary administrative scheme, as somehow distinguishing the Charter from all other treaties in its relation to subsequent custom.*

---

*As Hinsley put it, modern men seem not to suspect "that a single administrative and technological framework for political action would not necessarily produce a single political system: a successful international organisation or a world state." F. H. Hinsley, *Power and the Pursuit of Peace: Theory and Practice in the History of Relations Between States* 7 (1963).

It is perfectly plausible that the international system could function efficiently if these normative provisions of the Charter were on the same footing as all other treaties with respect to the possibility of supersession. Portions of the Charter, important though they are, do not necessarily relate to its constitutional character. The provisions concerning use of force and human rights are not essential to the UN organization's core functions; similar provisions have in fact been included in other treaties relating to both subjects. Why should Article 2(4) of the Charter be regarded as more immune from supersession by custom than, say, the Kellogg-Briand Peace Pact?* Professor Schachter has written that "[t]he resistance of a group of States to a rule of law, if sustained by their conduct and a denial of the obligatory effect of the rule in question, may have the consequence of carving out an exception to that rule."[5] It is hard to see why that consequence should obtain with respect to a customary rule but not a treaty rule—or, for that matter, to see why it should be limited to "carving out an exception" rather than supersede the rule altogether.

The suggestion that custom cannot trump the Charter is belied by the Charter itself. The Charter's own nonsupersession provision, Article 103, exempts the Charter only from supersession by subsequent *treaties,* not from supersession by subsequent *customary* norms.[6] If the drafters of the Charter wished to attempt to insulate the Charter from supersession by custom, they surely would have included custom, with treaties, in Article 103. That they did not include custom in Article 103 implies a belief that custom should not or cannot be rendered ineffectual by a prior treaty provision. Article 38 of the Statute of the International Court of Justice lists custom after treaties as a source of authority, but there is no indication that that placement is intended to

---

*The infamously ineffectual Kellogg-Briand Peace Pact of 1928 purported to outlaw war. Its parties declared "that they condemn recourse to war for the solution of international controversies, and renounce it as an instrument of national policy in their relations with one another." Art. I, Treaty Providing for the Renunciation of War as an Instrument of National Policy, art. 1, done at Paris, Aug. 27, 1928, 46 Stat. 2343, T.S. No. 796, 2 Bevans 732, L.N.T.S. 57. Among its parties were (actually, *are*; the Pact is still in effect, and states continue to ratify it) the United States, the United Kingdom, Germany, France, Italy, the Soviet Union—and virtually all other belligerents in World War II.

imply a hierarchical ordering. By what logic can states be disabled from consenting to a new norm through custom rather than treaty? Customary law traditionally has been seen as preceding and legitimating treaty-made law. As Hans Kelsen wrote:

> One of the norms of international law created by custom authorizes the states to regulate their mutual relations by treaty. The reason for the validity of the legal norms of international law created by treaty is this custom-created norm. It is usually formulated in the sentence: *pacta sunt servanda.*[7]

Thus it would seem strange if the Charter or any other treaty were deemed resistant to supersession by custom.

The contention that Charter principles governing use of force are peremptory norms—*jus cogens**—is not compelling. The argument finds its most forceful expression in the American Law Institute's *Restatement:*

> Some rules of international law are recognized by the international community of states as peremptory, permitting no derogation. These rules prevail over and invalidate international agreements and other rules of international law in conflict with them. Such a peremptory norm is subject to modification only by a subsequent norm of international law having the same character. It is generally accepted that the principles of the United Nations Charter prohibiting use of force ... have the character of *jus cogens.*[8]

To find this comment in the normally cautious *Restatement* is surprising. The concept of *jus cogens* has emerged only recently[9] and is "hotly controverted."[10] The International Court of Justice, in the *North Sea Continental Shelf Cases*, pointedly declined to "enter into, still less pronounce upon any question of *jus cogens.*"[11] It has not been universally accepted, though it did find expression (over

---

*In fact, the argument is made that not one but two peremptory norms are implicated—those governing use of force and also self-determination. See Natalino Ronzitti, "Use of Force, Jus Cogens, and State Consents," in *The Current Legal Regulation of the Use of Force* 147, 149 (A. Cassese ed., 1986).

the opposition of the United States[12]) in the Vienna Convention on the Law of Treaties, which requires that a peremptory norm be "accepted and recognized by the international community of States as a whole"[13]—a standard more rigorous that the *Restatement*'s, which would require recognition only by the "international community of states...." If the test for initial recognition of the rule is indeed consent by most states—and it is, after all, state consent that holds the international legal system together*—the question arises: Why cannot a majority, in effect revoking its consent, be permitted to end or amend the rule? Why would not the emergence of such a modifying norm constitute one that "has the same character," since it would necessarily relate to the same subject matter? The concept of *jus cogens* is at odds with the basic supposition of customary international law that norms are a function of the will of states. The reliability of states' commitments in expressing that will is fundamental to stability in international relations.†

Moreover, substantial disagreement exists among scholars as to what norms are *jus cogens*.[14] In light of the uneven record of state compliance, on what basis can it be claimed that the rules of the Charter partake of this character? Under the principle of *jus cogens*, violations—acts in derogation of the norm—have no effect on the norm's validity. But, by that token, why should the Kellogg-Briand Peace Pact not also have been seen as *jus cogens*? If the argument is that the character of the norm precludes derogation, it should hardly matter that normative provisions happen to be placed among institutional provisions in the same treaty. As discussed later, proponents of broad Security Council power conveniently forget their affection for *jus cogens* when the issue is whether the *Security Council* can ride roughshod over the Charter's limits on its

---

*The doctrine of positivism provides the intellectual scaffolding for modern international law, and that doctrine, J. L. Brierly wrote, "teaches that international law is the sum of rules by which states have *consented* to be bound, and that nothing can be law to which they have not consented." J. L. Brierly, *The Law of Nations: An Introduction to the International Law of Peace* 51 (6th ed. 1963) (emphasis in original).

†The notion of *jus cogens*, as one commentator put it, is "a means of undermining the sanctity of the pledged word...perfectly adapted to the idiosyncrasies of a hypocritical age." Georg Schwarzenberger, "International Jus Cogens?" 43 *Tex. L. Rev.* 455, 477–78 (1965).

power. Why are the Charter's limits on *state* power to use force peremptory but not its limits on the Security Council's power to do so? Why should the Charter's limits on the right of the Security Council to use force—set out in Articles 2(7) and 39—not *also* be seen as *jus cogens,* since those provisions are, after all, part of the same regime for the centralization of power that subsumes Article 2(4)? Even if the concept of *jus cogens* is accepted and Article 2(4) is seen as a peremptory norm, a new norm permitting use of force to stop internal genocide would seemingly represent a norm of the same character. The prohibition against genocide is, it must be remembered, perhaps the norm most widely accepted as *jus cogens* by those who endorse the concept.[15]

Reliance upon *jus cogens* is one tactic of those striving to save the Charter from the conduct of noncompliant states. Another is that such states are merely "interpreting" the Charter. It is insisted that state behavior is properly viewed not as a subsequent, independent source of custom but, rather, as a *practice* relevant to interpretation of a treaty. But this contention is more assertion than argument. It derives from statements such as that made by Judge Jennings in the *Nicaragua Case,* that "the behaviour of [states which are parties to the Charter]...and the *opinio juris* which it might otherwise evidence, is surely explained by their being bound by the Charter itself."[16]

It is understandable why one might jump to the conclusion that at least some acts of parties to a treaty reflect their belief as to what the treaty means. Writing about the Geneva Conventions, Professor Theodor Meron has pointed out that "[a]cts concordant with the treaty obviously are indistinguishable from acts 'in the application of the Convention.'"[17] A state's decision makers have many motivations. Compliance with a treaty may or may not be one. But a state's behavior surely cannot be explained by its treaty obligations alone. The obligation imposed by Article 2(4) of the Charter on NATO's 19 member states does not explain their military attack against Yugoslavia; other factors, as I will suggest later, proved far more salient. There simply is no reason to assume that state conduct necessarily is caused by perceptions as to what a treaty permits or prohibits. States act for reasons altogether unrelated to their treaty obligations.

Another argument of the Charter's defenders is similar— namely, that states' intent not to establish a new customary norm at odds with the Charter is properly inferred from their unwillingness to acknowledge violation of a treaty.[18] "[T]he United States did not preach what it practiced," Henkin claimed; "it did not seek to reinterpret the law to weaken its restraints."[19] A variation on this theme states the argument even more strongly by claiming that states cannot be deemed to intend to establish a new customary norm unless they actually *deny explicitly* (in Schachter's words) "the obligatory effect of the rule in question." The *Nicaragua Case* provides an example of such reasoning (in answer to the argument that custom provided support for U.S. support for the *contras*):

> If a State acts in a way prima facie incompatible with a recognized rule, but defends its conduct by appealing to exceptions or justifications contained within the rule itself, then whether or not the State's conduct is in fact justifiable on that basis, the significance of the attitude is to confirm rather than to weaken the rule.[20]

The rule is, in other words—to paraphrase one of the prime proponents of the scholastic approach, Thomas Franck—"Break it *and* fake it."[21]

The inference of state approval is not warranted. That a state argues a rule to be inapplicable does not imply that the state acknowledges the rule's existence; why should a state take a needlessly confrontational stance in questioning the existence of a rule when the state regards the rule as irrelevant to the case at hand? States, like individuals, rarely admit to law violations. When charged with breaching the law, whether customary or treaty, they inevitably defend by arguing that they complied with the law, even though that argument may entail contortions to justify aberrant conduct. As Oscar Schachter has written, "every time a government uses force or responds to such use by others, it invokes the law along with considerations of morality and humanity."[22] Or, as Brierly puts it, "when a breach of international law is alleged by one party to a controversy, the act impugned is…always [defended] by attempting to prove that no rule has been violated."[23]

This should hardly be surprising. Confrontation is not seen by states as being in their interest. In most situations, little is to be gained through a frontal challenge to existing law. To do so could lead to broader disorder, which few states see as in their interest, as well as to condemnation and possible reprisals. So it is wrong to infer that a state supports a given rule from a simple claim of compliance—let alone from its unwillingness to explicitly admit to noncompliance. Such a claim may connote approval of the rule, but it may also signify a rational desire not to incur unnecessary political or diplomatic penalties. Or a claim of compliance may merely represent an effort to shore up support. In many democratic states, political support for a given initiative would not be enhanced if the government were seen as thumbing its nose at international law—even though the legal consequences of violating use-of-force rules, as the United States showed following the *Nicaragua* judgment, are nonexistent. "[T]he legal justifications offered by states," Schachter properly notes, "are often perceived as rationalizations contrived after the decision to intervene has been made."[24]

The purpose of international law's insistence upon flat-out disputation of a disliked rule is to get at the noncomplying state's *psychology*—to ensure that the recalcitrant state in fact *believes* that it had the right to do what it did. But the state's action itself answers that concern. As Weisburd writes, "the very fact of the contrary practice provides evidence on that score ... [A]ction unaccompanied by any explanation, against the background assumption that restriction is not presumed, [is itself] evidence that the acting state sees no restriction affecting the action in question."[25]

To require that states must challenge existing law to establish a new rule is to misperceive state behavior on another level. If states legally justify their behavior at all,* they typically do so without specificity, so it is impossible to know their actual intent—to know whether they are challenging an existing rule or proposing the formulation of a new one. During NATO's action against Yugoslavia, for example, British Prime Minister Tony Blair repeatedly proclaimed that NATO was acting in accordance with international law.[26] NATO's "strategic concept," adopted at the time of its fiftieth anniversary celebration in Washington, reaffirmed that future action would be carried out consistent with international law. [27] But what *belief* reasonably can be inferred from such statements? That action was or is permitted by the old noninterventionist regime of the Charter? That the Security Council had approved?

---

* "Nations do not regularly explain the legal basis of their actions, nor is it clear how to determine the normative belief of hundreds of states, many of whom have never had the opportunity or need to express their opinion on a particular principle." J. Patrick Kelly, "The Twilight of Customary International Law," 40 *Va. J. Int'l. L.* 449, 470 (2000).

Or that a new regime tolerant of intervention is or should be put in place? In truth, there is no principled reason for inferring one *opinio juris* over another. Equally plausible—perhaps more plausible—is a third possibility: that state officials never really decided *what* they believed the rule was or should be; that they simply acted to advance the state's interest as they saw it; that they made a vague, *pro forma* reference to international law because the appearance of legality further advanced that state interest; and that they avoided specificity because a particularized interpretation of the rule could only limit their own freedom to act in the future. In the case of Kosovo, Blair may have concluded (quite rightly) that NATO was not acting at odds with international law inasmuch as international legal principles concerning intervention were a mess and provided no hard and fast rule that could be breached. That he declined to spell that out hardly "reinforces" existing rules, such as they were.

Finally, classic international law is arbitrary in its assignment of the burden of going forward. International law, again, infers from a state's silence in the face of noncompliant conduct that the state does not intend to create a new rule—that it continues to consent to the old rule that it has broken. If State A intervenes in State B and says nothing, A's silence, in other words, is seen as agreement with the prohibition against intervention. International law also insists that a state's consent to a newly emerging norm may be inferred from its silence. But why not infer the opposite? Why not assume that when a state *silently* breaks the law that it disagrees with the law? Why not assume that if a state says nothing in the face of a newly emerging inchoate norm that it in fact *disagrees* with the old norm and does *not* consent to be bound by it? States have, after all, never *said* that their silence should be construed as international law construes it. Judge Sofaer summed up the scholastics' acquiescence argument:

> [L]et Acheson, Dulles, Kissinger, Shultz, Baker, and Albright do as they will pursuing their Presidents' policies, so long as they and their lawyers do not attempt to question use-of-force rules as these professors see them, so that someday those rules might actually become operative. This is a poor formula for an effective or meaningful rule of law in any area of human activity, let alone one in which law is ultimately the product of state practice, not professorial pronouncement.[28]

It is, in short, a conceit of customary international law that a state's legally self-serving explanation of its own behavior inevitably reflects that state's agreement or disagreement with an existing rule. The conceit produces a self-validating international legal system, auto-immune from external data that might challenge its foundational assumptions. The system is blind to the reality that indifference to a rule, cloaked in traditional diplomatic niceties, often sounds the same as acquiescence or even acceptance. As Mark Weisburd observes, "to insist that the only legally significant element...is the violator's dishonest labeling of its action is to reduce the evaluation of legal rules to a matter of word games, unrelated to any effort to shape conduct."[29] Yet international lawyers pine for better ways to get "into the heads" of state decision makers, believing that if they can only find out what decision makers *really think* international law is, the problem will be solved. In his treatise on customary international law, Anthony D'Amato discusses at length the practicality of Myres McDougal's suggestion that decision makers be subject to "mass interview" using "current social science techniques" to identify the true content of international law.[30] The consistory is flatly unwilling to confront the possibility that many of those decision makers, if at all candid, would reply "Who cares?" or "There's no such thing." It is no accident that, as Louis Henkin put it, "the student of foreign affairs is skeptical about international law.... When he thinks of law at all, he sees it in the main as an esoteric subject for academic speculation by wishful professors, with little relevance to affairs between nations."[31] Doctrinally, international law reassures itself that they *must* care. "[T]he traditional view," D'Amato himself acknowledges, "seems to depend upon exact motivational analysis of state behavior."[32] But states' motivations—in reality, of course, the motivations of their decision makers—often are multiple, overlapping, contradictory, unarticulated, and undiscoverable. What quality of rules could a system reliant upon such premises reasonably be expected to produce?

It might be objected that the tendency of decision makers to avoid acknowledging law violations shows that use-of-force law in fact has some "bite" after all. Not so: This tendency derives from considerations that are diplomatic and political rather than legal. Diplomatic habits of mind form over long periods of time. Patterns of practice emerge from conduct that takes place within all the sub-regimes, not simply that governing use of force. It should hardly be surprising that decision makers accustomed to dealing with matters where law counts might stick with the same low-risk rhetoric when dealing with interventionism. Intervention occurs infrequently in the lives of decision makers—too seldom to justify an all-new rhetorical wardrobe. This is true even though, as the *Nicaragua Case* revealed, openly acknowledging a violation of the use-of-force subregime—which American officials in effect did on several occasions—can *legally* cost a state nothing. Confrontational costs in such a case are of course real, but those costs are, again, political and diplomatic, arising wholly apart from costs that may be incurred by virtue of supposed law violations.

The ultimate argument of the Charter's defenders is that subsequent custom can no more supersede the Charter than murder or rape can supersede the statutory prohibition against these acts. Oscar Schachter makes this point forcefully:

> Some commentators contend that the widespread and consistent violations of Article 2(4) constitute practice sufficient to supersede the Charter rules and their customary law counterpart. This argument is no more convincing than the assertion that if a large number of rapes and murders are not punished, the criminal laws are supplanted and legal restraints disappear for everyone.[33]

In fact, a critical difference exists between individuals and states that engage in unlawful conduct. States are lawmakers; individuals are not. Under the rules of the international legal system, states are empowered through their actions to create binding norms of customary international law. Under the rules of no domestic legal system are private individuals so empowered. Widespread and consistent state declarations that were at odds with the 1958 Law of the Seas Convention thus effectively superseded that treaty.

Schachter's real objection seems to be that however widespread noncompliant behavior may be, it cannot be regarded as law. But rape and murder are not good examples: Because of the centrality of these prohibitions to the criminal code, they would be among the last crimes to occur in sufficiently large numbers to justify a conclusion of desuetude, which is discussed later. A more reasonable example would be an offense where widespread violation is conceivable, such as the now repealed 55-mile-per-hour speed limit. What really was the law when the federal highway speed limit was 55? Of course, the statutory speed limit remained 55, even though everyone went at least 60. But if one asked "How fast can I go?" would the correct answer indeed be "55"? That really is the issue. As discussed later, Schachter regards law as something that circumscribes discretion, and it simply cannot confidently be asserted that the unenforced 55-mile-an-hour speed limit circumscribed discretion.

Schachter goes on to argue that "hundreds of political conflicts exist, and many if not most actions taken by states do not constitute illegal uses of force. Therefore, to conclude that some violations constitute 'practice accepted as law' gives 'practice' a peculiar meaning, quite different from 'widespread and uniform usage.'"[34] It is of course true that only illegal uses of force can constitute superseding custom; a legal act is consistent with the law and supersedes nothing. But the realist argument is not that "most actions taken by states constitute illegal uses of force"—which would be irrelevant even under international law's tilted analysis. The argument is that *many* such actions have taken place. As noted later, the conclusion is incontrovertible that Article 2(4) has been subject to widespread and repeated violation by a large and representative group of states. And that, I suggest, is legally significant.

B. Subsequent "Treaty" Practice—or Inconsistent Custom?

To reiterate, practice is seen by international lawyers as relevant in two different contexts—to inform the meaning of a treaty, and also as a component of custom. The difference is important. It goes to the question whether states see their obligation as stemming from a "new" custom or a potentially anachronistic treaty. Sorting out one from the other often depends upon contextual factors not easily quantified or even identified. These include elements such as the general state of relations between the treaty partners, whether the obligations imposed by the treaty have proven controversial domestically, and whether the treaty merely confirmed a prior pattern of dealing between the parties. In most instances, it is virtually impossible to determine for which of the two purposes state practice is pertinent. When state officials are silent with respect to a colorably applicable treaty, for example, and strong domestic opposition has developed to a given interpretation of a treaty, there is no basis in logic for assuming that state action evidences adherence to that interpretation even if that action is merely consistent with it. Here again, traditional international law doctrine superimposes a factitious mentalist template over state conduct—a presumed motive on the part of state decision makers—that conveniently provides coherence to the law's self-validating structure. But, as elsewhere, state motives are too diverse to permit facile inference and categorization. State officials may have acted utterly without regard to any treaty obligation and solely to advance an independent interest. If so, those acts fall more properly into the realm of custom as an independent source of authority—which is attended by its own conceptual difficulties. With respect to norms governing use of force, as D'Amato has suggested, at one level the distinction makes little substantive difference. "[S]tate practice since 1945—whether considered as simply formative of customary international law," he wrote, "or as constituting interpretation of the Charter under the subsequent-practice rule—has drastically altered the meaning and content of Article 2(4)."[35] At another level, however, the distinction is critical, for the question, again, is whether states continue to view the Charter's core provision—the "principal norm of contemporary international law"[36]—as binding law. If the Charter's use-of-force regime is no longer law, that's worth knowing.

C. Difficulties with the Concept of Custom

Thus far I have, for purposes of this analysis, accepted the core notion of custom uncritically, as international lawyers do, to show another, unseen dimension of the rules that NATO violated. Before proceeding further, however, it is appropriate to look more closely at the way customary international law is made with respect to use of force by states. The purpose here is to consider whether the *product* of that process is properly viewed as obligatory on states, including coalitions of states such as NATO. If the law is to be regarded as obligatory, it must provide one "best" answer. If the law's methodology provides more than one answer that is equally plausible, it provides no answer. If it provides no answer, as will be seen, a state is free to act as it wishes.

1. "Observance" of the Law: Empirical Problems with the Notion of State Practice

International law, it repeatedly is said, is generally observed. The proposition, indeed, typically is taken as an article of faith by international lawyers. Recent scholarship on compliance jumps quickly over the question *whether* international law is observed and proceeds to analyze *why* states comply.[37]

Perhaps international law is generally observed, by which is meant, presumably, that states act in ways consistent with its requirements and do not act in ways inconsistent with its prohibitions. But an examination of precisely what is meant by state "acts" and state "nonacts" reveals that the claim of purposive compliance is difficult to verify, one way or the other. That difficulty calls into question the soundness of the rules governing intervention that that process has produced—whether use-of-force practice is examined for the purpose of illuminating the meaning of a treaty, or as a component of custom.

a) The requirements of customary international law: Elasticity of a state "act."   On its face, the methodology of customary international law seems seductively straightforward. One merely identifies what states do, lines up the precedents, and inductively describes the result—which is then used as a rule against which the lawfulness of future state acts can be measured deductively. How states actually act provides the database from which it is inferred how states are required to act.

Would that it were so simple.

Set aside the conclusory leap from *is* to *ought* (a problem that has vexed philosophers for centuries but causes international lawyers little worry today*). The inescapable problem with the methodology of customary international law is that it provides, and can provide, no guidance in deciding upon the level of generality or particularity with which a given state act is described. Facts constituting the precedent can arbitrarily be described broadly or narrowly. No principle exists for separating text from context.[†] NATO's action against Yugoslavia is an example. What precisely

---

*See, for example, Hans Kelsen, *Principles of International Law* 20 (1952) ("States ought to behave as they have customarily behaved.")

[†]As Tom Farer put it, "The problem for practice claimed to have ripened into law is ... the complex, time-bound context of each of the precedents that constitute the practice. A new case is a unique pattern of facts (described in sufficient detail, of course, all cases are unique) arising in a new context .... " Tom Farer, "Conclusion: What Do International Lawyers Do When They Talk about Ethnic Violence and Why Does it Matter?" in *International Law and Ethnic Conflict* 326, 330 (D. Wippman ed., 1998).

was the "act" that NATO performed? What precedent was created? A moment's reflection reveals a number of possible formulations. Let us state only a few, from broad to narrow, adding elements as the description is further particularized:

- Use of force without prior Security Council authorization.
- Use of force without prior Security Council authorization **for the purpose of stopping genocide.**
- Use of force without prior Security Council authorization **against a nondemocracy** for the purpose of stopping genocide.
- Use of force without prior Security Council authorization **by a military alliance of democracies** against a nondemocracy for the purpose of stopping genocide.
- Use of force without prior Security Council authorization by a **50-year-old** military alliance of democracies against a nondemocracy for the purpose of stopping genocide.
- **Use of air power** without prior Security Council authorization by a 50-year-old military alliance of democracies against a nondemocracy for the purpose of stopping genocide.

Which of the preceding possibilities represents a "correct" or "accurate" or "true" description of what occurred? The answer, of course, is that each does. Each account is equally accurate; there is no one, "true" formulation of the precedent.* The precedent does not exist "out there;" it is a construct of the mind.

This simple demonstration may be taken as implying a general failing of custom as a principled, nonarbitrary source of law, but it is not. The failing is a failing of custom as a source of *international* law.† It is a failing of the *international* system in particular because

---

*This may be one reason why, in Thucydides' account of a famous peace negotiation, the Athenians quickly brushed off the Melians' suggestion that a precedent legitimating aggression would, sooner or later, come back to haunt Athens. "This," they replied, "is a risk that we are content to undertake." Thucydides, *History of the Peloponnesian War*, ch. 17. Of course, the Athenians may also have calculated—perhaps like NATO contemplating intervention in Kosovo—that their adversaries would not soon be in a position to avail themselves of *any* precedent, broad or narrow.

† The weakness of custom as a source of authority is particularly pertinent in the use-of-force subregime, because that subregime is particularly dependent

the international system, unlike domestic legal systems, lacks an authoritative interpreter of the law.*

There is no final arbiter of the scope of the NATO precedent. Contrast the use of custom in domestic legal systems, such as the United States, where a court determines authoritatively what facts comprise the precedents on which it will rely. Whether one sees international law as law or nonlaw because no such final arbiter exists is another question; the point here is simply that it's all in the premises: (1) there exists no international institutional structure for determining the scope of a historical precedent; (2) determining the scope of such a precedent is necessary for describing state behavior; and (3) without a nonarbitrary way to describe state behavior, no nonarbitrary rule can be identified. A state confronted with a string of such elastic "precedents" can therefore play them like an accordion to compose virtually any tune it desires.† "The past is infinitely various," writes Michael Howard, a prominent military historian. It is "an inexhaustible storehouse of events from which we can prove anything or its contrary ... . The trouble is that there is no such thing as 'history.' History is what historians write ... ."[38] Of course, they can't change what actually happened. But like lawyers, they can *select,* and it is their *selection* of facts in describing the given incident that tilt history as well as law one way or the other.

b) The prohibitions of customary international law: State nonacts as acts. To international law scholars, to do nothing is to do something. The requirements and prohibitions of which customary

---

continued

upon customary norms. In other subregimes, such as those concerning international trade or civil aviation, norms are primarily treaty-based.

*As Thomas Franck graphically put it, "In the absence of some universally credible fact-determination procedures, the effort to establish whether a use of force is illegal under Article 2(4)... is stymied by contradictory allegations of fact by the parties to the dispute and their allies. It is rather as if the law were to leave to the two drivers in a motor vehicle collision the sole responsibility for apportioning liability, helped only by the unruly crowd gathered around them at the scene of the accident." Thomas M. Franck, "Who Killed Article 2(4)?" 64 *Am. J. Int'l L.* 809, 817 (1973).

†For one of the more creative efforts to overcome these difficulties, see W. Michael Reisman, "International Incidents: Introduction to a New Genre in the Study of International Law," 10 *Yale J. Int'l L.* 1 (1984).

international law consists are inferred both from states' acts and nonacts. Two difficulties inhere in the methodology used to infer prohibitions. One is empirical, the other theoretical.

The empirical problem is that, at least in some circumstances, state silence or inaction connotes nothing. Classic international law doctrine infers from state inaction an intent to conform to a preexisting prohibition. The observation of J. L. Brierly typifies the thinking of international lawyers: "[T]he law is normally observed because, as we shall see, the demands that it makes on states are generally not exacting and, on the whole states find it convenient to observe it … . The laws of peace and the great majority of treaties are on the whole regularly observed in the daily intercourse of states."[39] If states have regularly declined to perform an act, in other words, a given state is prohibited from performing that act, *and the reason that it declines to act is that it is prohibited from doing so.* The assertion of Louis Henkin is, once again, representative of the thinking of international law scholars. "[T]he United States had a good record of compliance with the law of the Charter," he writes. "In general, it refrained from the use of force even in circumstances in which, in earlier times, that might have been a serious option."[40] In earlier times, the United States might have invaded Russia, as its expeditionary force did following World War I. Now it does not. Is the reason that it does not its desire to comply with the Charter? Is it possible that a bit more is going on here—such as the 20,000 nuclear warheads still in the Russian stockpile? No; to Henkin, because the United States "did not seek to reinterpret the law of the Charter so as to weaken its restraints there were no compelling grounds for questioning the commitment of the United States to the law forbidding the use of force."[41]

But correlation is not causation. That a state acts or does not act in a certain way is not necessarily attributable to international law.* Identical past state acts can be a product of different causes.[42] As Jack Goldsmith and Eric Posner put it, "[s]ometimes what appears to be acting in conformity with a customary international law norm may actually be a *coincidence of interest* … a behavioral regularity that occurs when nations follow their immediate self-interest

---

*As Nigel Purvis observed, the fact that states "[o]n occasion … seem to act [as] if they actually were 'complying' with international law" does not mean that they actually intend to obey it. Nigel Purvis, "Critical Legal Studies in International Law," 32 *Harv. Int'l L. J.* 81, 110 (1991).

independent of any consideration of the action or interests of other nations."[43] One state may decline to perform a given act because it is too poor to do so; another because its population is opposed to doing so; another because it benefits from another state's already having done so. To view "coincidence of interest situations" as "examples of norm-following" is an "error of induction."[44] It might be said that the added requirement of *opinio juris* precludes international law from mistaking a series of such acts as obligatory norms. But *opinio juris* is often ignored* and precisely the same sorts of inferences are made in establishing *opinio juris* as in establishing state practice—and those inferences are drawn from data that typically are used interchangeably in establishing either *opinio juris* or state practice itself. The Nuremberg tribunal, for example, reached conclusions about customary international law without ever examining state practice, instead looking only at state declarations.[45] The International Court of Justice followed a similar approach in the *Nicaragua Case*. "The World Court in the *Nicaragua* case," D'Amato wrote, "gets it completely backwards." Rather than looking first to state conduct to see whether there is in fact practice that could qualify as custom, the Court turned first to considering whether states had "accepted" the rule in question— finding affirmatively that they had done so and that the requirement of *opinio juris* was therefore met—while looking "only vaguely" at what states had actually done.[46] Thomas Franck expressed similar criticism of the Court's sloppiness in dealing with *opinio juris* in the *Nicaragua Case*. "What," he asked, "of the need to test *opinio juris* against state conduct, as, for example, in respect of the principle of the nonuse of force? While the majority opinion conceded that 'examples of trespass against this principle are not infrequent,' it still concluded that the rule nevertheless is part and parcel of customary international law. Why? The Court speaks vaguely of the existence of *opinio juris* and 'substantial practice'— but adds nothing more specific."[47] The Court's methodology is to *infer* purpose from silence or, as in *Nicaragua,* to detach purpose from (unestablished) practice and then to *substitute* purpose for practice. But there is no reason to infer any motive when a state says nothing about why it did nothing. Inaction coupled with

---

*See, for example, Louis Henkin's claim that the prohibition against use of force is generally observed, which discussed below.

silence means nothing. It is incoherent to talk of a state's purpose with respect to something it never did.

Similarly, there simply is no reason to view a nondatum as a datum—let alone to construct an entire theory of law based upon nondata. In U.S. domestic jurisprudence, the courts would give short shrift to the argument that legislative *inaction* somehow constitutes legislative *action*.* A court would "walk on quicksand" to equate the two, Justice Jackson wrote for the United States Supreme Court.[48] But international law says the opposite, in a linguistic sleight-of-hand that is part of its scholastic methodology of auto-validation: International law construes state *in*action as state *action* and regards state behavior that is merely *consistent with* a preexisting rule as reinforcing that rule—or actually as *creating* the rule (if the behavior is early enough). It is only by considering "the U.S. decision not to commit aggression against Canada" (to use Louis Henkin's example) as a state act that it is possible to aggregate such acts so as to accumulate a sufficient number to claim custom. But of course the United States did not act; there is no nonagressive behavior on the part of the United States vis-à-vis Canada from which to infer anything. As D'Amato put it, "At every moment in time, any state is *not* acting with respect to innumerable situations"[49]—and, one might add, for innumerable reasons, including "comity, courtesy, policy, disinterest, or sheer inertia."[50] It beggars logic to presume that the reason for unexplained state inaction (and it almost always is unexplained) is necessarily international law. Yet, to make their system work, international law scholars are willing to accord opposites the same meaning—which helps explain Tallyrand's dry observation: "Non-intervention is a word with the same meaning as intervention."[51]

---

*The "vast differences," Justice Rutledge said, "between legislating by doing nothing and legislating by positive enactment" made it improper to give effect to inaction. *Cleveland v. United States*, 329 U.S. 14, 22 (1946) (Rutledge, J., concurring). This principle of statutory construction is elementary. "The first question," Reed Dickerson wrote, "is whether legislative silence can constitute effective legislative action. It seems obvious that a legislature cannot legislate effectively by not legislating at all." Reed Dickerson, *The Interpretation and Application of Statutes* 181 (1975).

2. *The Illusion of* Opinio Juris

International law does not regard practice, standing alone, as constituting custom. Practice must be accompanied by a mental element, a belief on the part of states that the practice is followed as a matter of juridical obligation. The presence of *opinio juris* supposedly serves to distinguish norms that have the character of legal rules from mere habits of courtesy or comity. *Opinio juris* theoretically provides the vital link to the claim that the community of nations *intends* a particular practice to bind its members. It is for this reason that international lawyers examine "the reaction of the international community" after an incident occurs—the objective is to see what rule, if any, the international community regarded as law. And it is for this reason that international lawyers look to a state's *explanation* when it breaches an existing rule: Did the state intend that its act represent the first step in the formation of a new customary norm, or did the state excuse its conduct by claiming compliance with—and thus reaffirming the applicability of—an old rule? Oscar Schachter writes that "such violations as do occur are not 'accepted as law.' On the contrary, in virtually every case one state's use of force has been condemned by large numbers of states as violating existing fundamental law."[52]

But the notion of the international community's "intent" is pure fiction. The international community is not a unitary actor. It is difficult enough to determine what officials in one state "were thinking" when it undertook a given action.* There is no reason to infer the intent of the "community" from the intent of a handful of its members. The Indian delegate to the United Nations stated categorically that the Security Council does not represent the wider global community; the Council's membership is unrepresentative, he said, and its methods of work do not welcome or accept the views of the

---

* Even commetators generally comfortable with international law's traditional methodology have had difficulty with the glib treatment of *opinio juris* by the International Court. In the *Nicaragua Case*, the Court asserted that *opinio juris* may be "deduced" from "the attitude of the Parties...." Military and Paramilitary Activities (Nicar. v. U.S.), 1986 I.C.J. 14, 99–100, ¶ 188 (Nov. 26). "What," Thomas Franck asked, "does the Court mean by 'attitude'?" Thomas M. Franck, "Some Observations on the I.C.J.'s Procedural and Substantive Innovations," 81 *Am. J. Int'l L.* 116, 118 (1987).

wider membership.[53] "At most," Patrick Kelly writes, "acquiescence furnishes some evidence of the attitude of a few states. It is insufficient to demonstrate general acceptance unless the vast majority of states have failed to protest when a norm has been asserted against their immediate interests."[54] Nor is there any possible way of discovering what governmental officials in remote and diverse nations have "in mind" when a given event occurs.* One hundred ninety nations surely have no single, unified opinion formed in reaction to multiple and divergent news accounts that reach them concerning "what happened." Even if all nations agreed upon the same version of the facts, differing ideas and beliefs would cause those facts to be viewed dramatically differently. The prism of culture draws an ever-shifting line between text and context. To think that one can somehow discover objectively how "the facts" of an event were perceived by the "international community" represents breathtaking naïveté. The possibility of identifying a common denominator of agreement runs aground on the shoals of language and culture: Even if the verbal reactions of state officials could be had, and even if it were possible to infer from their rhetoric their true, heartfelt "reaction," verbal formulations inevitably differ so much that attempts to classify the data of such a survey would necessarily be enormously subjective and imprecise. Nonetheless, so fixated are international lawyers on the "reaction" of the "international community" that some actually go so far as to excuse unequivocal law violation if the "community" fails to condemn it.†

Nor is it realistic to expect state officials to "fess up" and acknowledge illegality when they act at odds with a disliked rule. International law, as discussed earlier, facilely assumes that a nation can and will simply assert its disagreement with the law when that nation finds its own interests or the command of justice to conflict.

---

*It has been 70 years since Max Radin debunked the myth of "the intention of the legislature," but international law has not, alas, caught up with modern analysis of domestic collective entities. See Max Radin, "Statutory Interpretation," 43 *Harv. L. Rev.* 863 (1930).

†See, for example, Mary Ellen O'Connell, "The UN, NATO, and International Law After Kosovo," 22 *Hum. Rts. Q.* 57, 68 (2000) ("To the extent that the international community has not criticized or opposed the Security Council's conduct, it should probably not be viewed as *ultra vires* or unlawful.").

"Of course," Louis Henkin writes, "a nation may assert that the law is or should be different, but it takes the risk that, unless its assertion is accepted, it will face the consequences of violation."[55] That is correct—and the rational course more often than not is to avoid incurring that risk, since the long-term payoff in law change is speculative, and the short-term payoff in penalty avoidance is certain. Moreover, it is a myth that states can always challenge the law and seek to change it. Custom forms too slowly for that process to work. By the time another state might act to challenge the law, penalties often will have been imposed, thus further deterring additional would-be challengers. Many customary norms are thus in fact static and for all practical purposes unchangeable, because the acts that comprise the custom simply fall too far apart temporally.

Nonetheless, with respect to incident after incident, international lawyers continue to look for the "international reaction." Faced more often than not with a dearth of data, they continue to infer community intent from a handful of its members, and they continue to infer a given member's intent from its unwillingness to act irrationally. Their theories need to be held up to the light of hard evidence.* To do so will entail disaggregating the international community and getting behind the fanciful notion of its unitary "intent." It will require, then, an empirical assessment of the actual record of state compliance with the international ban on intervention. Before examining that data, however, it is useful to conclude with a closer look at the issue of causation.

_____

* Hinsley, as usual, is on point:

> The seventeenth-century proposals, like the earlier ones, were advocated in a world that was quite different from the modern world.... We have not been content with ignoring the historical context of theories propounded long ago and with distorting the views of their critics. We have displayed a marked reluctance to test the theories against the actual development and operation of the system of relations between states in modern times. It is against the dangers and deficiencies of this system that these antiquated theories are still invoked. What those dangers and deficiencies are we take on trust, and whether the theories are even applicable to them is a question we never stop consider.

F. H. Hinsley, *Power and the Pursuit of Peace: Theory and Practice in the History of Relations Between States* 3–4 (1963).

Louis Henkin has taken the lead in arguing that "the norm against the unilateral national use of force has survived."[56] Reviewing the record, Henkin insists that "nations have not been going to war" and that "unilateral uses of force have been only occasional, brief, limited."[57] The prohibition against intervention, "seriously breached in several instances, has undoubtedly deterred intervention in many other instances."[58] "In any event, whatever the reasons, the fact is that the law against the unilateral use of force is commonly observed."[59] "The law works."[60] Henkin proceeds to give an example: U.S. refusal to proceed to "eliminate" or "displace" Fidel Castro at the Bay of Pigs.

> Surely, the statesmen who made the decision to limit U.S. participation in that enterprise, and refrain from attempting it again, decided that the national interest in maintaining legal obligations and avoiding the consequences of violation outweighed the interest in displacing Castro.[61]

Does the law "work?" Was the law "surely" the reason for leaving Castro in place? The law might or might not work, but one cannot reasonably infer that it does work—that it is "commonly observed"—for the reasons given by Henkin. The proposition that "nations have not been going to war" is false. The number of times that armed force has been used since 1945 (detailed below) in violation of the Charter is significant. Even if states' collective inaction has been consistent with the Charter, only by ruling out the possibility of contrary or irrelevant motive ("whatever the reasons") can one infer an intent to comply with the law. Potential causes of state inaction are countless. "Surely" the decision not to invade Cuba and eliminate Castro in 1961 did not derive solely from the proscription of Article 2(4); might the fear of provoking a nuclear exchange with the Soviet Union, or souring relations with other Latin American countries, or generating domestic opposition, have played a slight role in the decision?* Henkin presents no evidence to support the claim that the law "has undoubtedly deterred intervention." Nor could he adduce such evidence: State behavior, like

---

*In fact, as the Church Committee later revealed, no fewer than eight times following the Bay of Pigs did the U.S. attempt to assassinate Castro—in clear violation of the Charter.

human behavior, is far too complex to permit such facile assumptions of causation. But it is not even clear that Henkin is *open to* empirical data concerning the level of state compliance with Article 2(4). Henkin responded candidly to Franck's 1970 obituary for Article 2(4):* "For me, if Article 2(4) were indeed dead," Henkin wrote, "I should have to conclude that it rules—not mocks us—from the grave."[62]

Before concluding this chapter, it is important to note that traditional international law has a doctrine that captures the process by which a treaty is superseded by subsequent custom. That doctrine is called "desuetude." Considered in conjunction with three related doctrines—instant custom, *non liquet,* and the freedom principle—the concept of desuetude suggests that, even if traditional international law analysis were accepted on its own terms, a treaty becomes a dead letter when violation reaches a certain point.

D. Desuetude, Instant Custom, Non Liquet, *and the Freedom Principle*

The concept of desuetude describes the process by which subsequent custom or practice supplants a treaty norm, such as Article 2(4) of the Charter. The notion is captured by the maxim *leges non solum suffragio legislatoris set etiam tacito sonsense omnium per desuetudinem abrogentur*—roughly, "laws may be abrogated not only by a vote of legislators, but also by passive agreement through custom." The idea traces to Roman law, which recognized that a statute could be rendered void by lack of enforcement over a given period.[63] Hans Kelsen considered desuetude the "negative legal effect of custom."[64] The theory, equally applicable to prior treaties as to prior statutes, is that if the written instrument derived force by virtue of public acceptance, inconsistent custom must be given effect by the same principle.[65]

Still, the concept of desuetude is controversial, and for understandable reasons. Custom inconsistent with a treaty constitutes, at least initially, a violation of the treaty; desuetude seems to undermine the norm of *pacta sunt servanda.* Desuetude serves ultimately to

---

*See Thomas M. Franck, "Who Killed Article 2(4)?" 64 *Am. J. Int'l L.* 809 (1970).

legitimate the very acts that the treaty was intended to guard against. A number of delegates to the UN's 1968 Conference on the Law of Treaties, which produced the Convention on the Law of Treaties,[66] expressed such concerns in voting to strike from the Convention an article that would have incorporated notions of desuetude.[67] An earlier version of the article would have recognized that a treaty may be modified by "the subsequent emergence of a new rule of customary law relating to matters dealt with in the treaty and binding upon all the parties."[68] Explaining the proposed rule, the Commission commented that "in the application of a treaty account must at any time be taken of the 'evolution of the law.'"[69] This provision was eliminated from the article that was stricken in 1968, however, on the ground that the "question formed part of the general topic of the relation between customary norms and treaty norms which is too complex for it to be safe to deal only with one aspect of it in the present article."[70] When finally stricken, Article 38 set forth a one-sentence rule: "A treaty may be modified by subsequent practice in the application of the treaty establishing the agreement of the parties to modify its provisions."[71]

It is clear from the 1968 debate, however, that Article 38 was *not* stricken because the majority rejected the realism underlying the concept. The delegate from Italy, for example, stressed that that Article merely "reflected a legal fact that had always existed. International law," he said, "was not a slave to formalism and by reason of its nature must adapt itself to practical realities." He pointed out that a "glance at history could only make one thankful that, in certain cases, practice had modified treaties, which might otherwise have had tragic consequences."[72] Others expressed concern that the Article was added at the last minute and was inartfully drafted. The Israeli delegate did not question that the rule spelled out in the Article in fact existed in international law, but thought it covered by other articles.[73] The Swiss delegate stated flatly that the Article "was in conformity with international law … ."[74] It is hard to answer the argument of the delegate from Argentina: If the parties agreed to apply a treaty in a manner "different from that laid down in its provisions, where was the violation?"[75] The best conclusion seems to be that of the reporters of the American Law Institute's *Restatement (Third) of the Foreign Relations Law of the United States.* Desuetude, they wrote, is accepted in modern international law as applying to unenforced treaties or provisions of treaties.[76] If the rationale for law is consent, the changed consent of the parties must govern, whether it be expressed in the form of a new treaty that supercedes an older treaty or a new custom that supercedes an older treaty.

Though "desuetude" is not always so labeled, the doctrine is no stranger to domestic jurisprudence. "[T]here are times," Alexander Bickel wrote, "when law does not gain general consent merely by virtue of having been authoritatively pronounced, and lacking such consent it cannot be effective … . [T]he law may stay on the books for a while, it may even be observed in some parts … but if it is substantially abandoned in practice, that in the end is what really matters."[77]

There are reasons to give the doctrine even more weight in international law than it is given in domestic law. It might be argued that it makes little sense to think that the law prohibited NATO from doing what it did, but that NATO's very action made that same action lawful. Nonetheless, traditional international law principles suggest that a customary norm can quickly become inoperative in the face of massive noncompliance by powerful states. William W. Bishop argued that the acts of powerful states in the formation of a custom would be regarded as more significant than the acts of small states.[78] "[A] single precedent," Gilberto Amado wrote, "could be sufficient to create international custom."[79] Brierly believed that the customary norm of national sovereignty over airspace took effect "at the moment the 1914 war broke out."[80] In the *North Sea Continental Shelf Cases,* the I.C.J. propounded what has been called the doctrine of "instant customary law." The Court said: "[T]he passage of only a short period of time is not necessarily, or of itself, a bar to the formation of a new rule of customary international law."* Henkin himself has seemed to give weight to the notion of instant custom with respect to use of force. "Military intervention in civil war was not acceptable under traditional international law," he writes, "but that law may never have recovered from the wounds it suffered at many hands during the Spanish Civil War."[81] The law of Article 2(4), I will suggest, has not recovered from the wounds it suffered at many hands during the Kosovo War.

---

*The Court did indicate, however, that state practice "should have been both extensive and virtually uniform … and should have occurred in such a way as to show a general recognition that a rule of law or legal obligation is involved." 1969 I.C.J. 43.

One might reasonably conclude, therefore, that if massive violation does not actually *supplant* a preexisting treaty or customary norm, at a minimum such violation would create a state of uncertainty as to what the law is. *Non liquet* is another concept that goes back to Roman law. *Non liquet* means "it is not clear." The doctrine of *non liquet* refers, today, to an insufficiency in the law, to the conclusion that the law does not permit deciding a case one way or the other.[82] "Over time," Daniel Bodansky explains, "rules of the game have emerged through convergent practices (custom) and explicit agreement, bringing areas of international life within the rule of law. But, often, states differ and no rule gains acceptance one way or the other."[83] (That seems to describe precisely the current state of affairs concerning use of force.)

But the fact of legal uncertainty does not end the analysis. International law has a doctrine that addresses legal uncertainty—a rule for no rules. It derives from the famed *Lotus Case*, and it is called the "freedom principle." The freedom principle presumes that a state is deemed to be free to act unless it can be established that international law imposes some limitation or prohibition that circumscribes that freedom.* Obviously, the freedom principle has severe limitations as a guide to state conduct. The principle depends for its application upon an antecedent determination of the breadth of existing legal uncertainty. By particularizing that uncertainty, a narrow ambit of state power is produced; by generalizing it, a broader ambit is produced. The freedom principle thus relies for its application upon an answer to the very question that it seeks to resolve. Nonetheless, the freedom principle usefully reminds us that international law is not always clear, and that when a given question can be argued either way, a state is presumed to be free to act. Indeed, it could hardly be otherwise in any legal system. It is, as Kelsen wrote, a "fundamental principle that what is not legally forbidden to the subjects of the law is legally permitted to them."[84]

One could thus think of massive violation either as creating no law, or as creating new law that permits what is no longer a

---

* "The rules of law binding upon states ... emanate from their own free will as expressed in conventions.... [R]estrictions upon the independence of states therefore cannot be presumed." *Lotus*, 1927 P.C.I.J. (ser. A) No. 10, at 18.

violation,* or as throwing the law into a state of confusion and precluding any authoritative answer.† The final alternative, I believe,
best reflects the inadequacy of the legalist model's mode of analysis.
International law repeatedly asks the wrong questions. "No
answer," Alexander Bickel said, "is what the wrong question
begets."[85] But there is no practical difference among these perspectives. Whichever approach one takes, the conclusion follows that no
lawful impediment exists to state action. As will be seen, that is the
state of international law with respect to intervention by states.

E. Conclusion

Even if one accepts the scholastic tenets of international law doctrine, custom can arise with respect to the same subject addressed
by a treaty—even the UN Charter—and, if it is inconsistent, that
custom should effectively supercede the text of the treaty. If the custom is characterized as practice evidencing states' interpretation
of the treaty, the effect should be the same: The practice controls.
"A putative rule," as Weisburd aptly put it,[86] "cannot survive contrary practice no matter how that practice is characterized."

But the tenets of an outdated legalist schema can no longer
merit acceptance. Too often, as Hinsley notes, we have failed to
subject "our experiments in international organization to the test of

---

*This was the conclusion of the International Institute for Strategic Studies,
which in its 2000 report states flatly that "[t]he events in Kosovo and East
Timor suggest that humanitarian intervention is now established as an
important feature of international relations." International Institute for
Strategic Studies, *Strategic Survey 1999/2000*, at 28 (2000). It is hard to
seen how events in East Timor have any precedential effect since humanitarian intervention is by definition nonconsensual and, as the IISS itself
acknowledges, "the intervention force entered East Timor ... with the consent of Indonesia." *Id*. at 21.

†This is, in effect, Hans Morgenthau's answer to the question whether
those states that initiated World War II acted illegally. "[T]here is today no
way of stating with any degree of authority whether any nation that went
to war after [the conclusion of the Kellogg-Briand Peace Pact in] 1929 in
pursuance of its national policies has violated a rule of international
law ... ." Hans J. Morgenthau, *Politics Among Nations* 271 (4th ed. 1966).

our own experiences."* It is time for international law to move out
of the scientific age of Grotius and to test its theories against evidence. Peace and human dignity cannot be advanced by blind
adherence to an anachronistic methodology and the fantasy-land
rules it produced.† We need to ask, at long last, whether the rules
work, and if not, why not. We need to look not at words but at
deeds—not at paper rules but at real rules—not at *opinio juris* but
at practice. We need to ask whether the actual behavior of states in
supportive of, or contrary to, supposed norms.[87] To his credit, the
Legal Adviser of the U.S. Department of State recently took to task
the UN Human Rights Committee for its "cavalier approach" to
customary international law, an approach that substituted "conclusory" assertions for actual state practice.[88] Actual state practice
should be the starting point, not an afterthought, in legal analysis,
and it is actual state practice to which we now turn.

---

*He continues:

> Rousseau and Kant could judge what the results might be only in the light
> of their political theory. We have not only misinterpreted therir conclu-
> sions and failed to use the history of international relations to test our
> own. We have also ingnored or misinterpreted the practical results of inter-
> national experiments which we have accumulated in the last fifty year.
>
> This fact in its turn is not impossible to understand. A scientist
> would not try to make a weight move itself uphill; he would find out
> why it moves down. In politics, in contrast to the sciences. wishes and
> hopes, which always dictate the work man undertake, similarly domi-
> nate the post-mortems they conduct upon it.

F. H. Hinsley, *Power and the Pursuit of Peace: Theory and Practice in the
History of Relations Between States* 7 (1963).
†"[T]here are questions of intellectual honesty at issue here," Weisburd has
written. "Assertions that state practice is legally irrelevant are, in effect,
assertions that there is an easier way of creating international law than that
of generating a genuine consensus among states. There is no easier way,
and respect for the truth demands that we acknowledge that fact." A.
Mark Weisburd, "Customary International Law: The Problem of Treaties,"
21 *Vand. J. Transnat'l L.* 1, 46 (1988).

THREE

State Practice: The Charter and Interstate Violence

Having examined the inadequacies of the traditional international law framework for analyzing the effect of states acts and nonacts, let us turn now to what states actually have done. What has been the actual track record? The UN Charter permits use of force only in response to an armed attack. To what extent have states actually honored this prohibition?

A. Use of Force since 1945

Existing research, though surprisingly patchy, paints a sobering picture of state practice. Between 1945 and 1980, there were over 100 wars that have killed over 25 million people.[1] Arend and Beck list a noninclusive, "representative sampling through 1990," as follows:

The U.S. action in Guatemala (1954); the Israeli, French, and British invasion of Egypt (1956); the Soviet invasion of Hungary (1956); the US-sponsored Bay of Pigs invasion (1961); the Indian invasion of Goa (1961); the U.S. invasion of the Dominican Republic (1965); the Warsaw Pact invasion of Czechoslovakia (1968); the Arab action in the 1973 Middle East War; North Vietnamese actions against South Vietnam (1960–75); the Vietnamese invasion of Kampuchea (1979); the Soviet invasion of Afghanistan (1979); the Tanzanian invasion of Uganda (1979); the Argentine invasion of the Falklands (1982); the U.S. invasion of Grenada (1983); the American invasion of Panama (1989); and the Iraqi attack on Kuwait (1990).[2]

Nor have things been particularly peaceful since the end of the Cold War. Wallensteen and Axell count some 90 armed conflicts between 1989 and 1993. These involved 60 different governments—about one-third the UN's members.[3] Henkin himself lists Korea, the "recurrent Arab-Israeli hostilities of 1956, 1967, and 1973, the flurry between India and Pakistan over Kashmir in September 1965, the invasion of Czechoslovakia by Soviet troops in 1968," and "Ethiopia-Somalia and Vietnam-Cambodia-China in 1978–79."[4] To these might be added numerous other cross-border clashes including the Iran-Iraq War of the 1980s;* American air strikes against Iraq (1998–99); intermittent Israeli actions against Lebanon during the 1990s; the U.S. bombing of Sudan and Afghanistan (1998); U.S. air strikes against Libya (1986); the Pakistani incursion into Indian Kashmir (1999); the Uganda-Rwanda-Congo war (1997–99);[5] Ethiopia's attack on Eritrea (2000); and—most prominently, of course—NATO's air campaign against Yugoslavia during 1999.

A study conducted at the International Human Rights Law Institute at DePaul University spanned the period from 1945 to 1996 and broke down conflicts into international, noninternational, and internal. It reported the results as follows:

The study has found an estimated 285 conflicts globally from 1945 [to] 1996, of which, as of December 1996, forty-eight were ongoing. These conflicts are grouped, legally, as follows: 65 international, 38 non-international, and 182 internal. The estimated 65 international conflicts produced approximately 11 million deaths between 1945 and 1996. This is compared with the estimated 220 conflicts of a non-international, internal, and tyrannical regime victimization character, which produced approximately 87 million deaths. Taken together, conflicts occurring between 1945 and 1996 have resulted in an estimated 98 million casualties; 87 million of which were in the course of conflicts of a non-international, internal, and tyrannical regime victimization character, and 11 million of which were in the course of conflicts of an international character. The evidence thus is that since

---

*Here, Richard Falk noted, "[W]e witnessed for the first time since World War I an example of one country attacking another country—Iraq attacking Iran—while the world look[ed] on with indifference." Richard Falk, *Revitalizing International Law* 85 (1989).

World War II, conflicts of a non-international and internal character have produced a far greater level of victimization than conflicts of an international character.[6]

Other studies have documented even more numerous uses of force. Herbert K. Tillema counted 690 overt foreign military interventions between 1945 and 1996.[7] A report of the Carter Center in February 1998 identified 30 "major ongoing wars."[8]

Of course, not all war necessarily involves a use of force in violation of Article 2(4). Under traditional international law norms, a civil war does not violate international law, nor does intervention on behalf of a sitting government to put down an insurgency not amounting to civil war.[9] Truly international conflict, however, *would* necessarily entail an unlawful use of force inasmuch as not every participant can avail itself of the self-defense exception of Article 51. In a given case, it need not be determined which side acted lawfully. For purposes of assessing compliance with the Charter, it doesn't matter: The fact of cross-border violence in itself evidences a violation of the Charter by one party or another, since the Charter flatly prohibits nondefensive use of force and since a nondefensive use of force necessarily triggered hostilities in each case. Moreover, though the number of casualties has been enormous, that, too, does not matter for purposes of assessing compliance. The Charter prohibits any nondefensive force, not just nondefensive force that leads to casualties. That a given incident was bloodless, or nearly so, is of no consequence. The sole question is whether force was used or threatened in violation of the Charter. And the historical record shows that that occurred frequently. D'Amato alludes to instances where force was used in connection with "decolonization … humanitarian intervention, antiterrorist reprisals, individual as well as collective enforcement measures, and new uses of transboundary force such as the Israeli raid on the Iraqi nuclear reactor" in concluding that "[i]t is hard to fashion a *customary* rule of nonintervention from all these practices that are inconsistent with such a rule"—and, in the *Nicaragua Case*, as he points out, the Court did not even try.[10] It did not even try, one is forced to conclude, because practice does not support a customary norm against intervention. As Franck has written:

Traditionally, a normative principle has been thought to enter into customary law only after being confirmed by practice, that is, after it is demonstrably adhered to by the actual conduct of the large preponderance of international actors capable of violating it.

The customary norms cited by the Court [in *Nicaragua*] are adhered to, at best, only by some states, in some instances, and have been ignored, alas, with impunity in at least two hundred instances of military conflict since the end of World War II.[11]

B. Attempts at Categorizing States' Use of Force

Law cannot regulate acts that it is unable to place in categories. Categories make it possible for law to prohibit or permit. Regulation of a subject matter is impossible unless it comprises acts susceptible of being distributed into discrete categories. Some subject matters are more amenable than others to categorization. Distinct categories of trade barriers, for example, or of radio frequencies, make possible the regulation of international trade or telecommunications. If use of force is to be made subject to law, we must be able to sort it into categories.

The Charter attempted to establish two categories: defensive and nondefensive use of force. These proved inadequate for a number of reasons, one being that they failed to reflect actual state practice with sufficient accuracy and nuance. As a consequence, some commentators have sought to refine those categories further by seeking patterns in actual state practice concerning intervention, intending that the new categories based on these patterns could then be used either for interpretation of the Charter or in the recognition of developments in customary law. On one basis or the other (often the possibilities are not distinguished) their hope has been to justify a new norm permitting "humanitarian intervention." In the effort to do so, these commentators have looked, generally, at three features of each state act in question: its purpose, its effect, and the international reaction to it.

But these categories fail. I have already discussed the difficulty inherent in identifying the motive behind a state's act. International reaction is also a slim reed on which to base a given classification. As I discuss below, it too is subjective and easily manipulated to support virtually any predesired result.

Because of such difficulties, and because a given intervention can have salutary humanitarian consequences whatever its motive,* focus is sometimes directed at the *consequences* of an intervention.

---

* "[I]f people are subject to violence, disease, and starvation due to government abuses, intervention by another state that ultimately stops the abuse

However, similar problems attend efforts to identify the effects of a state's act. Effects, like purposes, are invariably numerous, and a humanitarian effect may be simply a salutary but unintended consequence, and one of many consequences at that. Few would view the 1941 German invasion of the Soviet-occupied Baltics, for example, as humanitarian intervention, though it had the consequence of bringing about the release of Soviet political prisoners. Moreover, modern historiography is leery about concluding that one event "caused" another.[12] Too many earlier factors are related to the occurrence or nonoccurrence of a later event to justify the claim that one of those factors "caused" the event. "Proximate" causation, all law students know, resolves the problem only by drawing an arbitrary line that rules out as "nonproximate" some factors but not others. An alternative to proximate cause analysis is to ask whether an event would have occurred "but for" the occurrence of another event. However, "but for" causation, so-called, is no less arbitrary.* Causation does not exist "out there;" it is a construct of the human mind, and speculation about the "causes" of my cold—or of the American Civil War, or of the collapse of the League of Nations, or of NATO air strikes against Kosovo, or even of Milocevic's capitulation—is fraught with difficulty. This is not to question Newtonian physics; actions of course have reactions. Nor is it to suggest that the probability of certain outcomes cannot be enhanced. But in the worlds of history, law, and politics, the number of actions and reactions in the web is vastly greater than the number in a physics laboratory—leading to an enormous gap in the capacity for prediction of the social sciences as compared with the natural sciences. A physics laboratory isolates individual factors; in the laboratory of society, isolation of individual factors is

---

continued
promotes human rights regardless of whether the intervention is motivated primarily by humanitarian concerns or self-interest." Note, "Humanitarian Intervention: The New World Order and Wars to Preserve Human Rights," 1 *Utah L. Rev.* 269, 302 (1994).
*Is the "cause" of my cold (1) sick George, who sneezed on me; (2) the virus he carried; (3) my decision to come to work that day, where I encountered George and the virus; (4) riding my bike to work in the rain—or thousands of other factors, tracing back to my parents having met at a dance? "But for" the occurrence of any one of those events, I would not have caught the cold.

difficult if not impossible. So causation is best approached charily in analyzing the "effects" of a given state action.

A cursory review of several "classic" cases illuminates the categorization problem. I examine the four incidents selected by Fernando Tesón in his book *Humanitarian Intervention*, on which he relies in arguing that the Charter permits such intervention.* They are Tanzania's 1979 intervention in Uganda, France's 1979 intervention in the Central African Republic, India's 1971 intervention in East Pakistan, and the United States' 1983 intervention in Grenada. In each case, I take pertinent facts from Tesón's own account to summarize his argument for categorizing each as a "precedent," and I then point out why that categorization is problematic.

1. Tanzania's 1979 Intervention in Uganda

The name Idi Amin has become a byword for "genocidal maniac." "With few possible exceptions," Tesón writes, "the crimes committed by Amin probably have no parallel in modern history."[13] The Ugandan head of state killed around 300,000 people, many of whom were tortured and killed in his presence.[14] Julius Nyerere, the President of neighboring Tanzania, felt "aversion" to Amin's "murderous practices."[15] On November 15, 1978, Tanzanian forces invaded Uganda, and in April 1979 they ended Amin's rule, forced him into exile, and halted the atrocities.[16]

True, but: In assuming power, Amin had overthrown a close personal friend of Nyerere, Milton Obote, whom Nyerere was committed to return to office.[17] Nyerere had earlier intervened in two other states—the Comoros in 1975 and the Seychelles in 1977—to oust regimes that he disliked.[18] The month before the Tanzanian invasion of Uganda, in October 1978, Uganda invaded Tanzania.[19] Amin proceeded to declare the annexation of occupied Tanzanian territory.[20] *Then* Tanzania invaded Uganda. When the Organization of African Unity attempted mediation, Nyerere specified cease-fire

---

*I select Tesón because his method of classifying is common in the literature. See, for example, Oliver Ramsbotham and Tom Woodhouse, *Humanitarian Intervention in Contemporary Conflict: A Reconceptualization* (1996); Anthony Clark Arend and Robert J. Beck, *International Law and the Use of Force* 113 (1993) (to qualify as humanitarian intervention, the "specific purpose must be essentially limited to protecting fundamental human rights").

conditions that included no demand that Amin step down or that he take any action to halt domestic human rights abuses.[21] "Admittedly," Tesón candidly concludes, "Nyerere most probably would not have invaded Uganda had not Amin engaged in his frivolous aggressive enterprise."[22]

The international community "was remarkably assertive in expressing the relief with which the fall of the Amin regime was received,"[23] Tesón concludes. In fact, a handful of states did express support for Tanzania, but their stated reasons varied; the United States did so on self-defense grounds.[24] There is no evidence that a majority of states took a position for or against the Tanzanian action.

2. France's 1979 Intervention in the Central African Republic

Jean-Bedel Bokassa was not Idi Amin, but his bloodlust was nearly as notorious. The head of state of the Central African Republic tortured and murdered schoolchildren and took reprisals against those who gave evidence to an investigatory commission.[25] In September 1979, a group of citizens, supported by 1,800 French troops, seized power in a bloodless coup.[26] The horror ended.

True, but: French economic interests remained strong in the Central African Republic following its independence from France in 1960.[27] An international consortium had signed an agreement in 1975 to explore uranium deposits in the country,[28] and the Bokassa government was no paragon of stability. The magnitude of human rights violations was questionable. Arend and Beck have written that the incursion "was not undertaken in response to a sufficiently widespread loss of life to be legitimately categorized as a 'humanitarian intervention.'"[29] "France had the encouragement, and perhaps even the approval, of the leading French-speaking African nations,"[30] Tesón insists—his only evidence being a "multinational report" prepared by "eminent African magistrates" that he claims had been accessible to some officials within the French government, coupled with the fact that only Libya, Benin and Chad condemned the French action.[31] Yet, as Michael Akehurst points out, "France tried to pretend that her troops arrived in the Central African Empire, at the request of the *new* government, *after* Bokassa had been overthrown."[32]

3. India's 1971 Intervention in East Pakistan

On March 23, 1970, following continuing tensions deriving from West Pakistan's economic and political domination of East

Pakistan, East Pakistan—later known as Bangladesh—declared its independence. Two days later, the West Pakistani army invaded East Pakistan and began the indiscriminate killing of unarmed civilians. The International Commission of Jurists reported "ruthless oppression ... the attempt to exterminate or drive out of the country a large part of the Hindu population; the arrest, torture and killing of ... activists, students, professional and business men and other potential leaders ... the raping of women ... the destruction of villages and towns ... and the looting of property."[33] The Indian army invaded Pakistan and on December 16, 1970, the Pakistani army surrendered.[34] The brutality ceased.

True, but: Pakistan may actually have attacked India prior to the Indian invasion.[35] Earlier, the population had fled East Pakistan en masse, an exodus that resulted in perhaps 10 million refugees who lived in horrifying conditions in makeshift camps in India.[36] Under the strain, India's economy had suffered severely.[37] "After some internal debate," one commentator observed, "the Indian government decided that it was cheaper to resort to war than to absorb the refugees into India's already troubled eastern region."[38]

International reaction, Tesón believes, supported India: The majority of states "implicitly acknowledged that the normative force of [Article 2(4)] is attenuated where acts of genocide are concerned."[39] In fact, India voted against the UN General Assembly's resolution on the matter because of its "lack of emphasis on the Pakistani repression against the Bengalis."[40] Tesón points to nothing adopted by the General Assembly remotely suggesting that it considered humanitarian intervention to be permissible under the Charter.*

4. The United States' 1983 Intervention in Grenada

In 1979, the parliamentary government of Grenada was overthrown in a bloodless coup headed by Maurice Bishop, who promised free elections.[41] Elections were never held. In October 1983,

---

*Oscar Schachter noted that the resolution adopted by the UN General Assembly "called on both India and Pakistan to withdraw troops from the other's territory but it was clearly directed against the Indian forces in East Pakistan. India strongly opposed the resolution but it was carried by 104 to 11." Oscar Schachter, "International Law: The Right of States to Use Armed Force," 82 *Mich. L. Rev.* 1620, 1629 n. 19 (1984).

another coup resulted in Bishop's overthrow.[42] On October 19, up to 200 people were killed, including Bishop and three former cabinet ministers.[43] Reportedly, the army opened fire on a crowd including women and children.[44] On October 25, following requests by the Organization of Eastern Caribbean States and Grenada's Governor General Sir Paul Scoon, a contingent of 1,900 U.S. troops landed, accompanied by 300 men from six Caribbean countries.[45] Three days later, the military operation was completed. Tesón writes, "Casualties included 18 Americans, 45 Grenadians, and 34 Cubans."[46] The U.S. Ambassador to the United Nations, Jeanne Kirkpatrick, said that the United States acted to restore "the rule of law, self-determination, sovereignty, democracy, [and] respect for the human rights of the people of Grenada."[47]

True, but: There was no pattern of brutality on the part of the government remotely approaching that in Uganda, the Central African Republic, or East Pakistan. Virtually all violence occurred on one day, October 19, in the turmoil incident to the second coup—something not uncommon when governments are forcibly overthrown. Official explanations of the U.S. purpose shifted, ranging from President Reagan's initial claim that the objective was to "protect innocent lives, including up to 1,000 Americans," to his claim ten days later that it was a "rescue mission" that "saved the people of Grenada from repression."[48] Oscar Schachter has observed that "[t]he Americans on the island were not hostages and threats had not been made against them."[49] Not mentioned by Tesón was the possibility that the new government being established would have been unacceptably friendly with Cuba. The State Department Legal Adviser said explicitly that the United States "did not assert a broad doctrine of humanitarian intervention" to justify its action.[50]

Tesón does not discuss the international reaction—except to note without elaboration that the "reaction of the United Nations majority and of ... critics does not do justice to the human rights cause."[51]

C. The Categorization Problem

I do not, of course, examine these cases to refute the view that intervention was permitted. To the contrary, for the reasons that I discuss, the most sensible view is that international law provides *no* satisfactory answer to the question. Rather, the facts of each "precedent," examined closely, yield—or rather confirm—three insights into the utility of trying to establish specific rules of law to govern the use of force from these "categories" of state practice.

First, states—in reality, state officials—act with multiple motives, not all of which can be identified and no one of which, often, is determinative. Julius Nyerere may or may not have invaded Uganda to restore a friend to power, to repel aggression, to stop genocide—or a for a host of other reasons that we may never know. French officials may have overthrown Bokassa to curb his barbarism—or to make the country safe again for French investors, or for some other reason. India may have invaded East Pakistan to halt geno-cide by the Pakistani army—or to halt the massive flow of Pakistani refugees that was dragging down the Indian economy. On what basis can one possible motive be selected over others? Who conceiv-ably can know what prompted these states to do what they did? Indeed, governmental officials sometimes themselves disagree as to why the state acted—witness the conflicting statements of the State Department Legal Adviser and UN Ambassador concerning Grenada.* Many proponents of humanitarian intervention, even those who accept the notion of national "motive," acknowledge that intervention is almost always carried out for mixed motives. "I submit that there is not a single case in the entire postwar era," Tom Farer has observed, "where one state has intervened in another for the exclusive purpose of halting mass murder, much less any other gross violation of human rights."[52] The same probably applies to the prewar period. "[C]lear examples of what is called 'humanitarian intervention' are very rare," Michael Walzer writes. "Indeed, I have not found any, but only mixed cases where the humanitarian motive is one among several."[53]

Some who discover mixed motives purport to be horrified, or discount altogether humanitarian concerns because they are sullied in the mix. Noam Chomsky, for example, believing that the

---

*Of course, the Legal Adviser may have been acknowledging only that the United States had not advanced the legal rationale that humanitarian inter-vention was consonant with the Charter (rather than suggesting that the United States did not act for humanitarian purposes). But that would only further underscore the difficulty of enlisting the Grenada "precedent" as supporting the lawfulness of humanitarian intervention: the refusal of the United States to embrace that justification should count against, not for, claiming Grenada as support.

American purpose in Kosovo was "the institution of the U.S. domi-nated global system," asks whether the "new humanism" in Kosovo was guided by power interests, or by humanitarian con-cern. "Is the resort to force undertaken 'in the name of principles and values,' as professed? Or are we witnessing something more crass and familiar?"[54] For Chomsky, the Kosovo intervention must have been guided *either* by power interests *or* by humanitarian con-cern; if it was not undertaken *solely* "in the name of principles and values," it was "crass."*

What prompted NATO to violate the UN Charter? No single answer will do. Henkin suggested various possibilities to explain why states *comply* with international law. "Considerations of 'honor,' 'prestige,' 'leadership,' 'influence,' 'reputation,'" he wrote, "which figure prominently in governmental decisions, often weigh in favor of obeying law."[55] In fact, with respect to NATO's action against Yugoslavia, considerations much like those probably weighed in favor of *violating* the law. No single factor can explain a single state's behavior, let alone that of 19 acting in concert. Joint statements issued in the name of all must be viewed skeptically. Such state-ments, particularly those issued in wartime, are often influenced by strategic considerations and sometimes can be little more than self-serving propaganda. "For every war," Gibbon wrote, "a motive of safety or revenge, or honor or zeal, or right or convenience, may be readily found in the jurisprudence of conquerors."[56] When issued on behalf of a coalition, particularly one such as NATO that operates under a unanimity rule, joint statements may not in fact represent the views of any given member.

Second, state acts have multiple effects, not all of which are intended and no one of which, as suggested elsewhere, is properly considered "primary." One apparent effect of Nyerere's invasion of Uganda was to remove from power an unstable and aggressive government that had designs on Tanzanian territory. Another was

---

*To Chomsky, "The factors that drive policy do not seem hard to discern": "If we deviate further from the marching orders that issue from Washington and London and allow the past to enter the discussion, we quickly discover that the new generation is the old generation, and that the 'new internationalism' replays old and unpleasant records." It's all "readily understood in terms of power interests." Noam Chomsky, *The New Military Humanism: Lessons from Kosovo* 15, 19 (1999).

to end Amin's genocide. But on what principled basis can Nyerere's act be categorized as one and not the other? Bokassa's overthrow ended his brutality, but it also restored the stability necessary for investment; why is French intervention properly categorized as "humanitarian" rather than "economic"? Why is the Indian invasion of East Pakistan called "humanitarian" when it too had undeniably salutary geopolitical consequences for India?* Suppose, in each case, the intervention had resulted in a much wider war and a number of deaths vastly greater than the number of lives saved: Would the intervention still qualify as "humanitarian"?

Moreover, while some "counterfactual" guesses are better than others,[†] no one can know how history would have turned out if something had *not* happened. Who is to say what would have happened if Tanzanian troops had not actually marched on Kigali and occupied the capital? Perhaps Amin would have been overthrown by his own people, who already were taking up arms against him. Similar questions could be asked in the other cases. Perhaps, chastened by international condemnation or lesser military or diplomatic sanctions, the miscreants would voluntarily have curtailed the most egregious human rights abuses. It simply is impossible to know what would have happened subsequently *but for* the occurrence of a certain event. To justify an act by its supposed "effects" is problematic, for it is always possible that the apparent effects would have occurred even if the apparently "causative" act had not.[‡]

---

*"India undoubtedly relished the thought of weakening its traditional rival by splitting it into two separate states." Note, "Humanitarian Intervention: The New World Order and Wars to Preserve Human Rights," 1 *Utah L. Rev.* 269, 303 (1994). "The gap between the two countries in nearly all elements of national strength increased substantially with the collapse of a united Pakistan in 1971 ... ." Naila Durani, "Air Power on the Asian Continent," *Def. & Foreign Aff.*, Apr. 1982, at 39.

†"With history one can never be certain, but I think I can safely say that Aristotle Onassis would not have married Mrs. Khrushchev." Gore Vidal, quoted in *The Sunday Times*, June 4, 1989.

‡For the use of counterfactual analysis to try to show that the legalist system "could have" prevented World War II, see Francis A. Boyle, *Foundations of World Order: The Legalist Approach to International Relations, 1898–1922*, at 148–49 (1999). The analysis is essentially a series of "what-ifs"—a list of hypothetically changed and presumed-to-be causal circumstances—to which any new, fanciful, better historical outcome can be

Third, classifying state acts on the basis of the "reaction of the international community" presents major problems. As pointed out earlier, the international community is not a unitary actor. It does not react as one. The international "community" says nothing *qua* community; if something is said, it is said by one or more officials of one or more states. A handful of states cannot speak for all states, and it is improper to infer agreement from silence. Many may disagree with the reaction of those that "react." It may not even be accurate to infer the reaction of a given state from a statement by a governmental official of that state. International law traditionally assumes that a government that controls territory and population speaks for the state. But if the government is a dictatorship, the inference that the spokesman represents the people of that state obviously is unwarranted. If the government is in turmoil—as was that of Russia, for example, following NATO's Kosovo intervention—its ministers may not even speak for their own government. (Recall the statement of the Russian foreign minister assuring the West that the incursion of Russian troops into Kosovo was an error and that they would quickly be withdrawn.) Even when numerous states do "speak," it is not always easy to gather all reactions. Western news organizations are notoriously indifferent to the Third World. As Patrick Kelly puts it, "Many states are unaware of the formation of custom unless their interests are specifically

---

continued

ascribed. Each what-if presupposes a context in which all other variables remain—unrealistically—the same. Boyle argues, for example, that "[i]f the habitually cantankerous and traditionally partisan Senate" had approved U.S. membership in the League of Nations, "there is perhaps a good possibility that the Second World War might not have occurred." *Id.* at 150. But for the Senate to have done so would have required that it *not* have been "habitually" and "traditionally" what it was—that American history and tradition would have been dramatically different. What would have made it so? How would a different history of the United States have affected the outcome of the *first* world war? Or the Civil War? How useful is it to hypothesize that the emergence of a Confederate States of America would have assured approval of the League and prevented World War II? Historical events are *dependent*, not *in*dependent, variables. Changing one inevitably involves changing countless others in unforeseeable ways. Counterfactual analysis is more usefully pursued by writers of science fiction than by serious historians.

affected. Even if aware of state practice inconsistent with their view, they may not perceive any immediate need to protest because they might not be aware that their silence binds them when their interests are not directly challenged."[57]

Further, not all official statements can be taken at face value. France initially dissembled following its overthrow of Bokassa. Sometimes states refrain from criticizing allies or go out of their way to criticize adversaries. Statements may have purposes other than legal explanation, such as gaining diplomatic advantage in negotiations, resolving unrelated disputes, or simply escaping blame. The 1979 Vietnamese invasion of Cambodia, overthrowing the regime of the notorious Pol Pot, is an example. Although occasionally cited as a case of humanitarian intervention that has added a gloss to the words of the Charter, Vietnamese officials in fact denied that their forces had even entered Cambodia, claiming that Pol Pot had been overthrown by the Cambodian people, not by Vietnam's military.[58] As discussed earlier, states simply do not articulate justifications that acknowledge a violation of international law—even though international lawyers insist that such an acknowledgment is crucial for establishing a new, supervening norm. As Tom Farer points out, in East Pakistan, Uganda, and Kampuchea, "all three invaders had solid ground on which to rest a claim of legitimate humanitarian intervention. Yet they ignored the doctrine, choosing instead to claim self-defense from an armed attack, a claim not one of them could persuasively sustain."[59] A state's leaders, in short, often speak out of both sides of their mouths. None wishes to be on the losing side of history. Consequently, it is often impossible to classify a speech as simply approving or disapproving a given initiative of another state.

Finally, commentators often take the opinions of nonstate actors as the equivalent of state reaction, looking to the approval or disapproval of scholars, newspapers, nongovernmental organizations and the rest as indicia of international opinion. But official state opinion may be very different: Why give weight to the views of others merely because they can make themselves heard? Not all states have the intellectual infrastructure to participate in global punditry, and those that do may not have the inclination. It is entirely plausible that many would-be critics as well as supporters of various state initiatives are silent simply because they believe that states powerful enough to carry out the acts in question really don't care what they think.

A practical illustration of these difficulties is presented by an effort to draw meaning from the debate in the United Nations General Assembly following the Kosovo crisis. At issue was a widely noted speech by the Secretary General, Kofi Annan, delivered on September 20, 1999. The Secretary General spoke approvingly of a "developing international norm in favor of intervention to protect civilians from wholesale slaughter ... ." The "core challenge" to the United Nations, he said, was "to forge unity behind the principle that massive and systematic violations of human rights—wherever they may take place—should never be allowed to stand."[60] The speech followed a report in which the Secretary General had opined that the "international community must remain prepared to engage politically—and if necessary militarily—to contain, manage and ultimately resolve conflicts that have got out of hand. This will require ... above all, a greater willingness to intervene to prevent gross violations of human rights."[61] On and off for a month after the speech was delivered, delegates commented on the issue of humanitarian intervention and, occasionally, on the Secretary General's speech and report. That is to say, *some* delegates commented: At least half of UN member states' delegations had nothing to say on the subject, one way or another. The language of diplomacy being what it is, categorizing the comments of those who did speak is like trying to nail Jell-O to a wall. Nonetheless, a close reading of the debate reveals that, of those delegates who did comment, roughly a third appeared to favor humanitarian intervention under some circumstances, roughly a third appeared to oppose it under any circumstances, and the remaining third appeared equivocal or noncommittal. Proponents, as one would expect, consisted primarily of Western democracies; opponents were primarily from Latin America, Africa, and the Arab world.

What conclusions can be drawn from such a line-up? Simple mathematics reveals that the "world community" as such has *no* view on the propriety of humanitarian intervention. If state "reaction" rather than state *action* is the point of reference, it is hard to see a "developing norm" of humanitarian intervention; an equal number of states oppose such a norm as support it. It is illogical to impute either support or opposition to the two-thirds that remained silent or noncommittal. It *may* be logical to discount the comments of nondemocratic states on the theory that their governments do not speak for their people, but such an approach would necessitate a major revamping of the UN system, which is premised on the sovereign equality of states notwithstanding their political systems. Thus, the President of the General Assembly, in attempting to summarize the debate up to October 2, was left merely to recap competing positions without even attempting a numerical analysis. And in New York City, the General Assembly does its work under galleries full of the world press, whereas in most member states' capitals "reaction" is unheard, unseen, and uncovered by international news media.

For all these reasons, efforts to establish a pattern of state conduct of the sort that might justify reliance upon a "custom" of intervention are doomed. Such efforts, to be successful, must depend upon a principled, nonarbitrary categorization of state acts. Is humanitarian intervention permissible? Customary international law, such as it is, provides no satisfactory answer.

The most pernicious consequence of reliance upon data concerning motive, effect, or community reaction is that it allows the assemblers of that data to mold the categories and resulting rules of law into anything they wish. In the parlance of international law, reliance upon such data conflates law's traditional categories of *lex lata,* the state of the law as it is, with *lex ferenda*, the law as it should be. Few commentators are more unabashed in their insistence that the law necessarily embodies their own personal moral insights than Fernando Tesón. Tesón's analysis is pervaded by a false-choice fallacy that repeatedly presents the legality of humanitarian intervention as the only conceivable analytic alternative. "Only the recognition of a right of humanitarian intervention," he writes of the French action in the Central African Republic, "can accommodate our intuition that the French action was morally justified."[62] In other words, the initiative of France, like that of Tanzania in Uganda, India in East Pakistan, and the United States in Grenada, could not have been morally justified if it had been unlawful. To justify the Tanzanian invasion of Uganda, Tesón writes, one must argue that there was a legal justification (like self-defense, which he does not believe works there). Otherwise, one must "declare the illegality of the Tanzanian action, in which case [it would be necessary to] accept that international law does protect genocidal rulers."

"An interpretation of the UN Charter and state practice that yields such a result is unacceptable."[63] Why is it unacceptable? Because it yields results that Tesón does not like. But that is of course the whole point of law—that the preagreed process of which it consists sometimes yields undesired results. If only "acceptable" results of that process warrant the appellation "law," why have a preagreed process—why not go straight to the "acceptable" result? What is "unacceptable" to Tesón—an absolute ban on interference in a state's internal affairs—was indispensable to others, including state interpreters of the Charter who spoke their minds quite frankly in the General Assembly. (Some of their comments are set out in Chapter 4.) "There must be something deeply wrong with an international system that protects tyrants such as Amin," he writes.[64] But of course in Tesón's view there cannot be anything wrong with the system; therefore, it cannot protect tyrants such as Amin. The instinct of China,* Russia, and other states—that there would be something deeply wrong with an international system that *permitted* intervention in their internal affairs—is simply not worth considering.† These states, and commentators who support them,

---

*See "China Has Consistent Policy on Kosovo Issue," *Xinhua General News Service,* Mar. 23, 2000, quoting Chinese Foreign Ministry Spokesman Sun Yuxi. "Such principles of the UN Charter as equality of sovereignty and non-interference in other country's [*sic*] internal affairs are far from outdated, he said. On the contrary, these principles still have great practical significance."

†The *N.Y. Times* described the dramatic impact of the Kosovo intervention on China's views of Western intentions:

> To China, Kosovo signified a major turning point. When the treatment of an oppressed minority became the rationale for military intervention, as Serbia's treatment of Kosovo's Albanians did, China felt vulnerable on its treatment of its own minorities, namely in Taiwan and Tibet. Some Chinese scholars see the war over Kosovo as a deliberate effort by the United States to divide Yugoslavia, and to assert a right to interfere wherever it likes.
>
> In a recent edition of Strategy and Management, a Chinese magazine, Zhang Wenmu wrote, "The problem now for China and other non-NATO countries is if NATO's scheme to dismember Yugoslavia is realized, then the United States and its allies may further apply this model to the Asia-Pacific and other regions to attack countries that constitute a 'threat' to its global control."

Seth Faison, "Beijing Sees U.S. Hand in Taiwan Shift on 'One China,'" *N.Y. Times,* July 15, 1999.

take a "dry legalistic approach"[65] devoid of morality. Better that they should adopt the "broad sense of political morality"[66] that he has, discarding preagreed process for (his) morally superior outcome: "To hold otherwise would amount to corrupting our foundations of moral good—and evil."[67] It seems not to have occurred to Tesón that adherence to that process could itself have moral dimensions.* But then, when legal analysis rests upon an "act of faith," as it does for him,[68] those who don't keep the faith don't count.

D. An Assessment of the Record

What lesson is to be drawn from this sorry record? It is impossible to avoid the conclusion that use of force among states simply is no longer subject—if it ever was subject—to the rule of law. The rules of the Charter do not today constitute binding restraints on intervention by states. Their words cannot realistically be given effect in the face of widespread and numerous contrary deeds. Richard Falk is correct: "The conclusion," Falk writes, "is that the legal effort to regulate recourse to force in international relations has virtually collapsed in state-to-state relations." He continues:

> [T]he [Charter's] formalized...renunciation of nondefensive claims to use force...provide little assured restraint upon state action. The decline of normative restraint can be seen in the broadening of the definition of self-defense and in the increasing resort to unilateral force by sovereign states. A consequence of this is to convert the rules of behavior embedded in the United Nations Charter into aspirational norms.[69]

Even if one accepts traditional international law analysis, there is no reason why the rules of the United Nations Charter that govern the rights and responsibilities of state parties should be immune from the operation of principles discussed in the last Chapter, the doctrines of desuetude, instant custom, *non liquet*, and the freedom

---

*"[T]he highest morality," Alexander M. Bickel wrote, "almost always is the morality of process." Alexander M. Bickel, *The Morality of Consent* 123 (1975).

principle. This is especially so, given the substantial number of state acts at odds with the noninterventionist regime of the Charter. At a minimum, therefore—under the scholastic approach itself—NATO's action in Kosovo pushed the old rules into a zone of twilight: a realm in which expectations have been confused, predictability has been lessened, and the contours of the law have been rendered uncertain. The validity of intervention now is less a function of formal rules than of the ebb and flow of global politics.*

NATO's action in Kosovo violated the *Charter,* but did it violate *international law*—which is more than just the text of the Charter? International law provides no satisfactory answer to this question. Its analytic tools simply are not up to the task. At least for the time being, therefore, the words of Justice Robert Jackson describe this transitional era: "In this area, any actual test of power is likely to depend on the imperatives of events and contemporary imponderables rather than on abstract theories of law.... If not good law, there was worldly wisdom in the maxim attributed to Napoleon that 'The tools belong to the man who can use them.'"[70] However one conceptualizes the state of the law—as nonexistent, as governed by a new customary norm that permits intervention, or as so confused that no burden of persuasion can be met that would establish a restraint or prohibition—the practical conclusion is, again, the same: No law currently prohibits intervention. Today, as Adam Roberts has written, "the fundamental question is not the legality, but the wisdom, of particular uses of force."[71]

International lawyers have long proceeded in a Platonic universe, ignoring actual practice, trying to explain it away, contending

---

*Pierre Hassner has written that the dual challenge to states posed by the "political reappearance of the world community" and "of domestic and transnational anarchy" can in a sense "be seen as a return to the Middle Ages, which, in turn, can be seen either as the reemergence of positive factors such as a universal community...or as the reemergence of precisely the private violence and the religious conflicts against which the modern secular states was invented." Pierre Hassner, "From War and Peace to Violence and Intervention: Permanent Moral Dilemmas under Changing Political and Technological Conditions," in *Hard Choices: Moral Dilemmas in Humanitarian Intervention* 11 (Jonathan Moore, ed., 1998). In the short run, these alternatives may not be mutually exclusive.

that it has no juridical implications.* For them, only the words of the Charter count; what has happened since 1945 is of no consequence. Nor do these scholars care whether the post–1945 regime is workable given earlier historical practice. They subsist in a world of forms: thinking, writing, and teaching not about what we can actually see—the shadows on the wall of the cave—but about idealized values that exist, *must* exist, somewhere. Theirs is a world of absolute and eternal ideals; the phenomena we can actually observe are merely an imperfect and transitory reflection of those ideals, unworthy of scholarly attention. They are true Platonists, and their effort to lead us to an ideal, less violent world has been a noble one.

The effort has also been a failure. Their effort has consigned international lawyers to a position of inconsequence in the making of life-and-death decisions by their governments. "[U]nrealistic standards have made international law wholly irrelevant in use-of-force decisions," former State Department Legal Adviser Abraham Sofaer has written. "National security officials—even the lawyers among them—are convinced that lawyers brandishing international law arguments have no credible role to play on use-of-force issues."[72] Their effort has led to utopian schemes like the Kellogg-Briand Peace Pact[†] that could have been recognized as unworkable from the outset had its authors taken the world as it is rather than as they preferred it to be. It is impossible to avoid the conclusion of Arend and Beck: Even the uses of force *acknowledged* by Henkin "would seem rather clearly to indicate that when a state judges other foreign policy goals to be at stake, it will generally *not* allow itself to be circumscribed by the prohibition of Article 2(4)."[73] Indeed, intervention among states has become so common that the Charter's use-of-force subregime may not properly be called a "system" at all. As Evan Luard suggested (in discussing the balance of power in pre–1815 Europe), "For anything like a 'system' to operate, it was necessary for one state to be able to rely on another

---

*"[I]n a clash between inadequate law and supreme national interests," Stanley Hoffman has written, "law bows—and lawyers are reduced to serve either as a chorus of lamenters with fists raised at the sky and state or as a clique of national justifiers in the most sophisticatedly subservient or sinuous fashion." Stanley Hoffman, "International Law and the Control of Force," in *The Relevance of International Law* 47 (Karl Deutsch and Stanley Hoffman eds., 1971).
†For a brief description of the Peace Pact, see Chapter 2.

responding to particular events and actions in a reasonably predictable fashion."[74] Who seriously would "rely" on a state to adhere to the proscription of Article 2(4) when that state's vital interests suggested a course at odds with the proscription? "[T]he high-minded resolve of Article 2(4) mocks us from its grave," Franck wrote.*

Henkin insists that the law "continues to provide strong support to forces opposing the use of force."[75] In fact, the effort to prop up dead use-of-force rules in the Charter has now become worse than a failure; it has actually undercut progress towards the more peaceful world that its adherents seek. More sensible, nuanced rules might have emerged.[†] But the Panglossian pretense that the Charter's

---

*Thomas M. Franck, "Who Killed Article 2(4)?" 64 *Am. J. Int'l L.* 809, 809 (1970). Franck's views may have modified since 1970, when those words were written, but his earlier assertion of the "demise of Article 2(4)," *id.*, was stated so forcefully that it is worth recalling. Franck continued:

The practice of these states has so severely shattered [mutual confidence in]...the precepts of Article 2(4) that...only the words remain.... In the twenty-five years since the San Francisco Conference, there have been some one hundred separate outbreaks of hostilities between states.... .

The failure of the U.N. Charter's normative system is tantamount to the inability of any rule, such as that set out in Article 2(4), in itself to have much control over the behavior of states. National self-interest, particularly the national self-interest of the super-Powers, has usually won out over treaty obligations. This is particularly characteristic of this age of pragmatic power politics. It is as if international law, always something of a cultural myth, had been demythologized. *Id.* at 809, 810–11 and 836.

Compare Thomas M. Franck, *The Power of Legitimacy Among Nations* 32 (1990) ("[T]he extensive body of international 'law' which forbids direct or indirect intervention by one state in the domestic affairs of another [and] precludes the aggressive use of force by one state against another ... simply, if sadly, is not predictive of the ways of the world.").

[†]"[An] absolute rule [of nonintervention]...will...be ignored, and we will then have no standards by which to judge what happens next. In fact, we do have standards [that]...reflect deep and valuable, though in their applications difficult and problematic, commitments to human rights." Michael Walzer, *Just and Unjust Wars: A Moral Argument with Historical Illustrations* 108 (2d ed. 1991).

limitations work*—international lawyers' gushing adulation of "the genius of the Charter"[76]—has distorted and misdirected the debate[†] and pushed the international community into an ever more lawless realm. The issue is not whether Article 2(4) is *jus cogens,* or whether states really, *truly* believed that their acts were lawful under a newly emerging norm, or whether states used an academically correct verbal formulation to justify noncompliance. Scholastic argument over such issues consigns international lawyers to the irrelevance that they deserve.[‡] The issue today is whether and how a *new* system can be developed that *does* work. William D. Rogers put it well:

> The web of undertakings that can restrain the use of force in international affairs ... is complex, going far beyond the simple words of the Charter. In the struggle toward a rule of law for the community of nations, the choice is not between the Charter norms and chaos. The choice is between the Charter and other means to fill in the corners of an incomplete canvas. These may be less ambitious. But they may also be more realistic. It probably makes little difference whether scholars classify these principles as law.[77]

---

*"Unlike the time of the League," Mary Ellen O'Connell writes, "the world is now accustomed to and generally supports an institution to administer rules restraining the use of force." Mary Ellen O'Connell, "The UN, NATO, and International Law After Kosovo," 22 *Hum. Rts. Q.* 57, 88 (2000).

[†]Henkin recognizes but rejects the possibility that the United States could decide that "it is undesirable—indeed, dangerous—to pretend that there is law when in fact there is none." Louis Henkin, "Use of Force: Law and U.S. Policy," in Louis Henkin et al., *Right v. Might: International Law and the Use of Force* 57 (2d ed. 1991). This would amount to "scuttling the law of the Charter" and would "reestablish Adolf Hitler as no worse than anyone else," *id.* at 58—as if the law of the Charter had not already been scuttled, and as if serious efforts at law reform necessarily meant embracing the legacy of Hitler.

[‡]As Arend and Beck write, "Given the weakened authority of 2(4) and its manifest lack of control, to use Article 2(4) in any way to describe the law relating to the recourse to force may simply be perpetuating a legal fiction that interferes with an accurate assessment of state practice." Anthony C. Arend and Robert J. Beck, *International Law and the Use of Force: Beyond the UN Charter Paradigm* 183 (1993).

The first step in painting on that "incomplete canvas" is to abandon the erroneous assumptions of the past, to recognize the prescience of some of the Charter's early critics* and to examine, without blinders, why the old system failed.

Such a review reveals that the Charter's use-of-force rules failed for a number of reasons. First, as discussed in the remainder of this chapter, contrary to the intent of its framers, the Charter did not create constabulary power in the Security Council to deal with the problem of interstate violence. The Charter thus did not stop the use of force by states. Chapter 4 analyzes the Charter's failure to deal effectively with the problem of intrastate violence, and the Security Council's ill-advised overreaching to remedy the Charter's omission. Chapter 5 examines gaping divisions over fundamental values which have effectively precluded the establishment of an authentic legalist regime to control the use of force among states. Chapter 6 notes the contribution of these factors to the decomposition of international rules governing use of force.

Despite these failings, the needs that the Charter was intended to meet continued; its failures thus invited action by states able and willing to act to fill the void. Each of these failures stemmed from an unwillingness of states to cede to the United Nations power sufficient to carry out the tasks envisioned for it. Ironically, as Chapter 6 suggests, the alternate system that has developed alongside the United Nations is grounded upon just such a ceding of power; the difference being that power is pooled among like-minded states that trust one another to apply power justly. This bifurcation has developed because an inflexible legalist model has proven resistant to the lessons of real-world experience in which states are now attempting to manage power more justly.

E. Why the Legalist Regime Failed to Control Interstate Violence

The Charter's use-of-force regime, Julius Stone argued, was premised upon an effective system of collective security.[78] That system

---

*See, for example, George Kennan, *American Diplomacy 1900–1950* (1951) (questioning whether the Charter's restraints could effectively suppress governments' bellicosity).

envisioned the establishment of a constabulary power on the part of the Security Council. It was contemplated by the framers of the Charter that the Security Council would have at its disposal standing or standby forces, contributed by member states under Article 43, to be used to put down any unlawful use or threat of force. But such forces have never materialized. Paralyzed by the veto during the Cold War, the Security Council never initiated the negotiation of the special agreements with member states pursuant to which forces were to have been provided.[79] (Secretary General Boutros Boutros-Ghali's 1992 *Agenda for Peace*[80] proposed the establishment of a permanent UN force, but nothing came of it.*) Thus, when confronted with the need to halt aggression, as in Korea or Kuwait, the Security Council was left to authorize the use of force by member states rather than to deploy forces under its own military staff committee.[81] So seldom has the Council succeeded in stopping ongoing interstate conflict, however, that states have been compelled to engage in self-help. Arend and Beck have noted the failure of alternatives to a constabulary Security Council, discussed earlier:

> Using the General Assembly as a substitute for the Security Council only really worked in the case of Korea. And in that case, the Security Council [had] already authorized the initial action. In subsequent uses of force, the Assembly has not been able to respond effectively to challenge an act of aggression. Similarly, the use of regional arrangements has not proved very successful. Such arrangements have responded only selectively to uses of force by states and have frequently been perceived as little more than a fig leaf for great power actions. Finally, peacekeeping, which developed in the wake of the failure of limited collective security, cannot be considered as a substitute. Peacekeeping

---

*At the outset of the Clinton Administration, support for the establishment of a standing UN army grew until General Colin Powell weighed in saying, "As long as I am Chairman of the Joint Chiefs of Staff, I will not agree to commit American men and women to an unknown war, for an unknown cause, under an unknown commander, for an unknown duration." "[T]hat was the end of the idea," a Pentagon official said. Ivo H. Daalder, "Knowing When to Say No: The Development of U.S. Policy for Peacekeeping," in *UN Peacekeeping, American Politics, and Uncivil Wars of the 1990s* 43 (1996).

explicitly recognizes that collective action to fight aggression is unlikely ... . In short, in the post-Charter period, international institutions have failed to deter or combat aggression.[82]

States thus have had no alternative but to use force themselves to fill the gap left by an unexecuted Charter. As Michael Reisman has written, "Article 2(4) suppresses self-help [only] insofar as the organization can assume the role of enforcer." When it cannot, "self-help prerogatives revive."[83] It has been objected that this analysis wrongly implies a dependence between Article 2(4) and Chapter VII of the Charter, and that in fact no such relationship exists: it never having been intended that a fully functioning Article 43 should serve as a condition precedent to giving force and effect to the Article 2(4) prohibition against nondefensive force.[84] But the objection misses the point, which is more functional than legal. Whatever the juridical implications, purely as a security matter, the vacuum created by a militarily feckless Security Council has invited state action that would not otherwise have occurred. As a purely political matter, the United Nations has surely been hobbled by having to play collective security chess without the queen of its own military force.

One reason that the Security Council has been unable to fulfill the role that the Charter's framers envisioned is that some member states are reluctant to place forces under its command, if indeed they are not prohibited by their constitutions from doing so. It is scarcely possible in this study to canvass all pertinent examples. One nation does warrant examination, however, by virtue of the centrality of its role in the Charter's collective security structure. That nation is the United States. Since Thomas Jefferson's first inaugural address, admonishing his countrymen to avoid "entangling alliances," Americans have been leery of involvement in military pacts with other nations, whether for the purpose of defending against perceived foreign threats or, later, of maintaining international security. That leeriness reflected itself in the U.S. refusal to join the League of Nations and, later, in the drafting of UN Charter provisions to reflect U.S. objections to the League 25 years earlier.

1. The Covenant of the League of Nations

The threat that the United States could be legally bound to use armed force without prior congressional approval penetrated to the heart of the debate in the United States over whether to join the League of Nations. Ambiguities in the League Covenant[85] on that point contributed directly to its rejection. Article 10 of the Covenant provided as follows:

> The Members of the League undertake to respect and preserve as against external aggression the territorial integrity and existing political independence of all Members of the League. In case of any such aggression or in case of any threat or danger of such aggression the Council shall advise upon the means by which this obligation shall be fulfilled.

Senator Henry Cabot Lodge, leader of the Senate forces opposing the League, proposed a reservation to the Covenant that stated:

> The United States assumes no obligation to preserve the territorial integrity or political independence of any other country or to interfere in controversies between nations—whether members of the league or not—under the provisions of Article 10, or to employ the military or naval forces of the United States under any article of the treaty for any purpose, unless in any particular case the Congress, which, under the Constitution, has the sole power to declare war or authorize the employment of the military or naval forces of the United States, shall by act or joint resolution so provide.[86]

President Woodrow Wilson opposed the Lodge reservation, arguing that it was unnecessary because the Covenant required unanimity.* "[T]here could be no advice of the council on any such subject," he said, "without a unanimous vote, and the unanimous vote includes our own, and if we accepted the advice we would be accepting our own advice."[87] He implied that he would not, in casting

---

*In fact, Wilson was correct in predicting that the Covenant would not be construed by League members as Lodge construed it. Hinsley apparently considers their interpretation of the Covenant erroneous and views their refusal to uphold their obligation to resort to war—to make the League an "enforcement machine"—as having brought about its collapse. F. H. Hinsley, *Power and the Pursuit of Peace: Theory and Practice in the History of Relations Between States* 318 (1963).

that vote, bind the United States in a situation where prior congressional approval was required to undertake the obligation in question: "I need not tell you," he said, "that the representatives of the Government of the United States would not vote without instructions from their Government at home, and that what we united in advising we could be certain that the American people would desire to do."[88] The Covenant, Wilson said, required no "surrender of the independent judgment of the Government of the United States ... ."[89] (He meant legal but not moral surrender.*) Yet Wilson's Senate supporters viewed the Lodge reservation as a "repudiation"[90] of the Covenant and voted against the resolution of ratification. The Senate defeated the Covenant (39 for, 55 against) with the Lodge reservation attached.[91] The view that the Covenant bound the United States to use armed force was shared by Herbert Hoover, Charles Evans Hughes, Elihu Root, and Henry L. Stimson, all of whom wanted it changed to remove the requirement.[92] "The ideal collective security system would allow no room for choice in any crisis; the law-abiding states would all be obliged to punish any transgressor.... It was precisely because these obligations were well understood by many U.S. Senators that President Wilson's design for the League of Nations was never realized."[93]

2. The United Nations Charter

This history was doubtless familiar to the framers of the United Nations Charter, particularly the Americans.[†] Secretary of State Cordell Hull said: "The biggest stumbling block that sent the Wilson movement in support of the League to utter destruction

---

*"[Borah said] it was his impression that the president intended Article X to be primarily a moral obligation, and asked if that was right. Wilson said that it was. Borah went on to ask whether it was not also a 'legal obligation.' No said the great idealist.... Was the article binding if it was not 'legal?' Wilson was asked. It was 'an absolutely compelling moral obligation,' he replied." Jon Willem Schulte Nordholt, *Woodrow Wilson: A Life for World Peace* 385–86 (1991).
†But not only the Americans. Sir John Simon said, "It is really essential that we should not enter into any extensive general and undefined commitment with the result that, to a large extent, our foreign policy would depend, not on this country, this Parliament and its electors, but on a lot of

in 1920 was the argument over this point, and no other political
controversy during our time had been accompanied by more
deep-seated antagonism."[94] From the beginning, preparations for
the negotiations in San Francisco reflected the felt need to avoid any
semblance of an automatic requirement to use armed force. In 1943,
the House of Representatives adopted the Fulbright Resolution,
expressing its support for the "creation of appropriate international
machinery with power adequate to establish and to maintain a just
and lasting peace, among the nations of the world, and ... favoring
participation by the United States therein."[95] That same year, the
Senate adopted the Connally Resolution, urging that the United
States, "acting through its constitutional processes, join with free
and sovereign nations in the establishment and maintenance of international authority with power to prevent aggression and to preserve
the peace of the world."[96] Beginning in early 1944, Secretary of
State Hull consulted with leading members of Congress on the developing plans for an international organization. Commenting on the
proposals that formed the basis of the U.S. position at Dumbarton
Oaks, Senator Arthur Vandenberg wrote in his diary:

> [T]o his credit, [Hull] recognizes that the United States will never
> permit itself to be ordered into war against its own consent. He
> has even gone so far as to suggest that we require this consent to
> be given by an Act of Congress. This is anything but a wild-eyed
> internationalist dream of a world State.[97]

Congress, in considering the Charter, assumed that forces would be
available for UN use only after Congress approved the terms of
their service in an Article 43 agreement. Even if such a contrary
argument were accepted, however, the central conclusion would
remain unaffected: Before casting a vote for Security Council action
under Article 42 authorizing the use of U.S. armed forces, the
President must get congressional consent if the use of force is not
one falling within his sole constitutional powers. As the *Harvard
Law Review* concluded, the "language [of] the United Nations
Charter ... clearly illustrates the neutrality of their obligations with

---

continued
foreign governments." John W. Wheeler-Bennett, *Munich: Prologue to
Tragedy* 355–56 (1948).

respect to the internal distribution of the war-making power."[98] Indeed, the same approach was adopted in subsequent treaties, leading to "general agreement that current postwar security treaties have not changed the relative powers of Congress and the President with respect to the use of the armed forces."[99]

The implementing legislation of the Charter was the United Nations Participation Act (UNPA).[100] The UNPA, its House floor manager said, "prescribes the domestic internal arrangements within our Government for giving effect to our participation in this enterprise and sets up the machinery for complying with certain of the major international commitments which the United States assumed upon ratification of the Charter."[101] Thus, the *Harvard Law Review* observed that "[t]he question which governmental department had power to determine for the United States the number of troops to be placed at the disposal of the Security Council was settled by Congress in the United Nations Participation Act … ."[102]

The prevailing view in Congress when the UNPA was enacted was that the only mandatory way for the Security Council to raise armed forces was pursuant to special agreements concluded under Article 43. (The Security Council has never concluded such an agreement with any member state.) The President, prior to directing an American vote in the Security Council requiring the use of force by the United States, was expected to seek congressional approval if that approval would otherwise be required. The Charter was seen as conferring no additional authority on the President to use United States armed forces in hostilities; the President could not, by an affirmative vote in the Security Council, confer upon himself power to use armed force that he would not otherwise possess. The text of the UNPA makes that clear, as does a review of its legislative history.

The text, in 22 U.S.C. § 287d., authorizes the President to negotiate special agreements under Article 43. Any such agreement must be approved by Congress "by appropriate Act or joint resolution."[103] The President is not required to seek further congressional authorization to make U.S. armed forces available for use by the Security Council under a special agreement.[104] A proviso to the section denies the President any authority to make forces available to the Council other than the forces made available under the special agreement. (The proviso contains one irrelevant exception: It permits an inference of authority under the succeeding section,[105] but that section applies only to activities "not involving the employment of armed forces contemplated by Chapter VII of the United Nations

Charter."[106] Because Article 42 is part of Chapter VII, no inference of authority may be drawn with respect to use of armed force by the Security Council under Article 42.)

The meaning of these provisions and related Charter provisions was explained to the House Foreign Affairs Committee by Under Secretary of State Dean Acheson. Referring to Article 43, he said:

[I]t means that we must work out with the Security Council a special agreement or special agreements in which we develop the number of troops, the type of troops, the location, the degree of readiness, and so forth, and that when we have done that and when you gentlemen have approved it, then, and only then, are we bound to furnish that contingent of troops to the Security Council—and the President is not authorized to furnish any more than you have approved of in that agreement.[107]

Under Secretary Acheson was then asked by Congressman Paul Douglas whether the President "would be unable to go beyond that with the unlimited force which Congress would still have to pass upon for unlimited war." The Under Secretary responded as follows: "Yes, beyond the amount which you have agreed in the special agreement. The President is not given authority to furnish any additional troops, and whatever happens after that is determined by the ordinary constitutional relations between the Congress and the President." Under Secretary Acheson later added that "the only reason that the President is permitted to make these [Article 43] forces available, after the special agreement has been approved, is to carry out the provisions of article 42."[108]

Both the Senate and the House reports on the UNPA emphasized that nothing in the Act authorized the President to make available to the Security Council any armed forces other than those provided for under an Article 43 agreement. Each contained the same paragraph:

In order that there may be no doubt about the availability of our armed forces, the committee believed it wise that the Congress should in this legislation confirm its view that the President has the power and obligation, in compliance with our understanding under the Charter, to make the forces provided in the agreements available to the Security Council. This act on the part of the Congress will contribute not only to public understanding within the United States but will also serve notice upon the world that as a nation we are prepared to carry out our obligations promptly and effectively. At the same time the Committee felt it important to make it clear that nothing contained in the statute should be construed as an authorization to the President by the Congress to make available to the Security Council for such purpose, armed forces in addition to such as may be provided for in the military agreements.[109]

In the Senate, the floor manager of the Bill, Senator Tom Connally, was asked by Senator Millikin whether there was any intent to transfer to the President the constitutional powers of Congress. "Where Congress does retain jurisdiction over a subject matter that might be voted upon by our delegate in the Council, to that extent the President would simply be a vehicle for issuing instructions in accordance with the retained powers and will of Congress. Is that correct?" Senator Connally replied: "Whatever the powers of Congress may be, if our constitutional duty reaches to that point, of course the President would be an instrument of Congress…. If such be the case, the President, I assume, would respect the authority of Congress and would act in accordance therewith."[110] Senator Wheeler then said that the legislation under consideration would give the President additional power to use force without congressional approval. "The bill," Senator Connally responded, "does not really give him any more power"[111] (although he conceded that the President's power under the Constitution was already broad). The most ardent Senate proponents of presidential power acknowledged that the President could vote in the Security Council for the use of United States armed forces only if those forces had already been provided under Article 43 agreements.[112] The rationale for this exception, Senator Connally quickly added, was that "[t]hese contracts must be submitted to the Congress. When the agreements are made with the Security Council, they must come back here."[113]

Members of the House evinced the same understanding. The floor manager of the bill, explaining its meaning, reassured House members that:

[t]he position of the Congress is fully protected by the requirement that the military agreement to preserve the peace [under Article 43] must be passed upon by Congress before it becomes effective. Also, the obligation of the United States to make forces

available to the Security Council does not become effective until the special agreement has been passed upon by Congress.[114]

In sum, the exclusive framework within which the President could introduce the armed forces into hostilities under the Security Council was the framework involving Congress established by Article 43. The possibility of an alternative framework not involving Congress was not seriously considered.[115] Corwin, not surprisingly, concluded that "the controlling theory of the act is that American participation in the United Nations shall rest on the principle of departmental collaboration, and not on an exclusive presidential prerogative in the diplomatic field."[116] The executive branch concurred. While arguing over the constitutionality of President Truman's use of force in Korea, it nonetheless conceded that the Act was directed at "withholding congressional authorization from the commitment of troops or forces beyond those specified in the agreements."[117] The UNPA, it has been pointed out, "does not apply to action taken by the President in the absence of such an agreement or upon the basis of a recommendation made either by the Security Council or by the General Assembly."[118]

F. Conclusion

The upshot for the Security Council of American insistence on having the final word was that any meaningful constabulary role was effectively ruled out. Swift and sure deterrence is the *sine qua non* of an effective collective security regime. A would-be transgressor must expect to meet an immediate and certain military response from the international community if the system is to work. But no such response is ensured if component states decline to delegate power to the Council to act without their consent. In effect, the Council is left as a mere conference of states with no power to mandate action by any of those states. The United Nations is relegated to the role of *convener*. No pooled authority to use force exists because none has been delegated. As a crisis arises, notwithstanding the Council's existence, member states must proceed to assemble "coalitions of the willing" as politics permit. As discussed later, effective pacific dispute settlement necessitates a gathering of *unlike*-minded states. For collective security purposes, however, it is not clear what is added by an institutionalized gathering of unlike-minded states: They agree to do nothing that they could not do in a noninstitutionalized setting. The point is made that this is the "fault" of the UN's constituent states, not those that happen to be members of the Security Council—which is true but irrelevant. The effect is the same: The Council has been hamstrung in exercising the constabulary power essential to persuading states to abandon self-help.

Collective security under the direction of the Security Council thus failed because the Charter did not permit the Council to requisition troops from individual states. The Council's hobbling was not the doing of the United Nations; individual states such as the United States considered the delegation of the requisitioning power violative of their own constitutional order. When it comes to using their own troops in combat, they trust their own judgment over that of the international community. And who can blame them? Vastly different political perspectives underlie the approaches of different members of the Security Council; it seeks to span disparities in values too enormous for any international institution to reconcile. It has been said that, as far as the prevention of war was concerned, "the League's successful functioning depended on conditions which, if they had existed, would have made the organization unnecessary."[119] Much the same is true of the UN's use-of-force regime: Because those conditions do not exist today, its use-of-force regime is ineffective. As Franck wrote in 1985, "its paralysis is an accurate reflection of the intense differences that divide nations."[120] The end of the Cold War notwithstanding, intense differences continue to divide nations. Until those differences become less acute, the resources of the international community are better directed at ensuring the stability of the geopolitical system that now governs the use of force. A stable geopolitical system, one that operates with predictability and shared expectations, is a necessary base on which to build a true legalist order.

It is ironic that many of those who argue that Article 2(4) must be accorded its originally intended meaning take precisely the opposite view when it comes to the meaning of Articles 39 and 2(7)—provisions limiting the power of the Security Council to use force. There, they suggest, it is *not* the intent of the framers of the Charter but subsequent practice that should be deemed controlling. The Charter's limits on the power of *individual* states to use force are written in granite, but its limits on that of the *Security Council* are scrawled in sand. As is discussed in the next chapter, precisely the opposite conclusion should follow: An organ delegated powers by other entities, as is the Security Council by individual states, should hardly be able, through repeated *ultra vires* actions, to expand unilaterally the scope of its authority. Such an organ is on a very different footing than the states that created it when it comes to the formation of customary international law, a process in which the latter regularly partake. Different principles apply to Security Council practice than to the practice of individual states when it comes to the effect of practice on the content of the law, as the next chapter elaborates. The transgressions of a *creature* of states, such as the UN Security Council, are entitled to far less juridical weight than the transgressions of the states that created it. Yet proponents of broad Security Council power to flout the Charter's limits often are the first to complain when the states that created it follow its lead.

The next chapter suggests that, like interstate violence, intrastate violence not only continued under the Charter but in fact proliferated. The Charter precluded the Security Council from intervening in the internal affairs of member states. The origin of the restraint, here again, was not the United Nations, but individual states that overwhelmingly refused to cede this central incident of sovereignty to a supranational organization—because here, too, they trusted their own judgment more than they did the international community's. Yet the effect was to place pressure on the Security Council to contravene the Charter's limits when, as the twentieth century drew to a close, leading states began to rethink the wisdom of the Charter's noninterventionist proscription. Like individual states, the Security Council thus felt impelled to ignore what appeared increasingly to be excessively rigid limitations of the Charter.

FOUR

Security Council Practice:
The Charter and Intrastate Violence

Can the Security Council label something a "threat to international peace and security" that is not a threat to international peace and security and thereby escape limits upon its power to intervene? "[P]roponents of a 'living Charter,' Louis Henkin has written, "would support an interpretation of the law and an adaptation of UN procedures that rendered them what they ought to be. That might be the lesson of Kosovo."[1]

If that is the lesson of Kosovo, it bodes ill for the rule of law, which counsels at least a minimal attachment to the received meaning of words and the intent underpinning legal instruments in which they are used. Central to the rule of law is the principle of limited power, the notion that an organ vested with coercive authority is restricted to those powers implicitly or explicitly conferred upon it by the instrument that creates it. The authority given such an organ is restricted to what its powers *are,* not what "they ought to be."

In the UN Charter, words establish limits on the coercive power of the Security Council. The Council is, in effect, precluded from intervening in the internal affairs of states absent at least a threat of cross-border violence. To "interpret" those limits out of existence through reliance upon the metaphor of a "living" Charter does violence to the rule of law. In the domestic context, an analogous debate on constitutional interpretation has occurred between "originalists" and "adaptivists"—between those who favor sticking with the intent of the Constitution's framers and those who would permit the document to adapt to changed times and circumstances in ways contrary to that intent. In the international realm, however, there has thus far been little such debate. Commentators have

assumed without analysis that the UN Charter—the "world's constitution"—is to be construed pursuant to the most extreme adaptivist
principles. "Principles" is, indeed, a loose description: they assume,
with Henkin, that the Charter can be construed simply to permit the
UN Security Council to do what it "ought" to do—as they define
"ought." States that take a different view, such as Russia, China,
India, and others—which represent a majority of the world's population—are confronted with a diktat from which there is no escape,
notwithstanding their protest that this is not the Charter that they
agreed to. If law constrains behavior, the approach of the radical
adaptivists is, in reality, not law at all but a form of the very
realpolitik that its adherents purport vigorously to reject.

A. Charter-imposed Limits on the Security Council

Tom Farer aptly captured the gist of the issue, recalling the story of
an irascible political boss of a city in New Jersey who was accused of
ordering his police force to violate the law. "That's impossible!" He
reportedly roared. "I am the law." "Is the Security Council," Farer
asks, "the only judge of the legality of its actions? Does it enjoy a ple-
nary discretion to interpret the breadth of its jurisdiction under the
Charter?"[2] Richard Lillich, along with numerous other proponents of
humanitarian intervention, would have answered yes. "[T]he Charter
is what (in this case) the Security Council says it is," he wrote.[3]
  But the UN Charter does not give the Security Council unlimited
power. Indeed, its power is limited by the Charter's most important
precepts. The Council is not given authority to intervene in states'
internal affairs. Like other international organizations and domestic
governmental entities, its powers are defined by the instrument that
creates it. An act beyond the scope of its authorized powers is *ultra
vires*. As even proponents of broad Security Council powers acknowledge, the framers selected only one of the Charter's principles—international peace—as a valid basis for use of force. As Farer put it:

> [T]he Charter sharply limits the power of the Security Council.
> The dominant states at the time, confident of their control of the
> Council, might, after all, have given it coercive authority in con-
> nection with all the principles and purposes of the Organization.[4]

But they did not give the Security Council *carte blanche*. "Nothing
in the *travaux préparatoires* suggests that the parties envisioned a

government's treatment of its own nationals as a likely catalyst of a threat or breach," Farer concludes.[5] Human rights, he continues, had only a "tenuous place" among the concerns of the Charter's framers, hardly sufficient to prevail as against explicit textual prohibitions and limitations:

> The Security Council's limited mandate; the overriding concern manifested in the *travaux* for the protection of national sovereignty; the explicit exemption from UN jurisdiction of matters of a primarily domestic character at a time when the domestic practices of many members, including the United States, were wildly inconsistent with one or another human rights norm; and the vagueness and generality of the duties concerning human rights imposed on states collectively offer a solid basis for concluding that human rights had only a tenuous place among the concerns of the founding members.[6]

The United Nations system has no judicial authority that has regularly "ridden herd" on this most powerful of the Charter's creatures. Whether the International Court of Justice can exercise review over the Council's action is unclear. The Court has not hesitated to tell other organs of the United Nations that they may not exceed their assigned powers. Advising the Council and the General Assembly that they had to respect the criteria (of Article 4 of the Charter) concerning the admission of new members, the Court said the following:

> The political character of an organ cannot release it from the observance of the treaty provisions established by the Charter when they constitute limitations on its powers or criteria for its judgment. To ascertain whether an organ has freedom of choice for its decisions, reference must be made to the terms of its constitution.[7]

But the International Court seems thus far to have left open the question whether it has authority to overturn Security Council acts that it considers invalid* Never has the Court declared any act of the Security Council invalid as beyond the scope of its authority—under Article 39 or any other provision of the Charter. A clash with

---

*In the *Certain Expenses Case*, a majority of the judges agreed that "the Court does not possess powers of judicial review or appeal in respect of the decisions taken by the United Nations organs concerned." 1971 I.C.J. 16.

the Security Council could pose fatal risks to an already feckless international judicial tribunal, yet a United Nations system devoid of checks and balances raises the threat of unbridled power wielded on an international scale with unfettered discretion.*

Whether the International Court can or does declare an act of the Security Council invalid is in any event irrelevant to the issue of the ultimate validity of such an act. The reason for Charter-imposed limits is to ensure that the Security Council does not exceed its delegated powers. Even if the Court were not willing or able to invalidate an unlawful act of the Council, the act would remain unlawful; the Council should respect limits on its power notwithstanding probable abstention by the Court. The Security Council cannot effectively collude with the International Court to remove restraints that the Charter imposes upon either organ. The limits of the Charter are binding on the Council whether they are enforced by the International Court or not. That "there is no mechanism for sanctioning the Security Council if it breaches the Charter," Mohammed Bedjaoui concluded, "in no way weakens the principle that the Council is subjected to the Charter...." To argue otherwise, he suggested, would be akin to giving "a prisoner...the keys to his jail, so that the obligation to remain deprived of liberty depended solely upon himself."[8]

---

continued

But see Questions of Interpretation and Application of the 1971 Montreal Convention Arising from the Aerial Incident at Lockerbie (Libya v. UK; Libya v. U.S.), *Provisional Measures*, 1992 I.C.J. 3, 114 (Orders of Apr. 14), where the International Court indicated that Security Council Resolution 748 is valid because Article 25 of the UN Charter makes Security Council resolutions adopted in accordance with the Charter binding on member states, and Article 103 makes obligations of member states under the Charter prevail over obligations undertaken pursuant to other international agreements. Since the Court did not look beyond the Charter to general international law, it did not decide whether the Security Council may override the legal rights of states.

*For an illuminating discussion of the issue, see "UN Checks and Balances: The Roles of the I.C.J. and the Security Council," in *Contemporary International Law Issues: Opportunities at a Time of Momentous Change*, Proceedings of the 1993 Joint Conference, American Society of International Law and the Nederlandse Vereniging voor Internationaal Recht 280–297 (1993).

Lillich—and a surprising number of others*—would have given the prisoner the keys. Farer, too, seems untroubled by *ultra vires* Security Council action, believing the Council analogous to the British Parliament; as he sees it, the Council's legislative supremacy persists only with state support.[9] There is some force to this argument. Generalized community approval may explain the *political* acceptability of the Council's actions. But the analogy does not adequately account for the perennial "tyranny of the majority" problem.† The Charter imposes limits on the Council that are far more specific than those imposed by the unwritten British Constitution on the Parliament. The purpose of those limits is, in part, to protect the right of weak states against intervention by the

---

*See, for example, Stanley Hoffmann, *The Ethics and Politics of Humanitarian Intervention* 28 (1996) ("The greatest recent progress has been the willingness of the Security Council to broaden the tent of 'threats to peace.'"); Anthony Parsons, "The UN and the National Interests of States," in *United Nations, Divided World: The U.N.'s Roles in International Relations* 104 (Adam Roberts and Benedict Kingsbury eds., 1993) ("The UN, without formal Charter amendment, is flexible enough to reinterpret the restriction in Article 2(7) on intervening in the domestic affairs of states ... . In the years to come Article 2(7) may well be seen as a dead letter similar to the military articles." *Id.* at 118.). Perhaps the most breathtaking adaptivist claim is that of Michael Reisman, who has argued not only that Article 2(7) has been changed, but that that change has also changed Article 2(4). See Michael Reisman, "Kosovo's Antinomies," 93 *Am. J. Int'l L* 860, 861 (1999) ("Kosovo does not erode Article 2(4). Article 2(4) was changed by the contraction of Article 2(7), which, by effectively eliminating for serious human rights violations the defense of domestic jurisdiction, removed from the sphere of the 'political independence' of a state the right to violate in grave fashion and with impunity the human rights of its inhabitants.").

†"[U]nless one is prepared to put the theoretical basis of international law on a footing other than consent, unless one is prepared to advocate the legality of majority rule on its own merits, one must reject the idea that custom has a role to play in the political organs of the United Nations.... [W]e are dealing with sovereign states which base their activity on consent ... . Consequently, it is fruitless to describe a consistent practice of the General Assembly or Security Council as creating international law. To do so would be to assume the surrender of sovereignty ... ." J. S. Watson, "Autointerpretation, Competence, and the Continuing Validity of Article 2(7) of the UN Charter," 71 *Am. J. Int'l L.* 60, 77 (1977); see also

strong. Without the guarantee that intervention would not be permitted—without the protection of a state's domestic jurisdiction from outside interference—the United Nations as we know it would not exist.

The Charter's primary limits on the Council are set forth in Articles 2(7) and 39. To take enforcement measures under Chapter VII, the Security Council must first find a "threat to the peace, breach of the peace, or act of aggression" under Article 39:

> The Security Council shall determine the existence of any threat to the peace, breach of the peace, or act of aggression and shall make recommendations, or decide what measures shall be taken in accordance with Articles 41 and 42, to maintain or restore international peace and security.

Article 2(7) removes from the Council's powers matters that are essentially within the domestic jurisdiction of any state:*

> Nothing contained in the present Charter shall authorize the United Nations to intervene in matters which are essentially within the domestic jurisdiction of any state or shall require the Members to submit such matters to settlement under the present Charter; but this principle shall not prejudice the application of enforcement measures under Chapter VII.

These provisions are, together, the linchpin of the Charter. Commenting on Article 39 in his initial report to the President on the San Francisco Conference, Secretary of State Edward Stettinius said: "If any single provision of the Charter has more substance than the others, it is surely this one sentence, in which are concentrated the most important powers of the Security Council."[10]

---

continued
D. W. Bowett, *United Nations Forces* 427 (1964) ("So long as the United Nations remains an organization based upon the co-operation of sovereign States for the preservation of international peace and security—and not a federal or 'supra-national' organization—it should in principle refrain from any form of coercion in respect of internal, civil disorders.").
*Article 2(7) of the Charter tracks Article 15, paragraph 8 of the Covenant of the League of Nations, which was actually less protective of state interests than the Charter in that it placed off limits only those matters that were "*solely* within [their] domestic jurisdiction … ." (emphasis added).

The meaning and purpose of these provisions is clear. "In ... purely 'civil' strifes," Derek Bowett writes, "when the problem is simply one of the internal order and stability of a State ... no United Nations Force should be used."*,[11] Even *with* the consent of the sitting government, he notes, Article 39 must be construed as precluding the United Nations from acting absent some threat to international peace. "[N]o consent of the territorial State," Bowett continues, "can authorize functions which do not stem from the necessity to maintain or restore *international* peace and security .... To embark upon such functions, even with the consent of the host government, would involve the United Nations Force in what is plainly a domestic matter and not one affecting *international* peace. It would involve a suppression of the right to self-determination ... ."[12]

But more than self-determination is at issue. As Frederic Kirgis has noted, the intent behind this limitation is to give some protection against arbitrary action by the Security Council.[13] The Article was "clearly intended to address ... traditional cross-boundary uses of deadly force by governments."[14] The combined effect of these provisions is to preclude the Security Council from taking any enforcement action absent a threat to the peace, breach of the peace, or act of aggression. Not only would such action not be authorized under Article 39; because it is not, such action would run afoul of the principle of nonintervention set out in Article 2(7)†

It has also been argued that the prohibition of Article 2(4) corresponds to the restriction of Article 39. The argument is that the phrase "threat of force" in Article 2(4), relating as it does to a threat of cross-border violence, in effect correlates with the phrase "threat to the peace" in Article 39. The upshot is that these provisions,

---

*Because "genocide [and] gross violation of human rights by arbitrary violence ... are likely to endanger *international* peace by producing exactly the conditions which would encourage intervention by outside Powers," UN action to suppress such measures would be justified. D. W. Bowett, *United Nations Forces*, 426–27 (1964). The inference seems dubious; in few instances have gross human rights violations incited intervention.

†Thus D. R. Gilmour has argued that if a situation is essentially internal, Article 2(7) precludes consideration by the Security Council. D. R. Gilmour, "The Meaning of 'Intervene' within the Meaning of the United Nations Charter," 16 *I.C.L.Q.* 330, 349 (1967).

construed *in pari materia,* effectively proscribe the use of force by the Security Council in internal situations.[15]

What of the qualifying exception of Article 39 ("this principle shall not prejudice the application of enforcement measures under Chapter VII")? Fairly construed, it can mean only that where valid enforcement action is undertaken, action that would otherwise represent intervention in a state's domestic jurisdiction would not. It would not constitute intervention in Iraq's domestic jurisdiction, for example, if, during the Gulf War, military bases within Iraq were bombed. The exception does not diminish the vitality of the prohibition against intervention absent valid enforcement action. If it did—if the Council could intervene in the internal affairs of a state merely by labeling its intervention as an "enforcement action"— the prohibition would be rendered meaningless and could be dispensed with semantically. No: the Charter imposes a double prohibition against unwanted Security Council action by setting out both a limited scope of authority—Article 39—and an explicit proscription against acts exceeding that authority—Article 2(7). Unless there exists a "threat to the peace, breach of the peace, or act of aggression," its action is invalid as a violation of a state's domestic jurisdiction.

What exactly *is* a "threat to the peace, breach of the peace, or act of aggression?" A reasonable construction of the phrase, construed in conjunction with Article 2(7), would be that it comprehends at least a threat of action by a state that is (a) violent and (b) has cross-border effects.

That that predicate contemplates at least a threat of actual violence (as opposed to, for example, mere refugee flows or human rights violations) is implicit in the connotation of the antonym of *violence, peace.* Action carrying no threat of violence does not threaten the peace. The peace is threatened only with a use of force or the threat of force. This has been the meaning accorded the phrase by the United States on a number of occasions.[16] At the time of the Berlin airlift in 1948, for example, the U.S. representative to the Security Council summarized the Article's meaning as follows:

What constitutes a 'threat to the peace' as that term is used in Article 39 of the Charter? A threat to the peace is created when a State uses force or the threat of force to secure compliance with its demands.[17]

The representative proceeded to state that the Soviet Union, "in illegally obstructing by threat of force the access of the three Western powers to Berlin creates a threat to the peace"[18]—suggesting, again, the need for some threat of force or violence before a threat to the peace can be found. Human rights violations not comprising force or violence thus cannot be classified as threats to the peace. In Goronwy Jones's words: "It was the evident intention of those who drafted Article 2(7) of the Charter that the United Nations should not interfere in questions involving a state's treatment of its own subjects, which covers the entire field of human rights."[19]

That the Article contemplates some form of transboundary activity is explicit in its terms: If the predicate set out in the Article is fulfilled, the Security Council is authorized to restore *international* peace and security, not peace and security lacking an international dimension. Consideration by the United States Senate makes clear that the phrase was taken by all to comprehend only action by more states than one. When Article 39 was discussed by the Senate Foreign Relations Committee, the phrase "peace of the world"—as opposed to simply "peace"—was used at least ten times in connection with the words "threaten," "endanger," and "threat to."[20] On the Senate floor, Senator Langer asked whether the Security Council could respond with force to a "revolt against England" by "the 400,000,000 people of India." The floor manager, Senator Connally, answered unequivocally that it could not. The dispute, he said, would constitute a "domestic matter within the jurisdiction of the British Commonwealth of Nations" under Article 2(7) of the Charter.[21] Use of the term "international" in Article 39 was taken to have special significance. "International peace" was distinguished from simply "peace." Senator Ferguson asked whether "'threat to the peace' and 'breach of the peace' may refer to an internal situation in a country."[22] Senator Burton replied that the entire Article referred to "international peace."[23] Senator Connally agreed, adding that the seeming discrepancy was "merely the result of a lack of conformity in the text; or to make use of the two expressions rather than use the same terms over and over again."[24]

The cross-border requirement was crucial not only to the U.S. Senate, however. Examining the origins of that limit, Sean D. Murphy notes that "[t]he phrase 'threat to the peace' arose at the Dumbarton Oaks Conference in the context of how to handle 'disputes' *among* states that could not be resolved peacefully."[25]

Insistence upon some transboundary effect makes sense. Cross-border violence is the element common to each of the three possibilities under which action is permitted by Article 39. As Henkin himself put it (albeit in earlier days):

In the absence of external intervention or the clear danger that an internal war will otherwise threaten international peace, the jurisdiction of the United Nations is open to question: It, too, is not supposed to intervene in strictly 'domestic affairs,' and presumably the strictly civil war, contained within national boundaries, would be deemed 'domestic.'[26]

Henkin later seemed to argue, inexplicably, that while civil war was deemed domestic, human rights violations were not.* Others have followed his lead,† though it is perplexing how one could find the Security Council empowered to intervene in, say, Tienanmen or Chechnya—or Los Angeles or Chicago—to stop the bloody

---

*In 1993 Henkin wrote:

I am not suggesting that there are no limits to what the Security Council can do. The Council has to act responsibly and intra vires; it has to interpret its Charter mandate honestly, scrupulously. Voting and the veto, and other political forces, shape and limit its actions. But the Security Council is master of its jurisdiction and its authority. Even that darling of champions of "sovereignty," Article 2(7), speaks not of "sovereignty" but of "domestic jurisdiction," i.e., of internal autonomy on internal matters. That is a truism. But that which is governed by international norms, which is subject to regulation by agreed international institutions acting within their authority, is not domestic but is within the social contract. The condition of human rights has long ceased to be domestic. "Ethnic cleansing" in Bosnia, even starvation in Somalia, is not essentially domestic.

Louis Henkin, "The Mythology of Sovereignty," *ASIL Newsletter*, Mar.–May 1993.
†See, for example, Lori Fisler Damrosch, "Commentary on Collective Military Intervention to Enforce Human Rights," in *Law and Force in the New International Order* 222 (Lori Fisler Damrosch and David J. Scheffer eds., 1991) (stating without support that "Article 2(7) of the Charter presents no barrier to action by U.N. organs in aid of human rights.").

suppression of disorder but not in Manila, Jakarta, or Teheran, when civil war raged in the Philippines, Indonesia, or Iran.

An argument occasionally is made that the framers of the Charter declined to define "peace," "breach," "security," and other key terms. They did so, it is contended, to afford the Security Council broad discretion is implementing its Chapter VII powers. It obviously is true that these terms are not defined. It is also true that there was sentiment on the part of some of the drafters of the Charter to give the Council flexibility in determining the near and far reach of its powers.* But, as Ian Brownlie has pointed out, there is a circularity in the claim that the Security Council has wide discretion in deciding upon ways and means.[27] Every agency, whether created by statute or by treaty, is responsible in the first instance for defining the scope of its powers. Day-to-day functioning would be impossible absent some self-prescribed assessment of the scope of delegated authority. The need to define powers at the margins, however, hardly implies the authority to define powers at the core. The propriety of determining whether action is permissible in hard cases by no means suggests that an agency can decide to *eliminate altogether* all meaningful limits on its power. It is one thing to determine whether an act falls on one side of a line or another, but quite another to determine to erase the line entirely. The former is an act of respect for the rule of law; the latter destroys it. That such reductionism is necessary to shore up the argument for Security Council interventionism merely highlights the argument's weakness.

A final argument sometimes is made that the Security Council should be permitted to intervene to carry out the "principles" of the Charter. But authority to enforce the Charter's amorphous principles would expunge all limits. And in any event the limits set out in Article 2(7) and Article 39 are surely among the Charter's most important principles. "The conclusion must be," Brownlie wrote,

---

*In fact, the record reveals that the seeming open-endedness of the formula was intended, at most, *not* to convey broader powers upon the Security Council than would tighter wording, *not* to obviate disagreement, *not* to eviscerate the force of the limitation, but rather merely to postpone the debate that everyone knew must some day occur. See Testimony of Lawrence Preuss, "Compulsory Jurisdiction of the International Court of Justice," *Hearings Before a Subcommittee of the Committee on Foreign Relations, United States Senate*, Jul. 12, 1946 (79th Cong., 2d Sess.), at 82.

"that the Security Council is subject to the test of legality in terms of its designated institutional competence."[28] That competence, he reminds us, is spelled out in the Charter. Article 2 provides that the "Principles" shall bind "the Organization and its Members."[29] Article 24, far from indicating an "unfettered conferment of powers," expressly stipulates that:

> In discharging these duties the Security Council shall act in accordance with the Purposes and Principles of the United Nations. The specific powers granted to the Security Council for the discharge of these duties are laid down in Chapters VI, VII, VIII and XII.

"A determination of a threat to the peace as a basis for action necessary to remove the threat to the peace cannot be used as a basis for action which (if the evidence so indicates) is for collateral and independent purposes... ."[30] Labeling something a threat to the peace that is *not* a threat to the peace does not make it one; the Security Council cannot expand its power through a semantic sleight of hand. To permit the Council to intervene in the domestic affairs of states would constitute nothing less than "the creation of a provision de novo."[31] To one mindful of the rule of law, the creation of a new rule is a task for the law's makers, not for law's interpreters. International law scholars, however much they may wish it otherwise, fall into the ranks of interpreters. Wisely or unwisely, those who made the law—the states that framed the United Nations Charter—made a rule that prohibited Security Council intervention in states' internal affairs. The reason behind that rule is not irrational. "We cannot dismiss as fantasy," Innis Claude wrote, "the anxiety that international organization might prove itself a new variety of tyranny, global in scope; in the long historical view, any tendency of international agencies to exhibit contempt for constitutional limitations is a bad augury."[32]

B. Security Council Practice

For the better part of its history, the Security Council respected the bar against intervention. Neither Pol Pot nor Idi Amin could provoke the Security Council to contravene the Charter's prohibition. In part, no doubt, the Council's inaction derived not only from the

Charter's explicit limits but also from a longstanding distaste on the part of the international community for involvement in a state's internal affairs. When the League of Nations was asked to intervene in the Spanish civil war, it responded by offering to store the Prado's paintings in Geneva.* In part, the Council's passivity also derived from divisions within it. For the better part of the postwar era, it stood paralyzed by the threat of a Soviet veto. Even when the Cold War thawed, however, the Council's members remained largely indifferent to governments' mistreatments of their citizens, restrained quietly but firmly by the belief that there, but for the grace of God, would go they. Hence Chechnya and Tienanmen Square.

Yet cracks began to appear in the old anti-interventionist regime. Although no armed attack had occurred, and although no interstate violence had broken out that posed any threat to the vital interests of any other state, in several situations the Security Council authorized use of force to set right states' internal affairs. As pointed out earlier, Kosovo did not mark the first time that the Charter's limits were transgressed because its allocation of power had proven unworkable. During the Korean War, when the Soviet Union's veto in the Security Council threatened to block prosecution of the war by the United Nations, the United States and its allies managed to shift the Council's functions to the General Assembly by getting it to adopt the "Uniting for Peace Resolution"[33]—even though the Charter gives the Security Council primary responsibility for the maintenance of peace and security and prohibits the Assembly, which is empowered only to discuss and make recommendations on a question,[34] from considering a matter which is being discussed by the Council.[35] (For reasons that are not clear,† no effort was made during the Kosovo conflict to

---

*Art. 15, § 8 of the League Covenant corresponded closely to Art. 2(7) of the UN Charter. It provided as follows:

> If the dispute between the parties is claimed by one of them, and is found by the Council to arise out of a matter which by international law is solely within the domestic jurisdiction of that party, the Council shall so report, and shall make no recommendation as to its settlement.

†The Foreign Affairs Committee of the British House of Commons received testimony that the Foreign and Commonwealth Office "was uncertain that the two thirds majority would have been achieved, and ... [that it] regarded the General Assembly as in any case a cumbersome procedure to use since

secure the approval of the Assembly under a similar resolution.*)
Still, the point remains: By intervening in the internal affairs of
states, the Security Council itself contributed to the erosion of the
Charter's constraints on use of force, beginning with Southern
Rhodesia and continuing with legally questionable interventions in
South Africa, Iraq, Somalia, Rwanda, and Haiti. Governments that
have come to justify humanitarian intervention by states acting in
the face of Security Council paralysis rely expressly on the Council's
own record.† A brief account of each follows.‡

---

continued

resolutions passed there could not easily be modified." House of
Commons, Select Committee on Foreign Affairs, Fourth Report ¶ 128
(May 23, 2000), http://www.publications.parliament.uk/pa/cm199900/
cmselect/cmfaff/28/2813.htm (last visited Feb. 23, 2001).

*The short-sightedness of the Uniting for Peace charade seemed largely to
have escaped American diplomats at the time, who apparently assumed
that the United States would retain a friendly majority in the General
Assembly for all time and would thus never need a veto—which can be
employed only in the Security Council. Within the space of two decades,
that majority had, of course, turned hostile, although the Assembly has not
again attempted the arrogation of the Council's executive powers. See generally Daniel Patrick Moynihan, *A Dangerous Place* (1978). After the
International Court's advisory opinion in the *Certain Expenses Case*, it is
doubtful whether the General Assembly has the authority claimed in the
Resolution. See John F. Murphy, "Force and Arms," in *The United
Nations And International Law* 97, 109 (Christopher C. Joyne ed., 1997).

†See, for example, Lloyd Axworthy, The Hauser Lecture on International
Humanitarian Law: Humanitarian Interventions and Humanitarian
Constraints, Address at New York University Law School (Feb. 10, 2000),
http://webapps.dfait-maeci.gc.ca/minpub ... n.asp?FileSpec=/
Min_Pub_Docs/103018.htm, ("The cumulative weight of international
human rights and humanitarian law, the global trend against impunity and
for accountability that led to the creation of the International Criminal
Court, *the precedents set by the Council itself*—all justify action in the face
of severe humanitarian crisis and Council inability to acquit its responsibilities.")(emphasis added).

‡Obviously this is neither a comprehensive account of Security Council
practice, nor an effort to parse every incident where the Council's authority
was controverted. It has been suggested, for example, that in the Congo in
the early 1960s "there was certainly no direct 'threat or use of force' by
one state against another," and no armed clash by outside powers appeared
imminent. N. D. White, *Keeping the Peace: The United Nations*

1. *Rhodesia*

The Security Council's first major intervention occurred in Rhodesia. In 1965, Southern Rhodesia's government declared its independence from Great Britain. The Security Council that same year called upon member states to sever diplomatic relations with the break-away regime[36] and, in 1966, authorized the use of force to exclude oil tankers from the ports of Mozambique (whence oil was transshipped to Southern Rhodesia)[37] and imposed selective mandatory sanctions,[38] referring in the latter two instances to a "threat to the peace" posed by the proclamation of independence.

Critics of the racist regime in Rhodesia hailed the UN action, but some were troubled by the Council's willingness to flout the limits of the Charter.[39] The *Washington Post* editorialized that the sanctions "amount to interference in the domestic affairs of another country merely because of the form of government practiced there."[40] "The white minority's transgressions," it said, "have occurred within the boundaries of one country … ."[41] Former Secretary of State Dean Acheson opined that "whatever the Rhodesians have done has been wholly within their own country … ."[42]

Enthusiastic about the policy objectives, defenders of the Security Council's action responded by effectively reading out of the Charter limits on the Council's power explicitly set out in Articles 2(7) and 39. Human rights violations are *never* a matter of purely domestic concern, Myres McDougal and Michael Reisman wrote:

> [T]he claim of "domestic jurisdiction" could not be invoked effectively to insulate the systematic deprivation of human rights in

---

continued

and the Maintenance of International Peace and Security 36 (1993). Nonetheless, the Security Council adopted a resolution finding a "threat to the peace." S.C. Res. 161, U.N. SCOR Resolutions 2 (1961). Does this incident belong on the list? I exclude it because, in the face of a civil war in which one side was supported by Belgium (Moise Tshombe) and the other (Patrice Lumumba) by the Soviet Union, a spill-over potential existed; the involvement of the superpowers loomed as a possibility. Moreover, the United States insisted that the government of the Congo had consented to the presence of foreign troops. Rather than enter into an extended discussion concerning such questions as the likelihood of cross-border effects or the extent to which local consent was actually given, I restrict the list to cases that raise the issue most prominently—without suggesting that the list is complete.

Rhodesia from the scrutiny and rebuke of "international concern … ."[43] [I]nternational peace and security and the protection of human rights are inescapably interdependent and … the impact of the flagrant deprivation of the most basic human rights of the great mass of the people of a community cannot possibly stop short within the territorial boundaries in which the physical manifestations of such deprivations first occur.[44] *Any* matter originating in one state with deprivatory effects going beyond its borders may become a matter of international concern.[45]

Lest there be any doubt that the Security Council can exercise jurisdiction over such actions, their argument continued, the Security Council has *said* that it has such jurisdiction, and that settles the matter: "[T]he fact that the situation in Rhodesia has been authoritatively found to constitute a threat to international peace makes irrelevant all conceptions of 'domestic jurisdiction … .'"[46] The limits of the Council's power, in other words, are determined by the Council; if it decides to expunge those limits, the limits are expunged.* The only procedural safeguards against abuse of power by the Council subsist entirely in voting procedures, "which require the concurring votes of the permanent members and a special majority of all members."[47]

2. South Africa

In 1977, the Security Council found a threat to the maintenance of peace and security with respect to South Africa. As in the case of Southern Rhodesia before it, it was the nation's policy of racial discrimination that triggered the Council's action. "Indeed," Murphy noted, "it is in the practice of the Security Council in respect of southern Africa as a whole in the 1960s that one can see the beginning of an expansive interpretation of what constitutes a 'threat to the peace.' There, the Security Council characterized two essentially

---

*For similar arguments, see N. D. White, *Keeping the Peace: The United Nations and the Maintenance of International Peace and Security* 37 (1993) ("Recent practice suggests that the requirement [of a breach or threat to the peace] is something of a formality, and that the Council is in reality concerning itself with purely internal situations."); J. P. Cot and A. Pellet, *La Charte des Nationes Unies* 665 (1985).

internal situations of human rights abuses related to systematic racial discrimination as threatening international peace and security ... ."[48]

The legal predicate with respect to South Africa was no more clear than it had been with respect to Rhodesia. The resolution referred to the country's internal policy of apartheid and called for an end to racial segregation; however, the resolution also referred to South Africa's "persistent acts of aggression against neighboring states,"[49] perhaps alluding to its armed attacks against Angola, Botswana, Zambia, Mozambique, and Lesotho.[50]

3. Iraq

The end of the Cold War accelerated the erosion of the Charter's restraints on the Council. Following the Gulf War, in April 1991, Iran and Turkey notified the Security Council that several hundred thousand Iraqi nationals were massing along their borders with Iraq and crossing into their territory. On April 5, 1991, the Council adopted a resolution that demanded that Iraq halt repression of its civilian population and permitted member states to enter Iraqi territory to carry out humanitarian operations. The Council noted its responsibility for the maintenance of peace and security and its concern that Iraq's repression had "led to a massive flow of refugees towards and across international frontiers and to cross-border incursions which threaten international peace and security."[51] These refugee flows, however, were the only cross-border activities, and hardly amounted to a threat to the peace—as was pointed out by representatives of Cuba, Yemen, and Zimbabwe, who voted against the measure, and of course Iraq itself. The resolution, the Iraqi representative said, was a "flagrant, illegitimate interference in Iraq's internal affairs" and a breach of Article 2(7).[52] China abstained. The Security Council, its representative said, "should not consider or take action on questions concerning the internal affairs of any State."[53] India also abstained; its representative urged that the Security Council "should not prescribe what should be done, for that would impinge on the internal affairs of the States."[54] Jane Stromseth has pointed out that "only ten of the fifteen Security Council members supported the resolution, and all of them emphasized the spillover effect of Iraq's repression *across borders*. Only France and Britain suggested that a state's violation of its citizens' human rights might by itself justify Security Council action if it reached a certain level of egregiousness. In sharp contrast, five members expressed great apprehension about a larger Security Council role in conflicts they viewed as essentially 'domestic.' "[55]

4. Somalia

No threat of cross-border violence arose in Somalia, but the Security Council was undeterred. In January 1991, the government of Somali President Said Barre was ousted, leading to widespread civil strife in which several local warlords fought for control. As famine threatened, the United Nations undertook humanitarian relief operations. Deliveries of food and medical supplies were disrupted, however, as internecine fighting spun out of control. (All violence, then as later, was internal, and no foreign interference of any sort was alleged.) The United States offered in November 1991 to provide military units to safeguard the deliveries. Secretary General Boutros Boutros-Ghali recommended that the U.S. offer be accepted, and the Security Council authorized use of force in Somalia in 1992.[56] The intervention probably halted a massive famine. Yet, as Frederic Kirgis observed, "[t]here was little evidence that the strife between clans in Somalia, devastating though it was for the people of that country, actually posed a serious threat to stability in neighboring states, at least in the short term."[57] Ruth Gordon concluded that "a humanitarian crisis with no discernible cross-border effects, or at least none that involved military consequences, triggered the most extreme measures the Council can undertake."[58] Arguably, the affront to Somalia's sovereignty was mitigated by the absence of a functioning government in the country at the time of the intervention. Still, as was true with respect to Haiti, the principles of sovereignty and self-determination had long been seen by international law as precluding outside interference of the sort undertaken by the Security Council.

5. Rwanda

Regular clashes between the Hutu and minority Tutsi tribes (the latter comprised approximately 15 percent of the population of 7.7 million) were common in Rwanda following its independence from Belgium in 1961. With the death of Rwanda's president in a plane crash in April 1994, however, the fighting dramatically escalated—even though a UN peace-keeping force was in Rwanda at the time to monitor a cease-fire agreement between the Hutus and Tutsis. (The Security Council reduced the mission's size and suspended relief flights into the country as the danger grew.) Radical Hutus took over the government and murdered the late president's prime minister, charging that he had been killed by the Tutsis. In a subsequent rampage, gangs of Hutus joined with militias and paramilitary groups in a mass slaughter of the Tutsi population. Many of the murders were carried out with machetes and sharpened sticks. By mid-summer, estimates of the dead numbered 500,000 to one million.[59] On June 15, 1994, French Foreign Minister Alain Juppe declared that France was prepared to intervene,[60] but he insisted upon a "green light" from the United Nations, which came on June 22 when the Security Council authorized the use of "all necessary means to achieve the humanitarian objectives" of its resolution of approval.[61] Within a month, a million Hutus had fled into Zaire. Violence broke out in the refugee camps, reportedly committed by Hutu soldiers.[62] As Murphy concluded, "[t]he deployment of French military forces into Rwanda in June 1994 was a use of force that normally would implicate Article 2(4) of the UN Charter. The reason given for the intervention was neither self-defense nor the protection of French nationals … . Even before the French intervention, the Security Council had declared the civil strife in Rwanda as constituting a threat to the peace, and had done so with emphasis more on the slaughter of Rwandan nationals than on their flight to neighboring countries."[63] Once again, the Security Council had intervened in purely internal strife that posed no threat to international peace or security.

6. Haiti

The decline of the old order was hastened, finally, with the Security Council's 1994 authorization of use of force in Haiti. The superpowers, in maintaining spheres of influence, had regularly flouted the old anti-interventionist order. In Haiti, the Security Council again followed their lead—as NATO would do five years later in Kosovo—without reflecting at all upon what new rules, if any, might be fashioned to take their place.

The Security Council's rationale for authorizing the invasion of Haiti was not altogether clear from the measure that did so.[64] But that resolution prominently mentioned the justifications put forward by the United States and set out no other legal rationale. One

U.S. justification not mentioned in the resolution concerned problems created for the United States by the flood of refugees. The Security Council dealt with the refugee problem not as a potential cross-border threat but, rather, in the context of humanitarian considerations. As in other situations in which the Council has acted under Chapter VII (involving, for example, Somalia[65] and Rwanda[66]), no armed attack had occurred. Indeed, no hostilities broke out apart from civil strife generated by domestic divisions that posed no threat to the interests of other states. Nonetheless, the Security Council chose to ride roughshod over Haitian sovereignty*—setting the stage for NATO to override Yugoslavian sovereignty. Like the Security Council, NATO too would not consider the rationale for continued ad hoc opportunism—or the impact of its improvised precedents on future attempts to avoid the piecemeal and move towards principle. Unlike the Security Council, however, NATO did not face Russian insistence on a geopolitical payoff as a condition for its support: In the behind-the-scenes back-and-forth on Haiti, the United States agreed to support Russia's demands for Security Council approval of its own peace-keeping force in Georgia.[67]

C. The Effect of Security Council Practice

There can be little doubt that the Security Council has acted in a manner inconsistent with the limits placed on its authority by Article 39 and Article 2(7) of the Charter. As Sean Murphy concluded after an extensive review of the Council's practice, "By considering essentially internal human rights violations and deprivations to be 'threats to the peace,' the Security Council is expanding the scope of its authority beyond that originally envisioned in Chapter VII of the Charter."[68] What is the effect of this

---

*Under traditional international law, it was irrelevant that the lawfully elected government had been displaced. With the possible exception of puppet governments installed by invaders, how a government comes to power has never been seen as relevant to the propriety of use of force against it. The classic view has been that it is for a nation's people to determine their destiny for themselves; whether they choose to do so by ballot or bullet is no concern of the international community, and their choice provides no justification for intervention.

Security Council practice on the Charter's meaning? Has it success-fully eviscerated the constraints placed on the Council by Article 2(7) and Article 39?

Two salient facts confront an interpreter of the UN Charter: It is a treaty, and it is a treaty that is said to partake in the nature of a constitution.

That the Charter is a treaty means that it is subject to accepted rules of interpretation applicable to all treaties. Those are set out in the Vienna Convention on the Law of Treaties.[69] The Convention provides that it applies only to treaties concluded after it entered into force, thus excluding the Charter.[70] Nonetheless, the Convention is widely viewed as a codification of preexisting princi-ples of customary international law.[71] This is true, in particular, with respect to Article 31 of the Convention. "Legal rules concern-ing the interpretation of treaties constitute one of the sections of the Vienna Convention which were adopted without a dissenting vote at the Conference and consequently may be considered as declara-tory of existing law."[72] Article 31 prescribes the basic rule for inter-preting treaties: "A treaty shall be interpreted in good faith in accordance with the ordinary meaning to be given to the terms of the treaty in their context and in the light of its object and pur-pose." A treaty's context is defined not to include subsequent prac-tice; rather, "[a]ny subsequent practice in the application of the treaty which establishes the agreement of the parties regarding its interpretation" is something that "shall be taken into account ... ."

Two aspects of this rule need to be noted. First, the subsidiary role accorded subsequent practice represented a repudiation of those (such as Myers McDougal) seeking to accord it a more promi-nent role in treaty interpretation.[73] Second, the rule inexplicably fails to distinguish bilateral from multilateral treaties. The Convention should have treated the two differently; practice subse-quent to a multilateral treaty raises more complex questions than practice subsequent to a bilateral treaty. Indeed, there may in some circumstances be reason to disregard altogether practice subsequent to a multilateral treaty. Judge Sir Percy Spender in the *Certain Expenses Case* wrote that while the subsequent conduct of state parties to a bilateral treaty may reveal their intent with respect to the meaning of ambiguous terms, "an element of artificiality" attaches when the meaning of a multilateral treaty such as the UN Charter is inferred from the actions of groups of states that are par-ties to that treaty. If the basis of interpretation is the intent of original members of the UN at the time they entered into the Charter, he asked, why should the subsequent conduct of other, newer members be examined at all to determine original intent? Moreover, one may add, even if the basis of interpretation is the intent of nonoriginal members, why should the subsequent conduct of one such member be examined to determine the intent of another—particularly if the other state was not even a party to the treaty at the time of the conduct in question? The Vienna Convention thus seems simplistic in its assumption that subsequent practice sheds as much light on the meaning of a multilateral treaty as it does on the meaning of a bilateral one.

Still, the substantive import of Article 31 is significant, for its rule gives no weight to subsequent practice unless such practice "establishes the agreement of the parties regarding its interpretation." This rather significant qualification is overlooked by commentators who argue for Security Council power to ignore all limits on its power* based on the assertion that the Vienna Convention "provides that the interpretation of a treaty may be influenced by practice."[74] Practice—even substantial practice—might exist but have no interpretive value. An example would be practice engaged in by only a small number of parties to a widely accepted multilateral treaty. The practice of a small minority of parties can hardly be regarded as "establishing the agreement" of all other parties to a treaty. In fact, that is precisely the situation with regard to the United Nations Charter. Even a unanimous Security Council would constitute only 8 percent of the total membership of the United Nations—hardly enough to "establish the agreement" of all 188 members that the Charter's most important safeguard had been expunged.

That the United Nations Charter is a "constitutive" treaty[75]—a treaty establishin norms and institutions whose object is to shape other norms and institutions—is said to argue for flexibility in its interpretation.[76] The United Nations, one commentator put it, is a "living global organization. It organs were designed both to implement important tasks and to interpret their own authority. Such

---

*See, for example, Mary Ellen O'Connell, "The UN, NATO, and International Law After Kosovo," 22 *Hum. Rts. Q.* 57, 68 (2000) ("To the extent that the international community has not criticized or opposed the Security Council's conduct, it should probably not be viewed as *ultra vires* or unlawful.").

organic growth is desirable and inevitable."[77] Americans in particular are familiar with the theory that a constitution must be a living
document. The United States Supreme Court has reminded us, since
the days of Chief Justice John Marshall, that our Constitution was
intended to endure for the ages and must be interpreted more flexi-
bly than, say, a code of civil practice. A constitution must have
"play at the joints," it must represent a statement of basic, lasting
principles that can be applied differently as society's needs change.
"The life of the law," Holmes said, "is not logic but experience."[78]
No people can be deemed to consent to rule of the cold hand of the
dead. These same considerations, the argument goes, counsel in
favor of a flexible approach* that considers subsequent practice in
interpreting the UN Charter, which is, at least in some respects,
analogous to a world constitution. "[W]e're returning to our global
constitution," said Soviet Foreign Minister Eduard Schevardnadze
as the Gulf War loomed, "the United Nations Charter."[79]

There is some force to this "adaptivist" approach. The world is
indeed a vastly different place than it was 50 years ago, when the
United Nations comprised less than one-third the number of member states that it does today. The framers of the Charter surely
could not have been expected to divine the needs of a world almost
so different from theirs. They painted the Charter with broad
strokes, intending that *some* of its gaps be filled by the reality test
of precedent and history. The Charter's dynamic quality thus
enables it to derive legitimacy from the intent, and consent, not
only from its original drafting signatories, but also from the continued participation of parties old and new in the lawmaking process.

Its appeal notwithstanding, adaptivism has a downside, and a
serious one at that: Carried beyond a certain point, it is at odds
with the notion of the rule of law. An extreme adaptivist approach

---

*See, for example, David J. Scheffer, "Commentary on Collective Security"
in *Law and Force in the New International Order* 101 (Lori Fisler
Damrosch and David J. Scheffer eds., 1991), who argues that "[t]he Iraq–
Kuwait crisis served to remind us that the Charter is a flexible document
and can be interpreted as such." *Id.* at 103. It is not clear why such a conclusion is justified in the context of the Gulf War. As Scheffer himself notes
on the preceding page, the United States regarded Security Council
approval as legally unnecessary and could have relied upon Article 51 had
the Council not acted. *Id.* at 102.

reduces the law to a wad of putty, to ever-malleable clay to be kneaded and shaped—and distorted—in response to every passing whim or caprice on the part of those strong enough to mold it. The approach robs the rule of law of its protective function, because the "interpreters" inevitably are the powerful, not the weak. It forsakes principle for expediency, predictability for arbitrariness, and the rule of law for the rule of men. The Charter, after all, spells out in plain words how it is to be amended; it says nothing about amendment by practice. Applied to the Charter, unbridled adaptivism would (to borrow a criticism of the U.S. Constitution) render the Charter all sail and no anchor.[80] This point was made forcefully by a number of delegates to the 1968 Vienna Conference that produced the Convention on the Law of Treaties. "[T]o admit that the parties could derogate from" specific provisions on the conditions of a treaty's revision, the French delegate opined, "merely by their conduct in the application of a treaty," would "deprive those provisions of all meaning."[81] Again, a simple counting reveals the manifest unfairness of the adaptivist argument. The Council consists of 15 members. There are now 188 members in the United Nations. On what basis can 8 percent of the parties to a treaty, through subsequent practice, amend the treaty for the remaining 92 percent?

Using custom to define the powers of one governmental organ as against another governmental organ is different from using custom to define the powers of a governmental organ *as against a nongovernmental actor in the system*. The difference is important in domestic law as well as international law. In domestic law, constitutionalists often refer to custom as a "reality test" to delineate the powers of the executive branch versus those of the legislative branch. That one branch has exercised a power in a given subject area, such as the realm of the recognition of foreign states, the making of international agreements, or the use of force, can inform the meaning of textual provisions that allocate power between the branches. So powerful is such custom that it can, under certain circumstances, take on the weight of a rule of law.[82] But far less weight is accorded custom when the power of the governmental entity in question is exercised against a nongovernmental actor— meaning, in domestic law, an individual. The question then shifts from a separation-of-powers issue to an issue of political freedom and civil liberty. The textual entrenchment of the right serves to put government on notice that power has been delegated to it by individuals, and only up to a point.

In the international system, the actors in the system are states, not individuals, but the principle is the same. Organs such as the Security Council that wield community power can exercise only those powers delegated to them by individual states. That those organs may have succeeded in carrying out acts detrimental to individual states in derogation of an entrenched right—such as the right against intervention entrenched in Article 2(7)—is of no juridical consequence. They, too, derive their powers from the entities within the system that created them. The principle of limited power is central. To abandon it would be to repudiate the most fundamental principle on which the United Nations system is founded. "We the peoples" begins the Charter, calling to mind the preamble of the United States Constitution—"We the people ... ." Both instruments remind us, in their first words, where the organs created therein get their power. They do not get it from themselves.

The idea of consent is the foundation of the legalist regime. Indeed, the system's requirement of state consent, as discussed later, has more than anything else been responsible for the collapse of the use-of-force subregime; a significant number of states manifestly do *not* consent to its proscription against intervention. It is equally a fiction to believe that all parties to the Charter somehow, through acquiescence, necessarily consent to the interpretation given the Charter by the handful of states that happen to be members of the Security Council. To do or say nothing is not necessarily to approve; most states lack the resources to monitor all developments to which they might conceivably wish to object. Moreover, states are not analogous to individuals for purposes of inferring consent to law that is made without their participation. Whatever the propriety of inferring an individual's consent to a constitution or other law made hundreds of years before his birth, no such guesswork is necessary with respect to a state's consent to a treaty. A state either ratifies a treaty or it does not. Its consent is not a matter of inference. The ratification process occurs, for each state, at a given point in time, a point at which the meaning of the treaty was discoverable by the ratifying state. Thus, the rights and obligations undertaken by the state can be determined by its specific action. Unless specified in the treaty, it is wrong to assume that the treaty may over time set out new rights and obligations not present at the time of ratification. This is so particularly when such treaty growth would impinge upon the domestic legal order of ratifying states or circumvent their ratification requirements.

Consent, it bears reiterating, *was* given to the text of the Charter. We know this: Instruments of ratification are on file. We do not know, however, that states have "implicitly" consented to principles at odds with those embodied in the text of the Charter that they ratified. When one state engages in an act at odds with the Charter and another is silent, we have no basis for assuming that the second state "believes" that the Charter has somehow changed its meaning. The suggestion that such an assumption is needed to avoid rule by "the cold hand of the dead" is mere rhetoric. In every legal system consent is inferred to rules made by others, even dead others; without such an inference, the rule of law would be impossible to administer. Constitutions, statutes, and treaties all oblige action or prohibit inaction by actors that played no role—and often did not exist—at the time of their making. There is better reason to infer community consent to legal rules that are formally adopted through universally accepted modes of approval than there is to infer community consent from the actions of a handful of members acting anomalously. Nonetheless, while radical adaptivists acknowledge that the Security Council has engaged in unarguable violations of the Charter,* they contend that those violations must somehow be overlooked because the "international community" has failed to condemn them.† The fiction of compliance is necessary, of course, to reinforce the illusion of an international rule of law governing use of force.

There is, in sum, a powerful reason to treat states differently from the Security Council in applying the doctrine of desuetude: States made the United Nations; the Security Council did not. It was the consent of states that created the Treaty, not the consent of the Security Council. States are the creators; the Security Council is a creature. If the Security Council's powers are to be changed, it is by the consent of states that change must be effected, not the consent of the Security Council.

---

*"The Security Council has ignored rules and principles; it has acted in some cases as though it were not itself subject to rules." Mary Ellen O'Connell, "The UN, NATO, and International Law After Kosovo," 22 *Hum. Rts. Q.* 57, 86 (2000).

†"To the extent that the international community has not criticized or opposed the Security Council's conduct, it should probably not be viewed as *ultra vires* or unlawful." *Id.* at 68 (2000).

If subsequent practice is to give life to the Charter, rather than to embalm it, three distinctions must be made.

First, practice is properly given greater weight in interpreting open-textured rules than in interpreting manifest ones. It is one thing to use practice to resolve textual ambiguities, but quite another to supplant clear prohibitions or limitations set out in the text. Subsequent custom can then be used not simply to fill gaps in the text, but to replace the text, to circumvent the amendment procedure that the Charter itself requires. A state has a right to expect that the treaty it ratified will be carried out in good faith by other state parties. And in a consent-based system, other states can hardly hold that state to rights or obligations to which it did not agree. This fundamental principle was written into United States law in 1988 in the so-called Biden Condition to the Treaty on Intermediate Nuclear Forces, which provided that the "United States shall interpret the treaty in accordance with the common understanding of the treaty shared by the President and the Senate at the time the Senate gave its advice and consent to ratification[,]" and that the United States "shall not agree to or adopt an interpretation different from that common understanding ... ."[83] (These principles apply as well to the NATO Treaty, which Deputy Secretary of State Strobe Talbot talked of "re-inventing"[84] so as to permit a wider latitude of operations.*) No "living constitution" worthy of the name, domestic or international, is so "alive" as to permit its most vital limits to be expunged through violation. That a practice occasionally arises from the repeated breach of a given prohibition or limitation is grounds not for celebration and emulation but for regret.[†] No legal regime can endure if the most important proscriptions that it imposes are capable of being revised through violation by its creatures.

---

*No reference was made to the need to get Senate approval for such a revision. On the need for Senate advice and consent, see Michael J. Glennon, "Interpreting 'Interpretation': The President, the Senate, and when Treaty Interpretation Becomes Treaty Making," 20 *U.C. Davis L. Rev.* 913 (July 1987), reprinted in *The ABM Treaty and the Constitution: Joint Hearings Before the Senate Committees on Foreign Relations and Judiciary*, 99th Cong., 2d Sess., 821–28 (1987).

†At the time the practice developed, it is worth noting, it was forcefully argued that abstention by a permanent member does not constitute a veto. See Myres S. McDougal and Richard N. Gardner, "The Veto and the Charter: An Interpretation for Survival," 60 *Yale L. J.* 258, 260–61 (1951).

It thus does not do simply to recite instances in which the Security Council took action "not in the Charter." Some provisions have "play at the joints"; others do not. Action consistent with the Charter, but not expressly authorized by it, is not the same as action inconsistent with the Charter—that is, explicitly or implicitly prohibited by it. There is broader room for adaptation in the direction of action not expressly proscribed than there is in the direction of action that is expressly proscribed. The limits explicitly imposed by Article 2(7) and Article 39 constitute express proscriptions. To argue for power to override express proscriptions is, in a very real way, to argue against the rule of law.

Nor does it do to retreat to the Charter's—or any other constitutive instrument's—"purposes," "principles," and "policies" as a way to escape the confinement of express textual limits and prohibitions. Any document like the Charter has multiple purposes, often conflicting. No one knows which trumps which. Overarching purposes can therefore be anything to anyone. The analysis of Myres McDougal and Michael Reisman is illustrative of the subjectivity of "purposive" interpretation. Referring to breadth of Article 39, they wrote:

The basic constitutional framework of an inclusive organization whose principal purpose is to maintain international peace and security could scarcely prescribe otherwise: if states were to be permitted to impede the organized community's efforts to rectify situations by claims that activities, however threatening, are immune from inclusive concern because they are within domestic jurisdiction, the principal purpose for which the whole constitutive structure is established and maintained could be easily defeated.[85]

Precisely the opposite conclusion to that McDougal and Reisman draw could just as easily follow from their argument. If the "principal purpose" of the United Nations is the maintenance of international peace and security (their assumption, not the Charter's; Article I lists no "principal" purpose, only four—with no hierarchy), why not infer that the whole point of protecting peace and security is to protect the peace and security of *states*—to protect *states'* ability to govern their territory and population as they see fit, free from outside interference? But why, for that matter, assume that the maintenance of international peace and security *is* the principal purpose of the United Nations? Article I also refers to "respect for the principle of equal rights and self-determination of peoples"; do the people of a state somehow lack power under the Charter to determine for themselves, as do the people of all other "equal" states, how they shall be governed? If the international system seeks a true rule of law, it must settle for more than result-oriented, arbitrarily shifting policy preferences.*

Second, as these considerations suggest, practice cannot present a back-door method of circumventing domestic constitutional requirements of legislative approval. The constitutions of some states, such as the United States, require legislative consent to treaties. Amendments to treaties, at least in the United States, also require such approval. (In the United States, of course, the Constitution requires Senate advice and consent.[86]) If modification effected by formal amendment to a treaty requires Senate approval, back-door modification effected by practice (to say nothing of a back-room "gentleman's agreement" among the Security Council's permanent members, which is recommended by Henkin[87]) cannot be exempt from the requirement of Senate approval. To permit presidential evasion of the requirement of Senate advice and consent for formal, textual amendment of a treaty by informal, customary modification would elevate form over substance and effectively read the Treaty Clause out of the Constitution. Not surprisingly, concerns such as these surfaced regularly during debates on desuetude at the Vienna Conference on the Law of Treaties, discussed earlier. The French delegate observed, for example, that "the principle of formal parallelism" required that modifications of a treaty at the domestic level should follow the same procedure as the original text; if the manner of a treaty's application itself modified the treaty, "that requirement of parallelism could hardly be met."[88] What of the amendment processes set out in a treaty? "Could an official who did not possess treaty-making authority," the Spanish

---

*Tom Farer, among others, sees the hierarchy quite differently: "Anyone who considers with some measure of objectivity the Charter's normative logic, its allocation of coercive jurisdiction and its omissions, as well as the preferences manifested by most participants in the drafting process and their immediately subsequent behavior, cannot help concluding that the promotion of human rights ranked far below the protection of national sovereignty and the maintenance of peace as organizational goals." Tom J. Farer, "Human Rights in Law's Empire: The Jurisprudence War," 85 *Am. J. Int'l L.* 117, 119–20 (1991).

delegate asked, "nevertheless modify the special revision or modification clause?"[89] The delegate from Venezuela quoted the Special Rapporteur: "[P]ractice contrary to a treaty constitutes a violation, not an interpretation of the treaty."[90]

The danger of circumventing domestic ratification requirements is compounded when the amendment process can operate even without the participation of the United States—as is true of the Security Council. The United States of course has a veto, but the United States need not necessarily be present on every occasion on which it might wish to cast a veto. In such a situation, the obligations incurred by the United States under the UN Charter would effectively be altered without even *presidential* consent, let alone Senate consent. Those obligations could, under such circumstances, be altered by the treaty-*created* entity, the Security Council, whose practice would have been initiated or reinforced with no participation by the state incurring those obligations. Other states may have no problem with such an arrangement. But the United States could never constitutionally become a party to a treaty that permitted its obligations to be altered without its consent. This possibility was considered in 1955 by the Senate Foreign Relations Committee. The Committee rejected the suggestion that the President could "alter drastically the nature of our commitments in the United Nations":

> In the United States there is little doubt that our Government would follow the regular treaty procedure outlined in the Constitution and secure the advice and consent of the Senate before ratifying a proposed amendment since any other course would be a subversion of the treatymaking process. Certainly it would be illogical if the President, after securing a two-thirds vote of the Senate approving the ratification of the original charter, could then proceed to alter drastically the nature of our commitments in the United Nations by accepting amendments without referring to the Senate for approval.[91]

In the 1980s, the Senate insisted upon the principle that a treaty means what it said when the Senate gave its approval.* The Senate

---

* "A general rule is that words used in a treaty should be read as having the same meaning they bore when it came into existence." Certain Expenses Case of the United Nations, 1962 I.C.J. 151 (July 20) (separate opinion of Judge Spender).

resisted the efforts of the Reagan Administration to "reinterpret" the ABM Treaty so as to permit what was seen by the Senate as being prohibited—deployment of the Strategic Defense Initiative—at the time of its 1972 ratification. This same principle precludes interpreting the UN Charter as today permitting what it was seen by all to prohibit—intervention—at the time of its 1945 ratification. As the Senate Foreign Relations Committee elaborated in 1955:

> [C]harter growth through interpretation can only proceed within well-defined constitutional limits. The United Nations is not a superstate. It...must function within the specific limitations laid down in the Charter. However broad an interpretation one might place upon the charter, the United Nations—under the limiting language found in article 2, paragraph 7—is not authorized to intervene in matters essentially within the domestic jurisdiction of any state.[92]

The reason that the Security Council must function within the Charter's limits was aptly stated by the French government in the *Certain Expenses Case*: The Charter is a contract in which states agreed to give up some of their power, "but nothing more":

> The States Members of the United Nations have subscribed...to the undertakings of the Charter but nothing more. The Charter is a treaty whereby states have alienated their powers only to the strict extent that they have consented to do so. Since the beginning of the functioning of the United Nations, no customary rules or practices contrary to the Charter can have been created unless those customary rules or those practices have been consistent and non-controversial.[93]

Hence it was with good reason that Judge Sir Percy Spender observed that the "nature of the authority granted by the Charter to each of its organs does not change with time."[94]

Third, practice by organs of the United Nations should accordingly be given lesser weight than practice by state parties to the Charter. The most thoughtful analysis of the question is, again, the famous opinion of Judge Spender in the *Certain Expenses Case*. Judge Spender wrote that while the subsequent conduct of individual state parties to a bilateral treaty may reveal their intent with respect to the meaning of ambiguous terms, "an element of artificiality" attaches when the meaning of a multilateral treaty such as the UN Charter is inferred from the actions of groups of states that are parties to that treaty. Judge Spender noted that the "essential fact" is that the Charter is a multilateral treaty. He continued:

> It cannot be altered at the will of the majority of the Member States, no matter how often that will is expressed or asserted against a protesting minority and no matter how large the majority of Member States which asserts its will in this manner or how small the minority.

Judge Spender went on to consider the specific case of intervention. He said:

> [I]f the General Assembly were to "intervene in matters which are essentially within the domestic jurisdiction of any State" within the meaning of Article 2(7) of the Charter, whatever be the meaning given to these words, that intervention would be entering into a field prohibited to it under the Charter and be beyond the authority of the General Assembly. This would continue to be so, no matter how frequently and consistently the General Assembly had construed its authority to make intervention in matters essentially within the domestic jurisdiction of any States. The majority has no power to extend, alter, or disregard the Charter.

Of course these same principles apply to the Security Council and other organs of United Nations.* As though a reminder were necessary—other provisions explicitly limit its power—the Security Council is ordered in plain terms to act in accordance with the Charter. Article 24(4) provides that "[i]n discharging [its] duties the Security Council shall act in accordance with the Purposes and Principles of the United Nations." One cannot, therefore, assume that simply because the Security Council has carried out an act, even more than once, that act is perforce lawful. This is the implicit

---

*Americans who are, because of the veto, sanguine about Security Council adaptivism might reflect that there is no reason why the same adaptivism ought not prevail in other UN agencies in which the United States exercises no veto.

assumption of those who maintain that the Security Council and other UN organs are somehow empowered to "interpret their own authority."[95] That the Charter imposes no meaningful checks on *ultra vires* action by one or more of its organs does not mean that the organs have unlimited power to redefine the scope of their own power—a distortion of principles of governance to which constitutions everywhere are susceptible. An effort in an earlier era to do that—the "attempt … to make the League [of Nations] more radical than the initial obstacles would allow"[96]—brought about the organization's collapse. Who could be surprised if China, Russia, India, or some other state, recalling the limits in the Charter that it agreed to, turned its back on an organization that traduced those limits one time too many? During the Vienna Conference on the Law of Treaties, delegates recalled the concern of the Soviet delegate that permitting treaties to be amended by subsequent practice "could be to prejudice the recognition of fundamental freedoms and rights and the principles enunciated by the United Nations Charter."[97] One need only imagine the reaction of the United States if a new rule were announced that the "living" UN Charter had, say, evolved to the point where the United States could no longer exercise a veto. Who seriously would contend that the United States had agreed to such an instrument?

It is worth noting, in this regard, the response of states to the Secretary General's suggestion that "massive and systematic violations of human rights—wherever they may take place—should never be allowed to stand."[98] As described earlier, only about half of the General Assembly's members addressed the issue, and a third of those that did disagreed. Among those that did disagree, a number were particularly adamant that the Security Council should refrain from interference in their internal affairs—including how they define and deal with human rights issues. Typical were delegates from these countries, who commented as follows:

> *China:* "The issue of human rights is, in essence, the internal affair of a country, and should be addressed mainly by the Government of that country through its own efforts … . Sovereign equality, mutual respect for State sovereignty and non-interference in the internal affairs of others are the basic principles governing international relations today."[99]
>
> *Indonesia:* "[W]e have the spectacle of a Security Council—when not paralysed by the veto of a permanent member—venturing to

take over the work of other United Nations organs in such fields as human rights, democracy and humanitarian aid ... . [W]e fully agree that massive and systematic violations of human rights, wherever they take place, should not be tolerated or condoned. But we cannot agree that this problem can be solved only by sacrificing the principle of national sovereignty and sovereign equality among nations. There must be a solution that does not threaten to demolish a principle on which the United Nations itself was founded."[100]

Cuba: "What would we have left to defend ourselves in the future if we poor countries were no longer able to rely on such principles as respect for sovereignty and self-determination, the sovereign equality of all States and non-interference in the internal affairs of other nations? ... In a unipolar world, attempts to impose notions such as the limitation of sovereignty, and humanitarian intervention, do not advance international security: they pose a threat to the countries of the Third World, which have neither powerful armies nor nuclear weapons. Such attempts must therefore be brought to an end: they violate the letter and the spirit of the Charter."[101]

Iraq: "The most dangerous phenomenon witnessed during the present decade ... is the advocacy of so-called humanitarian intervention. This doctrine, which has no place in international law, stems from an organized infringement of the most fundamental rules of the present international order, such as sovereignty, political independence, territorial integrity and non-interference in internal affairs ... . The universalization of the concepts of this doctrine would mean the complete denial of the will of the vast majority of States, with the result of destroying the present international order."[102]

Libya: "[M]y country strongly rejects intervention by a State, or a group of States, in the domestic affairs of another State under any pretext, including so-called humanitarian intervention."[103]

Pakistan: "[A] clear distinction must be maintained between humanitarian crises as a result of wars, conflicts or disputes which by their very nature constitute threats to international peace and security and other human rights issues. The latter fall within the purview of the United Nations human rights system and outside the competence of the Security Council ... . [F]or humanitarian interventions to find general acceptance they ... must fully conform[104] to the provisions of the United Nations

Charter and be undertaken only with the explicit authority of the Security Council, after a clear breach of, or threat to, international peace and security has been established."

Egypt: "Chapter VII … necessarily requires the existence of a conflict or situations leading to a conflict … . [The Security Council] should not intervene in matters that are within the domestic jurisdiction of States, as set out in Article 2, paragraph 7, of the Charter … . The international community must also see to it that the Council abides by the main criterion defined by the Charter for its intervention by force under Chapter VII. Article 39 gives the Council the power to determine the existence of any threat to the peace or breach thereof, so a given conflict, especially if it is internal, must be tantamount to a threat to international peace or a breach thereof."[105]

North Korea: "Sovereignty is the lifeline of every country. Non-intervention in the internal affairs of others and mutual equality are fundamental principles that should never be violated on any account … . [T]he Security Council should not take measures that might infringe upon the sovereignty of Member States … . [I]ntervening in their internal affairs should not be allowed."[106]

Whatever the shortcomings of the Charter, and they are many, it is not a bait-and-switch scheme, an instrument that cynically drew states in and, once their ratification was secure, revealed itself to be something altogether different, something they would never have agreed to. To suggest that it is not only demeans the memory of its framers, but will ill serve future efforts to develop an *effective* legalist order to control the use of force—which will depend, in the end, on assuring member states that what they agree to is what they get.

D. Stability versus Justice?

The relationship between stability and justice is complex. At one level, a trade-off exists between the two. To the extent that the international system is stable, it sacrifices justice, for a measure of instability inevitably attends the redistribution of rights and obligations inherent in the enhancement of justice. Conversely, a completely just system is unstable to the extent that a continuing readjustment of rights and obligations is permitted. At a superficial level, stability *competes* with justice.

At another level, though, the relationship between stability and justice is more symbiotic than oppositional. At that level, stability and justice do not compete, but go hand in hand and reinforce one another. The even-handed enforcement of norms is essential to both justice and stability. "Peace is a coin which has two sides," John Foster Dulles wrote. "One is the avoidance of the use of force and the other is the creation of conditions of justice. In the long run you cannot expect one without the other."[107] A grossly unstable order is likely to be unjust, and a just order implies a minimal level of stability. Intervention can thus, in certain circumstances, conduce to both justice *and* stability. As Hedley Bull observed, "[i]f ... an intervention expresses the collective will of the society of states, it may be carried out without bringing ... harmony and concord into jeopardy."[108] Not to intervene—to permit conditions of domestic barbarism to continue unabated—can undermine both justice and stability, as Stanley Hoffman pointed out in connection with Kosovo:

To tolerate this ferocious combination of ethnic cleansing and quasi genocide [in Kosovo] is to give other potential ethnic cleansers a green light in a world of fragile states and ethnic conflicts, and to invite world disorder on a grand scale. For there can be no order, no "stable structure of peace," to use Kissingerian language, without a modicum of moderation, especially in areas that are powder kegs.[109]

Nonetheless, the framers of the Charter proceeded on the assumption that, in fashioning a rule on interventionism, they needed to choose *between* stability and justice, to discard one value at the expense of the other. They chose stability. The Charter therefore bans completely the nondefensive use of force by states as well as Security Council intervention—regardless of the justness of the objective. In so doing, it chooses stability over justice in any instance in which they may collide. One of the earliest critiques of this feature of the Charter was that of Julius Stone, who noted the "absurdities and injustice to which it would lead" and objected to its "steady and repeated stress on the requirements of justice."[110]

In this regard, the Charter reflects the influence of the Great Powers, particularly the United States. These states were in general both satisfied with their fundamental situation in the world and dismayed at the disruption of world order in the two wars.* The legalist model that emerged from the postwar conferences embodied that disposition. It "implies that these are all states like our own," Kennan wrote,

> reasonably content with their international borders and status, at least to the extent that they would be willing to refrain from pressing for change without international agreement. Actually, this has generally been true only of a portion of international society. We tend to underestimate the violence of national maladjustments and discontents elsewhere in the world if we think that they would always appear to other people as less important than the preservation of the juridical tidiness of international life.[111]

Underestimating "the violence of national maladjustments and discontents" in places like Rwanda, Somalia, and Haiti has led international law to impose order prematurely. "[M]odern international law," William V. O'Brien observed, "has sacrificed justice in its attempt virtually to eliminate the competence of the state to engage in war unilaterally."[112] No cause, however worthy, however moral, however just, can—under the Charter—support the nondefensive use of force. As Myres McDougal put it, the Charter permitted use of force only for "value conservation," not for "value extension."[113] Anthony Clark Arend and Robert J. Beck accurately described that choice:

> [T]he value choice underlying the Charter framework for the use of force was that maintenance of international peace was to be preferred to the pursuit of 'justice'. Justice—the promotion of human rights, the encouragement of self-determination, the rectification of economic problems, the correction of past wrongs, and the equitable resolution of a host of other problems—was to be sought. In fact, the United Nations Charter established mechanisms to facilitate the pursuit of various 'just' goals. Justice, however, was not to be sought at the expense of peace. Undergirding the Charter was a belief that greater harm would be done to the

---

*"To the American mind, it is impossible that people should have positive aspirations, and ones that they regard as legitimate, more important to them than the peacefulness and orderliness of international life." George F. Kennan, *American Diplomacy, 1900–1950*, at 83 (1951).

international system by using force to promote justice than by living with a particular injustice. If peaceful means for seeking justice failed, and the choice was between peace and justice, peace was to prevail. Any threat or use of force against the political or territorial order, no matter how just the cause, was to be considered unlawful.[114]

It is open to question whether such repression should have been tolerated in 1945—whether the balance struck between stability and justice was right for the world that had just emerged from World War II. Even then, that balance was questioned. Argentina's Foreign Minister, in a 1945 diplomatic note, wrote: "[A] multilateral collective action, exercised with complete unselfishness by all the other republics of the continent, aimed at achieving in a spirit of brotherly prudence the mere reestablishment of the central rights, and directed toward the fulfillment of freely contracted juridical obligations, must not be held to injure the government affected, but rather it must be recognized as being taken for the benefit of all, including the country which has been suffering under such a harsh regime."[115]

It is not open to question whether the balance struck in 1945 is right for the world of 2000. It is not. The most farsighted among the Charter's framers saw their handiwork not as a finished and final product (as it is portrayed today by its more zealous defenders[116]), but only as a tentative and initial effort, the first sketch of what inevitably would be a work-in-progress. Senator J. William Fulbright, the leading congressional supporter of the United Nations during the founding period, had no illusions about the likely need to go back to the drawing board. "The one error," he said, "which we must not, above all others, make, is to assume that this organization is the last word." Fulbright knew that the Security Council, as constituted by the Charter, could not be counted on to keep the peace. "On the contrary," he said, the United Nations "is certain to be merely the first modest and hesitant step, sufficient to point the direction, but utterly inadequate to achieve the goal of lasting peace."[117]

The question is whether the defenders of the United Nations will continue to regard criticism as opposition and to avert their eyes from the Charter's glaring shortcomings.[118] Criticism is *not* opposition; criticism is an expression of hope and belief that the organization can do better. "There was a time when the United Nations was criticized solely by its enemies," said one of its stalwart supporters, Senator George Aiken, in 1962. "I think it is perfectly proper for the old, long-time friends of the U.N. to insist that it so conduct its affairs that it may live and be effective far into the future."[119] Unless it does so conduct its affairs, the United Nations will continue to stagger down the road to oblivion. For those who believe that a legalist system is ultimately mankind's best hope, that fate would, indeed, be tragic.

E. Conclusion

At the time the Council's domestic interventions were undertaken, their precedential effect seemed limited. But the inescapable conclusion nonetheless remained: The Security Council had pierced the veil of state sovereignty. It had approved use of force where no state had threatened international peace or security. The UN Security Council, the ultimate guardian of the noninterventionist regime, had itself flouted the regime that it had been established to protect. The floodgates were open.

Given the emerging post–Cold War belief that intrastate barbarism was no longer to be tolerated, and given the Charter's constraints both on individual states and on the Security Council itself, the Council confronted a dilemma. In the court of world opinion, unauthorized intervention by the Council facilitated unauthorized intervention by individual states. "Laws," Burke said, "like houses, lean on one another."[120] But *nonintervention* by the Council, paradoxically, could have had the same effect. Security Council inaction could have enhanced the incentive for individual states to intervene, particularly where the "CNN factor" weighed heavily on popular opinion. Faced with a no-win situation whichever way it turned, the Council sometimes opted to intervene and sometimes did not*— and with either choice laid bare the Charter's Faustian bargain.

---

*"The list of places in which the international community has not forcibly intervened in recent years, despite widespread starvation and/or extensive internal violence against civilians, is quite long (and likely incomplete): Afghanistan, Algeria, Angola, Bhutan, Burundi, Chad, Cuba, Djibouti, El Salvador, Equatorial Guinea, Eritrea, Ethiopia, Ghana, Guatemala, Indonesia (East Timor), Iran, Mali, Mauritania, Mozambique, Myanmar, Niger, Sierra Leone, Sri Lanka, Sudan, Tibet, Togo, Western Sahara, Yemen, and Zaire." Sean D. Murphy, *Humanitarian Intervention: The United Nations in an Evolving World Order* 296 (1996).

The pressures confronting the Council were understandable. Just as generals supposedly refight the last war, the draftsmen of the Charter responded to the crises precipitating World War II,[121] rather than foreseeable future problems, in fashioning its grand limitations on state power.* The *idée fixe* at which the Charter's core prohibitions are directed is invasion, the paradigm being the 1939 German invasion of Poland. The transcendent problem, it was thought in 1945, was interstate conflict.[†]

But the recurrent problem today is not invasion. The problem today is intrastate violence, not interstate violence.[‡] NATO Secretary General Lord Robertson has pointed out that "the nature of conflict is changing":

> More and more conflicts are taking place within states, rather than between them. During the Cold War, there were an average of about ten internal conflicts ongoing every year, be they civil wars, state collapse, or massive state oppression of minorities. Over the last decade, that number has grown to twenty-five intra-state conflicts per annum.[122]

---

*"[O]ne should not forget that the Charter is one war behind. It presupposes an aggression of the classic kind, such as it had been hypostatized by Hitler." René-Jean Dupuy, "The International Community, War and Peace," in *The Current Legal Regulation of the Use of Force* 271, 275 (A. Cassese ed., 1986).

†"In formulating the Charter provisions on the use of force, the framers were primarily concerned about overt acts of conventional aggression—instances where a state sends regular troops into another state or launches air strikes or a naval attack against another state. Those were the types of conflict with which the delegates at San Francisco were most familiar. The Second World War had begun because Germany, Japan, and Italy had invaded other states. Consequently it was conflict of this nature that the framers sought to regulate... . [I]n the world since 1945, however, most conflict has not been of this nature." Anthony C. Arend and Robert J. Beck, *International Law and the Use of Force: Beyond the UN Charter Paradigm* 37 (1993).

‡Secretary General Boutros Boutros-Ghali noted this phenomenon in 1995. See *Supplement to an Agenda for Peace: Position Paper of the Secretary-General on the Fiftieth Anniversary of the United Nations*, U.N. GAOR, 50th Sess., U.N. Doc. A/50/60 (1995).

Martin van Creveld observed in 1991 that not one of 20 major conflicts since the end of the Cold War was between states.[123] Indeed,
intrastate violence has been a far greater cause of human death and
suffering during this century than war itself.* *The Economist* calculated that 170 million civilians were killed by governments during
the twentieth century, excluding civil as well as international wars,
which accounted for only 37 million deaths—military as well as
civilian.[124] The focus of UN peace-keeping has reflected this shift,†
but the problem still is not addressed effectively by the Charter.
Thus intervention was authorized by the Security Council to deal
extra-legally with internal violence, long regarded under the Charter
as beyond official international concern.

The conclusion that the Security Council transgressed the
Charter may seem implicitly to consign the people of Rhodesia,
Somalia, or Haiti to oppression. Not so. That the Security Council
breached the restraints of the Charter does not, of course, mean
that the international community should have remained indifferent
to the often stomach-wrenching atrocities that gave rise to its
action—any more than the conclusion that NATO breached the
Charter means that indifference to Serb ethnic cleansing in Kosovo
would have been appropriate. The circumstances of each intervention are set out, again, not to suggest the impropriety of those interventions, but to highlight the dilemma in which the Charter placed
both the Council and NATO—providing literally no lawful means
of stopping humanity's most heinous brutality so long as it
remained within the perpetrators' own borders. The Security
Council's shoddy record in dealing with such crises no doubt flows

---

*Over 150 million people have been killed by 15 states alone in various
pogroms and mass political murders. See R. J. Rummel, *Death by
Government* 1–28 (1994).

†"Of the five peace-keeping operations that existed in early 1988, four
related to interstate wars and only one (20 per cent of the total) to an
intrastate conflict. Of the 21 operations established since then, only 8 have
related to interstate wars, whereas 13 (62 per cent) have related to
intrastate conflicts ... . Of the 11 operations established since January 1992
all but two (82 per cent) related to intrastate conflicts." *Supplement to an
Agenda for Peace*: *Position Paper of the Secretary-General on the Fiftieth
Anniversary of the United Nations*, U.N. GAOR, 50th Sess., U.N. Doc.
A/50/60, S/1995/1 (Jan. 3, 1995).

in no small part from the fact that it was not established to undertake such missions. The framers of the Charter never contemplated
that the Security Council would or should constitute a mechanism
for righting domestic wrongs without the consent of the sitting government. The Council was intended to represent a tool to prevent
and control clashes between states, not violence entirely within
them. The Council's initiatives to alleviate intrastate violence have
in many ways been laudable. Their creditability notwithstanding,
those efforts ought not be allowed to take on a specious legality. As
is true in considering NATO's laudable attempts to do justice
notwithstanding the Charter's disapproval, the Council's attempts
must themselves be critiqued with the same rigor. The objective is
not to distort the law to fit desirable policy outcomes; the objective
is to identify desirable policy outcomes, to determine whether the
law permits those outcomes, and, if it does not, to think through
how the law can be changed to permit such outcomes. Stretching
the law to fit preferred outcomes would accomplish nothing—other
than rendering the law useless when it is later needed as a safeguard. The analogy is old but still apt: To bend the law for necessity's sake is like blasting a hole in a fortress wall to be able to
shoot through it. Convenience may be had in the short term, but in
the long term, the hole provides a breach through which adversaries
can march. Better to build new walls with holes in the right places.
    There was no reason to assume that the only hope for oppressed
peoples lay in action by the Security Council. The suggestion that it
did exemplifies what military planners call the "fallacy of the last
move"—the assumption that history's web of events would have
ended with the last event identified, here, Security Council inaction.
The assumption is counterfactualism run riot, purporting to foresee
with perfect knowledge how history would have unfolded had a
given event not taken place. Again, this mode of analysis is insup-
portable. Who is to say what the reaction would have been to the
Council's nonenforcement of a nonlaw?* Perhaps regional organizations would have acted. Perhaps individual states would have set
matters right. Perhaps pressure would have mounted to give the

---

*"I know no method to secure the repeal of bad or obnoxious laws so
effective," Ulysses S. Grant said, "as their stringent execution." Inaugural
Address (Mar. 4, 1869).

Security Council power to act in such circumstances, thus benefiting humanity in the long term. As it was, the Security Council's extra-legal interventions merely provided an example for individual states to emulate. "Our Government is the potent, the omnipresent teacher," Justice Louis Brandeis said. "For good or for ill, it teaches the whole people by its example."[125] In the international system, the Security Council is as close to government as there is. When government breaks law, it takes the whole legal system down with it.

FIVE
———

The Collapse of Consent: Is a Legalist Use-of-Force Regime Possible?

This, then, is the state of things: International law provides no clear standards by which to assess the lawfulness of intervention by states, but it does set out a standard by which to assess the lawfulness of intervention by the Security Council—a standard that precludes intervention in states' domestic affairs. This groundwork having been laid, it is now possible to ask whether the construction of a true legalist use-of-force regime is feasible. The answer will depend upon what constitutes an authentic legalist order, and whether one now exists.

A. Is it Really Law? (Does it Really Matter?)

Perennial questions pervade international law, and the perennial of perennials is whether international law is really law. The question is all the more salient after NATO's action in Kosovo. The UN Charter prohibits what NATO did. But NATO acted anyway, undeterred, without fear of punishment. How can a system indifferent to prominent and massive noncompliance rightly be called a system of law?

In one sense, it should matter little what label is attached, whether "law" or something else. If the object is to appraise the system's utility, inquiry should focus not on what it is called but on whether the system performs the function it is intended to serve. If we are to talk about *things* rather than *words,* we ought to be concerned about labels only when they matter. This was in essence the famous 1945 response of Glanville Williams to John Austin (who had claimed that international law was not really law because it lacked sanctions commanded by a sovereign[1]). Williams argued that the debate was merely a quibble over a definition.[2]

In a larger sense, however, whether something "is the law" very much does matter. It matters because, at least in the common understanding, whether "it's the law" determines whether we have complete discretion to act as we wish. If "it's the law" that one cannot smoke in a restaurant, we think that we cannot smoke; if it's not, we can. So if something falls into the category "law," consequences obtain. Freedom to act is circumscribed.

1. Law as a Limit on Self-Dealing

The same applies whether the universe in question consists of individuals or groups, and whether those groups are corporations, organizations, or states. The notion of law as *obligational* is pervasive to the point of being intuitive.[3] Oscar Schachter put it succinctly: "[U]nless there is some limit to the discretion of States to decide whether they are bound, it cannot be said there is binding law."[4] The element of obligation does not imply a binary, law or no-law analysis. Rather, it suggests a spectrum that falls between opposite poles of obligation and lack of obligation. As suggested earlier, the law concerning use of force by individual states falls close to the "no obligation" end of that spectrum.

The preclusion of self-exemption is a necessary element of obligation and therefore of law. If the system is a system of law, no actor within it can decide not to be bound. Whether and when one is bound is decided beforehand; restraints upon behavior are preagreed. Preagreement requires a minimal measure of consensus on basic values underpinning the regime.

The notion of the rule of law thus comprehends, at its core, a preagreed, principled procedure for decision making, the objective being to prevent self-dealing. That there is prior agreement ensures that the results of that procedure will be honored; that the procedure is principled precludes results that are arbitrary because of self-judging. Hence, procedure was said by the late Judge Harold Leventhal to be the "first outpost of the law." The roots of these concepts are ancient. The Magna Carta (1215) reined in the institutionalized arbitrariness of an unbridled royal prerogative used to the Crown's advantage. John Sadler in *The Rights of the Kingdom* (1649) wrote that the idea of lawmakers as "judges of their own cause" is one "which our Law, and Nature itself ... avoiddeth and

abhorreth ... ."[5] John Locke underscored that the rule of law precludes "extemporary dictates" and is, rather, characterized by
"measures set down which may guide and justify [men's] actions."*
In separating actor from rule maker, law serves its most magisterial
function of providing an abiding check on the abuse of raw power.
Law, in its universality, applies to rule maker and actor alike. Law
is in this sense not unlike science. Science insists that the results of
an experiment should be the same wherever it is run, by whomever
it is run. Legal knowledge, like scientific knowledge, does not exist
unless it is the same for everywhere, for every one. To universality,
law, like science, owes its life.

Universality implies equality. "Equal justice under the law,"
"equal protection of the laws," "equal treatment"—these and other
notions of universality imply that all actors within the system are
subject to the same rules. All are, to the same extent, unable to
waive the application of those rules to themselves. No one is, in
this sense, above the law. "An insistence on equal subjection to the
law," Ian Brownlie has noted, "is a shared characteristic of the
opinions of a variety of constitutional law theorists."[6]

2. Sovereignty: Myth and Reality

The equality of states has therefore been seen as implicit in the
concept of sovereignty. Formalized in the 1648 Treaty of
Westphalia,† the sovereign equality of states has been seen as the
cornerstone of the international legal system.[7] Pufendorf believed

---

*"[W]hatever form the commonwealth is under, the ruling power ought to
govern by declared and received laws, and not by extemporary dictates and
undetermined resolutions, for then mankind will be in a far worse condition than in the state of Nature if they shall have armed one, or a few men
with the joint power of a multitude, to force them to obey at pleasure the
exorbitant and unlimited decrees of their sudden thoughts, or unrestrained,
and till that moment, unknown wills, without having any measures set
down which may guide and justify their actions." John Locke, *Second
Treatise of Civil Government* § 137 (Gateway Edition 1955) (1690).
†Actually, as Judge Luzius Wildhaber points out, the sovereign state began
to take shape in the seigneurial structures of the Normans in the tenth and
eleventh centuries. Luzius Wildhaber, *Wechselspiel zwischen Innen und
Aussen: Schweizer Landesrecht, Rechtsvergleichung, Völkerrecht* 19 (1996).

that "every man should esteem and treat another man as his equal by nature, or as much as man as he is himself."[8] From the equality of men was inferred the equality of states: "[N]ations composed of men," Vattel wrote, "are naturally equal, and inherit from nature the same obligations and rights. Power or weakness does not in this respect produce any difference. A dwarf is no less a man than a giant; a small republic is no less a state than the most powerful kingdom."[9] As Chief Justice Marshall wrote in *The Antelope*, "No principle of international law is more universally acknowledged, than the perfect equality of nations."[10] Not surprisingly, the principle of equality is central to the structure of the United Nations Charter. The first principle on which the organization is based is "the principle of the sovereign equality of all its Members."[11] From this architectonic sovereign equality flow the concepts of self-determination, jurisdiction over population and territory, the capacity to engage in diplomacy and treaty relations, nonintervention, and, indeed, the ban against force itself. If states were unequal, the legalist regime of the Charter would make no sense.

   Legalist dogma notwithstanding, the reality has always been different—even from the start of the state system. Evan Luard has pointed out that during the period from the Peace of Westphalia in 1648 to the Congress of Vienna in 1815—the period within which the notion of sovereignty originated and initially took shape—intervention in the internal affairs of states still was common:

   It was normal for governments to seek to influence political affairs in other states. Often they had, as we saw, many prominent politicians directly in their pay. France was the most often able to influence events in that way: A substantial number of politicians in Sweden, the United Provinces, England (including the Stuart Kings) and other countries received regular payments from her. The British were active in some countries: Both Catherine II before she became empress, and Bestuzhev, the most powerful Russian minister, were in British pay during the 1750s. Occasionally alliances could be disrupted and ministries overturned by direct approaches to local politicians. Thus, according to one historian, the "decisive influence" in causing England to abandon her alliance with France and make peace with the United Provinces in 1674 was "a campaign of clandestine Dutch intervention in English domestic politics": A campaign that "established a pattern of intervention by rival European powers that continued until 1688." The French government intervened equally actively in the reverse direction: To ensure that English politicians did not decide to go to war against him. They established "clandestine connections with leaders of the Country opposition, bribing some of the most active to wreck Danby's policy of pressing for entry into the war against France," and later assistant opposition leaders to make a "lethal attack" against Danby which caused him to be dismissed. Later Louis [XIV] "systematically and regularly intervened in politics of other Western European states: French diplomats encouraged and subsidized opposition groups to obstruct government policy that conflicted with those of France.... The technique of intervention...the giving of "presents" to minor rulers and ministers everywhere was a matter of routine and accepted as legitimate." Not only monarchs, through their diplomats and other agents, but also politicians of other kinds would seek to influence foreign governments. For example in 1710 the States-General of the United Provinces presented a memorial to Queen Anne, asking her not to dissolve the British Parliament: Though this caused some indignation in England it was by no means exceptional by the standards of this day.[12]

International law as it has evolved thus deals with the incidents or attributes of *theoretical* sovereignty—not sovereignty as it has actually existed in the reality of day-to-day state practice. State practice concerning use of force in the twentieth century, outlined above,* further highlights the gap between theory and reality.

For all the recent controversy concerning interventionist encroachments on sovereignty, international lawyers seldom deal with the critical antecedent question: Why *sovereignty?* Why posit *sovereignty* as *the* organizing principle of the international system? Why sovereignty rather than, say, a state's political system, or its religion, or its economic structure? Sovereignty has not always been the organizing principle; before the Thirty Years' War, that principle was religion. During the Kosovo crisis, at least one NATO state seemed to believe that the time had again come for a different organizing principle. "In the 21st century human rights will be the fundamental basis for defining international relations," the Polish Foreign Minister said. "Relations between nations can no longer be

---

* See pages 67–70.

founded on respect for sovereignty—they must be founded on respect for human rights."[13] The dubious rationale for elevating sovereignty above all other possible group characteristics as a source of legal entitlements becomes visible when two issues are addressed. First, what produces "sovereign equality"? And, second, are the assumptions consonant with reality?

A realistic look at the origins of sovereignty reveals why some groups enjoy its benefits while others do not. The notion of sovereignty, Kennan wrote, "ignores the tremendous variations in the firmness and soundness of national divisions: The fact that the origins of state borders and national personalities were in many instances fortuitous or at least poorly related to realities."[14] Michael Howard elaborates:

> It is hard to think of any nation-state, with the possible exception of Norway, that came into existence before the middle of the twentieth century which was not created, and had its boundaries defined, by wars, by internal violence, or by a combination of the two. These wars, in many cases, had been fought not between peoples but between princes asserting claims to what they regarded as their personal property.... The harsh fact is that state structure as it exists today is not the result of peaceful, teleological growth, the evolution of nations whose seeds have germinated in the womb of time and have come to a natural fruition. It is the result of conflicts that might, in very many cases, have been resolved differently.[15]

That being the case, an obvious question arises: Should the members of one group be legally disabled from receiving outside assistance to halt their genocidal extermination, while another group living in a neighboring country can seek such assistance, solely because the territory in which the first group lives happens to have been conquered 700 years ago by a given prince—who failed to conquer the territory in which the second group lives?

The answer given increasingly by Western governments is: Of course not. But precisely the opposite answer is given by traditional international law. The answer given by international law is that the only proper reference point is sovereignty. If a group lives in a sovereign state and its government chooses to exterminate it because its religion is incorrect, under international law intervention by any outside state on behalf of that group is impermissible. Sovereignty prevails over justice. In sovereignty, all states are equal. And equality,

since its enshrinement two centuries ago in the American
Declaration of Independence and the French Declaration of the
Rights of Man and of the Citizen, like sovereignty, has taken on the
status of a "given"—not only in the domestic life of modern nations
but in international relations as well.

As a battle cry, the statement that "all men are created equal"
has galvanizing power. As an empirical observation, however, the
statement has many meanings, some true and some demonstrably
not. Applied to states, the proposition that all are equal is, similarly,
open to challenge by evidence everywhere that they are not—neither
in their power, nor their wealth, nor in their respect for international order or human rights. As Kennan has pointed out, the
notion of equality is a myth; disparities among states "make a
mockery"[16] of the concept. "To suggest," Kennan wrote, "that any
of the smaller members of the United Nations—or any of the larger
ones either, for that matter—possess under the term 'sovereignty'
anything akin to the sovereignty once exercised by the emperors of
China or Byzantium is to stretch a point beyond all plausibility."[17]
Yet international lawyers have long viewed states as equally
empowered to make customary international law; the practice of
Liechtenstein and Bhutan counts for as much as the practice of
China or the United States when it comes to connecting the dots
of historical precedent and identifying custom. Neither population,
nor wealth, nor respect for the order of the community or even the
well-being of their own people goes into the equation. Only one thing
counts: sovereignty. Each sovereign state is equally able to partake in
the making of customary international law binding on all others.

3. The Security Council veto and sovereign equality

The rule of law thus counsels that states be treated as equals, but
reality reveals that they are anything but equal. Ideal and reality
cannot be reconciled. The UN Charter tried to effect a reconciliation
by giving each of the five Great Powers of 1945 a veto in the
Security Council—and in the process rendered itself incoherent.
By repudiating the principle of equality in Security Council decision
making, the veto makes nonsensical the Charter's organizing principle of sovereign equality and thus rules out any possibility of
authentic international governance. As Hans Morgenthau put it,
"[w]ith but one permanent member dissenting there can be no international government of the United Nations."[18] In the veto, the

Charter institutionalizes a form of self-dealing that is, indeed, anti-thetical to very notion of the rule of law. The veto establishes a process for authorizing use of force that is neither preagreed nor principled. It is not preagreed in that the procedure does not lead to an outcome to which all participants are bound; five preferred participants may object after-the-fact and cause the results to be undone. It is not principled in that the results, subject as they are to the veto, can be rendered inapplicable by an interested party. (The Charter purports to mitigate these difficulties by precluding use of the veto "in decisions under Chapter VI" by a "party to a dispute,"[19] but it sets out no effective enforcement mechanism, and in situations such as the invasion of Panama by the United States, the veto has been used notwithstanding that prohibition.[20]) That five members of the United Nations, and no other members, have a veto makes it hard to argue that the United Nations Charter constitutes an authentic legal regime. As Martin Wight put it, "The British argument to justify the veto, that no enforcement action could be taken against a Great Power without a major war, and that in such circumstances the UN 'will have failed in its purpose and all members will have to act as seems best in the circumstances,' marked a retrogression from the standards of the Covenant, a recognition that the rule of law is unobtainable in international relations."[21]

The presence of the veto thus undercuts the legalist system's claim to authenticity. At the same time, the need for the veto explains why an authentic legalist order governing use of force is not now possible. The risks inherent in a universal state system that provides no escape from lawfully centralized coercion continue to remain greater than the risks of a state system that lacks coercive compliance mechanisms. Deep divisions within the international community have made it impossible to devise safeguards sufficient to meet reasonably foreseeable dangers that coercion will be misdirected to undermine the values that it was established to protect.* Until such

---

* "[B]ecause the simple truisms that hold good for individuals do not hold good for states, and the factual background to international law is so different from that of municipal law, there is neither a similar necessity for sanctions … nor a similar prospect for their safe and efficacious use… . Hence the organization and use of sanctions may involve fearful risks and the threat of them add little to the natural deterrents." H. L. A. Hart, *The Concept of Law* 214 (1961).

safeguards are devised, a legalist use-of-force regime will remain a dream.*

B. The Collapse of Consent

According special treatment to the five permanent members of the Security Council represented an effort by the framers of the Charter to replicate the existing power structure. Their impulse was sound: No legalist regime can work if it ignores the actual distribution of power that its seeks to manage. But the power structure that exists in the world today cannot be replicated in an authentic legalist use-of-force regime. The effort to do so is an effort to square a circle. The incompatibility of the Charter's most fundamental precepts highlights the incompatibility of the values that the Charter seeks to reconcile. Equality—the assumption that Iraq, Libya, and Syria should have an equal say in world affairs with the United States, Britain, and France—is not, in fact, a principle that is accepted by all states, the rhetoric of the Charter notwithstanding.†

Moreover, the Charter's own terms belie the claim that its system is based upon states' consent. Article 2(6) establishes *de facto* obligations for nonmembers of the United Nations. It provides that

---

*UN Secretary General Kofi Annan has proposed that the Security Council be reformed to allow nine Security Council countries to overcome the veto that a single country can impose. "UN Security Council could see reform within a year, Annan," *Agence France Presse,* July 16, 1999. Given fundamental attitudinal differences among Security Council members, however, abolishing the veto would increase, rather than decrease, the danger of misdirected coercion. It was this danger that led Senator Tom Connally, an American delegate to the San Francisco conference, to declare that the delegates could kill the veto if they liked, but there would be no United Nations if they did. United Nations Information Organization, *United Nations Conference on International Organization* 2: 493 (1945–46).

†While the Soviet Union was the prime user of the veto during the UN's early years, its use by the United States accelerated afterwards with the formation of coalitions unfriendly to the West. From 1946 to 1986, the Soviet Union cast 121 vetoes to the United States' 57. Some 77 of the Soviet Union's vetoes were cast during the Organization's first ten years, whereas nearly all of those cast by the United States—45—were cast during the final ten years of that period. Sydney D. Bailey and Sam Daws, *The Procedure of the UN Security Council* 209 (2nd ed. 1988).

the "Organization shall ensure that states which are not Members of the United Nations act in accordance with these Principles so far as may be necessary for the maintenance of international peace and security."[22] At first blush, this provision may seem to accord with the basic requirement of customary international law that the direct effects of a treaty be limited to the parties to the treaty. But the Charter complies more in form than in substance. A nonmember state faces coercion, possibly in the form of a threat or use of force by the Security Council or UN member states acting at its behest, if the nonmember declines to act in accordance with Charter norms. That coercion may be exercised by the UN in response to a good faith disagreement by the nonmember. The nonmember may, for example, reject with the prevailing view that humanitarian intervention or anticipatory self-defense is unlawful. It can scarcely be maintained that a nonmember "consents" to be the subject of an armed attack if it should act pursuant to its own insight rather than that of the United Nations. Suppose OPEC states were to agree to "act in accordance with" the principles of a boycott agreement "so far as may be necessary for the maintenance of" a global, OPEC-established supply schedule, aimed at propping up the price of oil, and suppose a non-OPEC member sold oil below the OPEC-established floor. It cannot seriously be argued that that non-OPEC state "consented" to be the subject of an OPEC oil embargo. Yet this is precisely the logic behind the contention that the use-of-force system established by the United Nations is "consent-based."

That the Charter itself is not fully committed to the principle of consent is significant. Consent, as noted earlier, is the cornerstone of the legalist system. It is commonly said that that system is one in which obligation arises from the consent of the state that is bound.* These principles trace ultimately to John Locke's justification for the overthrow of the Stuarts in the 1688 Revolution, "which remains basically the theory of constitutional government and of popular sovereignty among the Anglo-Saxon peoples."[23] According to Locke, "man surrenders his natural rights to the political community, not absolutely, but to the extent necessary for the common good."[24] Rights not surrendered are retained, and the political

---

*See, for example, Georg Schwarzenberger, "The Fundamental Principles of International Law," 87 *Rec. des Cours* 195 (I, 1955) (consent is "coterminous with the existence of universal international law itself").

community can act collectively only to the extent that actors within it, through their consent, agree that it may do so.

The central condition to formation of the polity, therefore, is that consent be given to the extent necessary to maintain and preserve minimal public order. Governance by law requires common agreement concerning the basic elements of such order. Absent a consensus as to how the polity should function—absent agreement on what tasks it should undertake and what tasks should be left to individual actors—the formation of public authority is impossible. And such a consensus does not exist. As David S. Yost has written, "[T]he difficulty with the Kantian and Wilsonian model of international order is that, despite its enduring attractions, it does not offer a genuine alternative to balance-of-power politics; it is illusory, a fateful mirage, given that the conditions that might make it work are not available, and that (in part because of the absence of those conditions) governments will not behave as the model demands."[25]

That is the principal reason why legalist controls on the use of force have failed. Law requires agreement among the governed on basic values. Use of force raises questions about the most basic value of all—the value of human life. There remains, as the *New York Times* lamented, a "yawning gap between the West and much of the rest of the world on the value of a single human life."[26] Differences as to what constitutes "civic virtue" do not stop at human rights. Traits appropriate for participation in civil society are still seen very differently by clashing cultures. In some, for example, flexibility and compromise are valued; in others, rigid insistence on principle and fidelity to the memories of aggrieved ancestors is held high. This was brought home most vividly by ethnic strife in the Balkans and dramatically different reactions to it by peoples and their governments. During the Kosovo War, Russia supplied Belgrade with radar information on incoming NATO aircraft.[27] Scotland's national newspaper reported that a Russian spy penetrated NATO's command structure and passed information on to Yugoslavia that helped Belgrade's anti-aircraft units bring down an American Stealth fighter.[28] "Through the centuries," Henry Kissinger has noted, "these conflicts have been fought with unparalleled ferocity because none of the populations has any experience with—and essentially no belief in—Western concepts of toleration. The principles of majority rule and compromise that underlie most of the proposals for a solution have never found an echo in the Balkans."[29] Different estimations of the importance of forgiving one's enemies versus that of avenging age-old wrongs continue to separate cultures. The Kosovo War, opined Michael Wines of the *Times*, "only underscored the deep ideological divide between an idealistic New World bent on ending inhumanity and an Old World equally fatalistic about unending conflict."[30]

That divide is not new. The *rapporteur-général* of the Universal Peace Congresses wrote in 1900 that "Russia could not have a place in a true United States of Europe because of her régime and her lack of common culture with the rest."[31] Two years later, an English proponent of world federation wrote that "we can scarcely picture Russia as a reliable member of such a union;" the "best thing for Europe," he wrote, "might be that Russia ... should be regarded as a serious danger to all the civilized powers of the West."[32] The history of Russia is well borne in mind:*

> Ethnic cleansing and forced migration are not exactly unknowns to Russians. Pogroms forced 1.5 million Russian Jews to flee at the turn of the century. And Nikita Khrushchev forcibly moved so many Russians to Kazakhstan that by 1959 native Kazakhs made up less than a third of the population. From Stalin on, Soviet policy was to dilute the Soviet Union's 80-odd ethnic groups by moving Russian citizens onto their territories, evicting them from homelands and drawing borders so as to split large ethnic groups in two.[33]

The attitudinal gap between Russia and the West has closed little since the end of the Cold War—even as Russia ostensibly adopted notions of private property ownership and free markets. On October 19, 1999, *Izvestiya* of Moscow noted an alarming new tendency in Russia: In the absence of effective enforcement of property rights, people simply grab what they think should be theirs. It gave the example of the Barrikady agricultural cooperative in the Volgograd region, where peasant shareholders, claiming a combine harvester and a herd of cows as their own, seized them from a neighboring village. "This is how bloody slaughters have started in Russian history, leading in the end to two revolutions and the placing

---

*Compare Noam Chomsky, *The New Military Humanism: Lessons from Kosovo* 4 (1999). ("One will search in vain for credible attempts to provide evidence or argument for the critical distinction between enlightened and disorderly, surely not from history.")

of Russia outside the civilized world for the entire 20th century," the paper said.[34] The wholesale slaughter of civilians in Chechnya and the carpet bombing of its capital, Grozny—recommenced in the fall of 1999 following an infusion of IMF loans and other Western capital— provided a chilling end to the century in which humanity supposedly discovered international human rights. The problem, we are beginning to realize, was not simply communism; the problem was Russia.

China, unfortunately, is no closer than Russia to sharing basic civic values with the West. After Russian President Boris Yeltsin met with President Jiang Zemin in Beijing in December 1999, the Russian foreign minister reported that "President Jiang said he completely understood and fully supported Russia's actions… ."[35] Until the Kosovo conflict, many in the West believed that China and the industrial democracies would naturally continue to grow steadily closer, as they had since Presidents Nixon and Carter had opened up trade relations between China and the United States in the 1970s. They were wrong. Many Americans no doubt found it hard to watch scenes of the American embassy in Beijing being stoned by angry Chinese mobs without thinking that this was not the China that they thought they knew. Following the U.S. bombing of the Chinese embassy in Belgrade, for which President Clinton (and numerous other American officials) apologized as a mistake,* Chinese state-run media declined to report the U.S. apology for four days. During that period, the U.S. ambassador, unable to leave the embassy, referred to himself as a "hostage."[36] In the southwestern city of Chengdu, protestors set fire to the U.S. consul's residence. Chinese President Jiang Zemin told President Clinton that the protests were a spontaneous reaction of outrage. "This was reasonable," Jiang was quoted as saying.[37] United States Ambassador James Sasser never received an apology for the attacks.[38]

Differing attitudes toward the value of human life create differing attitudes toward sovereignty and intervention, which often are lost on Americans—including American international lawyers. "One accusation rarely noted in the U.S. press," the *New York Times* observed, "but extensively accepted as truth abroad, was that the bombing of Yugoslavia was a flagrant violation of

---

*"Stacks of taunting faxes came into Clark's office that day. 'Dear Gen. Clark,' many of them began. 'We've moved. Our new address is… .'" Dana Priest, "Bombing By Committee: France Balked at NATO Targets," *Wash. Post*, Sept. 20, 1999, at A1.

sovereignty and international law. In the Third World, where
boundaries are often in dispute and governments weak, these principles are held to be virtually sacred."[39] The President of the
Organization of African Unity saw sovereignty as a an important
means of defending the interests of the weak against the strong.
"We do not deny that the United Nations has the right and the duty
to help suffering humanity," said President Abdelaziz Bouteflika of
Algeria. "But we remain extremely sensitive to any undermining of
our sovereignty, not only because sovereignty is our last defense
against the rules of an unequal world but because we are not taking
part in the decision-making process of the Security Council."[40]
Algeria's opposition to humanitarian intervention is shared by
much of the developing world. Nelson Mandela criticized the United
States and Britain for their action in Kosovo and for not seeking
"explicit permission" from the Security Council before the bomb-
ings. "The message they're sending is that any country which fears a
[UN] veto can take unilateral action," Mandela said. "That means
they're introducing chaos into international affairs: that any country
can take a decision which it wants."[41] In April 2000, 114 member
states of the Non-Aligned Movement condemned humanitarian intervention.[42] It had "no legal basis under the Charter," they said.[43]
Colombian President Andrs Pastrana, speaking at the meeting, said
that "[a]ny humanitarian intervention should be carried out in the
framework of the principles of the U.N. Charter."[44] Sergey Lavrov,
Russia's UN representative, candidly described the chasm. One group
of countries, he said, will not "sit with [their] arms folded" and "wait
for a decision of the UN Security Council" in the face of "ethnic
cleansing and massive violations of human rights," whereas another
group of countries believes "that force cannot be used no matter what
the circumstances, apart from those that are defined in the Charter."[45]

 I have earlier reviewed the negative response of several states to
the suggestion of the Secretary General that the Security Council
might appropriately undertake humanitarian intervention. To these
might be added—so as to fill out the picture of the irreconcilability
of global opinion on the issue—the views of representative UN
member states* that oppose intervention by individual states and

---

*See also the critical remarks of delegates from Afghanistan, Angola,
Bahrain, Belarus, Ghana, Laos, Myanmar, Gambia, Sri Lanka, Tunisia,
and the United Arab Emirates.

coalitions of states, such as NATO, without Security Council approval. The following delegate comments might be borne in mind when evaluating the suggestions of Louis Henkin and others that a "new informal consensus of nations"[46] has developed concerning the propriety of humanitarian intervention of the sort undertaken by NATO:

Russia: "The founding fathers of the United Nations made provision for a law-based response to violations of peace and security. The international community can take also coercive measures, but this should be done in accordance with the Charter and following a decision by the Security Council. Unlawful means can only undermine rightful ends."[47]

Mexico: "[T]he Mexican Government reiterates the value of the peaceful settlement of disputes and firmly rejects the existence of an alleged right to intervene, particularly when it is proclaimed outside the framework of international law."[48]

Viet Nam: "The unilateral military attacks against the territorial integrity of sovereign States in the Balkans and the Gulf have set a dangerous precedent in international relations, running counter to the purposes and principles of the United Nations and in violation of the fundamental principles of international law, especially those of respect for the independence, sovereignty and territorial integrity of Member States."[49]

Kenya: "In accordance with the United Nations Charter, the Security Council has the primary responsibility to determine the existence of any threat to international peace and security.... There can be no derogation from this primary responsibility. In the fulfillment of this principle, it must be borne in mind that the principle of non-interference in the internal affairs of Member States remains a cardinal element in the conduct of international relations, as spelt out in the Charter."[50]

Jamaica: "The Security Council has the primary responsibility. It should not be ignored and disregarded in favor of unilateral action on the part of any State or group of States."[51]

Iran: "A lack of consensus in the Security Council does not entitle any country or small group of countries to act unilaterally in dealing with conflicts, particularly when gross violations of the sovereignty of other States are involved. In our view, the use of force or any other violation of the very basic principle of international law—respect for the integrity and sovereignty of other States—undermines the goals and principles of the United Nations Charter."[52]

Malaysia: "[W]hatever the merits of the argument in support of humanitarian intervention, we should not lose sight of the necessity of securing the authorization of the Security Council for any use of force against States."[53]

Peru: "The Security Council, charged with maintaining international peace and security, is the sole body that can authorize the use of force … . The unilateral use of force, ignoring the Council's jurisdiction, is therefore difficult to accept, because it undermines the foundations of the civilized coexistence of States in the modern world … . For Peru, full adherence to the purposes and principles of the United Nations Charter, which govern the international system, is fundamental—not only in words, but in deeds."[54]

Yemen: "The principle of State sovereignty is a well-established principle in international relations. We cannot accept the notion that this principle is outmoded and has been superseded by international developments … ."[55]

Cyprus: "If we accept interventions outside the United Nations, we may be opening a Pandora's box, for there will always be those leaders who will cover their sinister designs for expansion through aggression with a pretext of humanitarianism and the protection of minorities and ethnic groups."[56]

Colombia: "We consider it unacceptable that a regional defence organization took military action [in Kosovo] without the authorization of the Security Council."[57]

Ivory Coast: "The situation in Kosovo leads us to reflect on the growing danger of seeing regional organizations go beyond the limits of regional action imposed by Article 53 of the Charter. The use of force without Security Council authorization is a serious threat to international peace and security."[58]

Contrast these views with those of NATO leaders. "This operation is the first signal of the coming century," Polish Foreign Minister Bronislaw Geremek said during NATO's Kosovo operation. "In the 21st century human rights will be the fundamental basis for defining international relations. Relations between nations can no longer be founded on respect for sovereignty—they must be founded on respect for human rights."[59] Václav Havel described his support for NATO's action in an address to the

Canadian parliament:

> [T]here is one thing no reasonable person can deny: This is probably the first war that has not been waged in the name of "national interests," but rather in the name of principles and values ... [NATO] is fighting out of concern for the fate of others. It is fighting because no decent person can stand by and watch the systematic state-directed murder of other people .... The alliance has acted out of respect for human rights, as both conscience and legal documents dictate. This is an important precedent for the future. It has been clearly said that it is simply not permissible to murder people, to drive them from their homes, to torture them, and to confiscate their property ... .[60]

British Prime Minister Tony Blair, in a speech in Chicago (hailed by the British press for its unveiling of the "Blair Doctrine") said:

> No one in the West who has seen what is happening in Kosovo can doubt that NATO's military action is justified. Bismarck famously said the Balkans were not worth the bones of one Pomeranian Grenadier. Anyone who has seen the tear-stained faces of the hundreds of thousands of refugees streaming across the border, heard their heart-rending tales of cruelty or contemplated the unknown fates of those left behind, knows that Bismarck was wrong.[61]

"We need to enter a new millennium," Blair said later, "where dictators know that they cannot get away with ethnic cleansing or repress their peoples with impunity. In this conflict we are fighting not for territory but for values. For a new internationalism where the brutal repression of whole ethnic groups will no longer be tolerated."[62]

These sentiments were expressed following evidence that a growing number of states no longer assert that sovereignty can shield everything done within their borders, however heinous.[63] Javier Pérez de Cuéllar declared in 1991 that the principle of noninterference in a state's internal affairs could no longer justify protection of massive human rights violations:

> It is now increasingly felt that the principle of noninterference with the essential domestic jurisdiction of States cannot be regarded as a protective barrier behind which human rights could be massively and systematically violated with impunity.[64]

The Secretary General's views found support the following year in the 1992 Helsinki summit declaration of the Organization for Security and Cooperation in Europe. The OSCE asserted that human rights commitments are "of direct and legitimate concern to all participating States and do not belong exclusively to the internal affairs of the State concerned."[65] Another international organization to endorse the emerging norm was the Organization for Economic Cooperation and Development. The high point of the OECD summit in November 1999 was the signing of a revamped Charter for European Security, which provides that the human rights record of one member nation is the business of other members.[66] Judge Sofaer bluntly summarized the implications of such sentiments for the United Nations Charter: "If the Charter cannot provide a legal basis for such actions [as NATO undertook in Kosovo], then its already tenuous, theoretical exclusivity as the source of authority to use force must be lost."[67]

Thus, as the millennium drew to a close, the gap in values actually widened. "If anything," Hinsley observed, "a successful international organization has become even more difficult to achieve in the twentieth century, in a world that comprises multifarious communities with disparate histories and at violently different stages of growth," than it was when it was possible to imagine "the unity of a Christian Europe."[68] "Disparate history" is a large part of the explanation. Francis Boyle summarized the intellectual and cultural tradition of the states that founded the legalist order:

> All the major actors except Japan shared a cultural heritage schooled in the Old Testament, Greece, Rome, medieval Christendom, the Renaissance and Reformation, the European Enlightenment, the Industrial Revolution, the French Revolution and Napoleonic Wars, and the tradition of a "concert" of European powers determining matters of world politics by mutual consent and negotiated agreement throughout the nineteenth century.[69]

It should surprise no one that actors estranged from that heritage might be less than enthusiastic about the values of compromise, accommodation, toleration, individual rights, and humanitarianism that flow from it.

Of course, it is always tempting for observers from any cultural perspective to believe that the values of their own culture are and should be universal—to think (in the words of Shaw's Caesar) "that the customs of his tribe and island are the laws of nature."[70] Non-Western cultures impart a very different conception of the public good. The primacy of the "group" rather than the "individual" is a notion that pervades African and Asian perspectives. In many African societies, land is owned communally and there is no "right" to individual ownership.[71] Personhood is intelligible only in terms of group membership, in contrast to notions of "individualism" in the West.[72] Community and obligation come before individual and right.[73] Only members who belong to the community are entitled to have their "rights" protected.[74] Governmental efficiency and the promotion of common economic prosperity is valued over the protection of individual liberty.[75] Freedom to speak is a communal right, subject to limitation when it involves disrespect of authority[76] or undermines the common good. The Western emphasis on freedom from restraint is alien in cultures such as Islam.[77] Even where Western societies do focus on the group as a source of rights, the identity of the group is different. Whereas the "nuclear" family is now the fundamental unit of Western society, non-Western societies such as China see larger "kinship" groups as more natural.[78] These societies—which comprise most of the world's population—see the West, not themselves, as out of sync. Western materialism, vulgarity, and selfishness are to be resisted, not emulated.

Samuel Huntington's *The Clash of Civilizations* explores the phenomenon of cultural and civilizational division. "The fault lines between civilizations," he has written, "are replacing the political and ideological boundaries of the Cold War as the flash points for crisis and bloodshed."[79] Recent research by Richard Nisbett has revealed that cultural differences may stem not only from *what* different peoples think, but the *way* they think. The studies, carried out in the United States, Japan, China, and Korea, suggest that East Asians "think more 'holistically,' paying greater attention to context and relationship, relying more on experience-based knowledge than abstract logic and showing more tolerance for contradiction. Westerners are more 'analytic' in their thinking, tending to detach objects from their context, to avoid contradictions and to rely more heavily on formal logic."[80] Asians seem less susceptible to the "fundamental attribution error, the tendency for people to explain human behavior in terms of the traits of individual actors, even when powerful situational forces are at work."[81] They pay greater attention to background and circumstance than do Americans. (As noted later in this book, the implications of these findings for perceptions of customary norms may be profound.) Yet these differences do not seem genetically based; "Asian-Americans, born in the United States, are indistinguishable in their modes of thought from European-Americans."[82]

This research supports the speculation of Immanuel Kant. Although such differences seem in recent years to have grown, Kant believed that, over time, cultural differences narrow. Kant was the first philosopher to consider seriously the consequences of globalization. "Nature," Kant wrote, "employs two means to keep peoples from being mixed and to differentiate them, the difference of *language* and of *religion*. These differences occasion the inclination towards mutual hatred and the excuse for war; yet at the same time they lead, as culture increases and men gradually come closer together, towards a greater agreement on principles for peace and understanding."[83] It has recently been theorized that we are today witnessing the emergence of a global "cosmocrat" class, a new trans-national élite that is cosmopolitan in taste, Anglo-American in outlook, and more meritocratic than we have ever seen.[84] But convergence implies more than intermingling at the top; it requires a genuine coming together of fundamental values held by the mass of humanity. Recognizing that convergence in this sense was years away, Kant viewed supranational organization as unattainable and urged its rejection.

It is thus accurate, but insufficient, to blame the failure of international institutions such as the United Nations or the League of Nations on a failure of "political will" on the part of the states that they comprise.* Such organizations often are sold to member states' publics on the promise that they provide *added* value. The promise is that they do *more* than member states could do in their absence. But such organizations can provide only process, not enhanced political will. A. J. P. Taylor wrote that "[t]he League, like other international systems, provided a tolerable machinery by which the Powers could conduct their peaceful relations, so long as they wished to remain peaceful. No more could be expected of it in

---

*Compare Lord Robertson, NATO Secretary General, *Law, Morality and the Use of Force*, Address before the Institut de Relations Internationales et Stratégiques, Paris (May 16, 2000), in which NATO's new Secretary General argues, similarly, that the refusal of Russia and China to go along with NATO's action against Yugoslavia must be discounted by the fact

a world of sovereign states."[85] States lack political will for many reasons—one reason being, as discussed earlier, a genuine and well-founded distrust of the capacity of any centralized, international authority to use troops drawn from their own populations in a manner consonant with the values of those populations. (This doubt does not even reach the graver concern of states that such an authority might in fact operate *against* their own populations.) It is ironic but true that the very conditions necessary for the success of a legalist regime tend to lessen the need for one.

Still, more *can* be expected of an organization like the League *if* it is situated at the convergence of states' political wills. Nothing inherent in the concept of sovereignty precludes such a convergence. The point is, rather, that a convergence of states' wills is a necessary basis for an organization formed to execute the product of their joint will. The organization cannot be expected to supply that will itself. "In politics as in mechanics," John Stuart Mill said, "the power which is to keep the engine going must be sought for outside the machinery; and if it is not forthcoming, or is insufficient to surmount the obstacles which may reasonably be expected, the contrivance will fail."[86] "Power outside the machinery"—a confluence of values, attitudes, and interests that have their source in social and cultural forces predating institutionalized processes—has been responsible for the triumph of every successful legalist entity. The United States itself, the framers of its Constitution recognized, owed its foundation not to that Instrument but to the integrated political community that came before it—to "the same ancestors, speaking the same language, professing the same religion, attached to the same principles of government, very similar in their manners and customs ... ."[87]

One consequence of such ties is the formation of cross-cutting loyalties among divergent groups, who come to see common interests as predominating over firmly held interests of the group.* Such groups come to expect justice from the whole, not simply from their

---

continued

that "they did so because of their own domestic political concerns"—as though a government's compliance with the views of the governed represents an illegitimate basis for its diplomacy.

*"It is almost a truism," wrote John Westlake in 1894, "to say that the mitigation of war must depend on the parties to it feeling that they belong

own *part* of the whole, and are therefore comfortable placing coercive power in the hands of the whole, even at the (short-term) expense of the part.[88] The success of the United Nations was premised upon the presence of such bonds among the Great Powers. Secretary of State Cordell Hull told Roosevelt that the "entire plan" is based on the assumption that the "major powers will ... cooperate with each other ... ."[89] No machinery, he later said, "can produce this essential harmony and unity."[90]

Sovereignty thus need hardly be eliminated before the international management of force can be effective. Sovereign states are fully able to retain their sovereignty while permitting intervention to stop gross and widespread human rights abuses. The adoption of a new international "ordering principle" different from sovereignty is not a necessary condition for a more humane world. But the gap that divides sovereign powers over basic issues must narrow before the phenomena of community cohesion necessary for that effectiveness can occur on an international level. "[T]here is no longer," Hans Morgenthau wrote, "an international moral consensus from which quarreling nations can receive a common standard of justice for the settlement of their disputes."[91] Until the gap in fundamental values does narrow, it will be impossible for an international legalist system to reflect satisfactorily the realities of the international political system. A correspondence of *legal* expectations with *geopolitical* expectations, at least with respect to nerve-center security issues such as intervention, is essential if the legalist model is to be anything more than window-dressing. As Stanley Hoffman put it, success for the UN "depends on the convergence of its members' preferences and imperatives, especially those of its more powerful members ... ."[92] The gap today between those "preferences and imperatives" is now too wide for law to bridge. Law, today, can produce only platitudinous principles that dissolve when the heat of controversy (such as Kosovo) requires operational definition. When an effort is made to bridge the gap with specifics, as was done in the UN Charter with Article 2(4), the result is an unwieldy

---

continued

to a larger whole than their respective tribes or states, a whole in which the enemy too is comprised, so that duties arising out of that larger citizenship are owed even to him." John Westlake, *Chapters on the Principles of International Law* 267 (1894).

instrument too blunt and too rigid to manage conflict effectively. Kennan realized this 50 years ago. He wrote:

> The function of a system of international relationships is not to inhibit this process of change by imposing a legal straitjacket upon it but rather to facilitate it; to ease its transitions, to temper the asperities to which it often leads, to isolate and moderate the conflicts to which it gives rise, and to see that these conflicts do not assume forms too unsettling for international life in general ... for this, law is too abstract, too inflexible, too hard to adjust to the demands of the unpredictable and the unexpected.[93]

"The deepest problem of the contemporary international order," Henry Kissinger has written, "is a differing philosophical perspective." It is no answer to say, as Secretary General Kofi Annan has said, that "Members of the United Nations should have been able to find common ground"[94] on Kosovo, that the differences *should* go away.* The differences among nations are profound, and legalist institutions, however well intentioned and ingeniously conceived, will not make them go away. "This is our world," Paul Kahn ruefully concluded, "and speaking the language of law is not going to make it any different."[95]

The effort to force a legalist use-of-force system on a world that is not ready for it has had a number of perverse effects. One is most prominent in that it will make it more difficult for the international community to move to an authentic legalist order when the conditions develop to do so: The effort has fostered increased resort to systems of validation other than law. Other validating systems include notions of justice, morality, legitimacy, and the like. Libraries of course have been written about these ideas; their evolution in many ways constitutes the backbone of Western political thought. For present purposes, I wish to focus only on two aspects of such systems. First, none is based upon consent, which is the element of law from which it derives universality. That is, there is no single, authoritative statement that all actors within any such

---

*The Secretary General's remark calls to mind the ordinance adopted by a town in colonial New England that prohibited pigeons from alighting on the town's window sills.

system have accepted as defining its meaning. Second, none of these
alternate systems *is* universal, inasmuch as there is nothing other
than consent from which universality might be derived. None has
any objective validity. Justice, morality, legitimacy, natural law, and
the like lie in the eye of the beholder. The upshot is that, however
much rhetoric may dress them up, power and preference underpin
each of these alternatives, and power and preference are all that
remain in the absence of law. NATO's intervention, in other words,
may be *labeled* "just" or "moral" or "legitimate," but these concepts have no objective force; claims of objective validity ultimately
are products of the same cultural variables that account for the attitudinal divide that the legalist model itself proved unable to bridge.

   A closer look at one such system reveals their shortcomings as a
substitute for law. Because it is only the common element of subjectivity that is relevant, I discuss "justice" as a stand-in for other systems of validation that are not based upon consent—recognizing, of
course, that in other respects those systems are different.*

   Justice and law are not identical. The UN Charter itself does not
regard justice and international law as coextensive. The Preamble
identifies, as an end of the United Nations, "to establish conditions
under which justice and respect for the obligations arising from
treaties and other sources of international law can be determined."
"If justice is identical with international law," Hans Kelsen noted,
"one of the two terms is superfluous." More likely, Kelsen suggested, the concepts "may be in opposition to each other." Since the
Charter does not say which should then prevail, a choice is necessary, "which practically means that the Charter does not strengthen
but weakens the respect for the obligations of international law."[96]

   It is easy to understand the attraction of concepts like justice.
Such notions permit reference to a wider range of criteria than does
law, offering a broader choice of standards to judge the propriety

---

*Henry Kissinger is careful to distinguish justice from legitimacy in his clas-
sic work, *A World Restored* (1962). He uses the term "legitimacy" narrowly, as encompassing only an international "order whose structure is
accepted by all major powers." See *id.* at 1, 5, 145. Of course, in
Kissinger's lexicon such an order need not necessarily be just, as it is not in
Franck's. See Thomas M. Franck, *The Power of Legitimacy Among
Nations* 208–210 (1990).

of actions (such as intervention) than is made available by more "technical," legal analysis. Defining w*hich* criteria count is of course the problem. The history of Western philosophy has in large part been an effort to get away from the subjectivity of that definitional process and to identify objective means for assessing what is just. Alas, a cursory glimpse at that history discloses that the Holy Grail of objectivity has never been found; justice continues to mean different things to different people.

In earlier times, justice was thought to be a command of natural law. In Plato's Republic, there were no laws; the philosopher-kings did justice wholesale with knowledge and wisdom. The French king did not make law but rather "discovered" it. The father of international law, Hugo Grotius, believed—with Vattel[97]—that when law lags behind justice, the commands of natural justice must prevail.[98] Through the eighteenth century, the "law of nature and of nature's God"[99] was still thought to provide discoverable guidance for the regulation of human affairs. The preferred method of that century's *philosophes* was thus to collect and analyze scientific data; the laws of nature, it was thought, embodied first principles on which all must agree. In modern times, moral philosophies that lay claim to ineluctability have come to rely less upon external, empirical evidence and more upon internal, mental processes. The archetype of such approaches is Immanuel Kant's, set out in his *Critique of Practical Reason*. From premises that all reasonable persons must accept, Kant argues, comes the famous "categorical imperative": Act according to a maxim that can be adopted at the same time as a universal law of human conduct.[100] We must, in other words, apply the same rule to another's act that we apply to our own act. Persons unwilling to do so effectively acknowledge that their own behavior is impermissible by refusing to posit the moral principle necessary to legitimate their own conduct. Lying is thus impermissible in that one would not wish all others to lie.[101] The actions of collective entities such as nations are equally subject to the same precepts: The impermissibility of shooting down an unarmed civilian aircraft that has strayed over a state's territory, for example, is demonstrated by states' unwillingness to allow their own meandering aircraft to be shot down.

The methodology suggested by John Rawls[102] provides a conceptual paraphrase of Kant. To shape a just society, detach yourself mentally from your position in your own society and assume the "original position" in which no one yet has *any* position— economic, social, political, or even physical or psychological. Behind a "veil of ignorance"—not knowing in which position you might ultimately find yourself—design all societal positions, as well as the governing law. The process of so designing a society is akin to the process of formulating maxims of conduct under the categorical imperative. In the "original position," assuming equal odds of ending up in any of the positions you design, you might not make all positions equally attractive so as to build in incentives. Nonetheless, you would infuse each with the highest possible measure of autonomy (or, in the case of states, sovereignty) because you don't know what characteristics and preferences you'll end up with, and you would want make it as easy as possible to be "fulfilled" in whatever position you ultimately occupy.

Objectivist, deontological philosophies such as Kant's and Rawls'—that is, philosophies claiming that certain conclusions follow from the mere fact of existence, *a priori* philosophies that proceed from principles that are said to exist prior to empirical data—have of course generated volumes of commentary. For present purposes, it will suffice to point out three of the core problems that characterize such philosophies, the first being a problem shared with customary international law.

That is the level-of-generality difficulty—the problem inherent in characterizing the "act" in question. Is the act a "lie" or statement made, say, under duress to save a settlement from attack? Any act can be generalized or particularized almost infinitely so as to include or exclude almost any attendant circumstances, and the breadth of the "maxim" that derives from universalizing the act will very accordingly.* Neither Kant nor Rawls nor anyone else has told us how to decide what facts go into the "correct" formulation of a given act because there *is* no single, "correct," abstracted reality. "[A]bstractions," Barzun wrote, "form a ladder which takes the climber into the clouds, where diagnostic differences disappear," adding that "at a high enough rung on the ladder of abstraction, disparate things become the same: a song and a spinning top are, after all, but two ways of setting air waves in motion."[103]

---

*This same difficulty is discussed in connection with customary international law in Chapter 2.

In fact, recent research reveals that cultural differences may affect one's inclination towards particularity versus generality. Asians are more likely than Americans to take note of background and context, the studies show, raising the question whether Asians might thus incline to qualify "precedent" more heavily and to view precedent as controlling or even apposite in fewer circumstances. In fact, Americans and Europeans might also "find themselves on different sides of the *high and low context* divide," writes the Norwegian sociologist Torbjørn Sirevåg, building on the work of Edward T. Hall.[104] A "high context culture," Sirevåg writes, is one in which "much background information (many words) is not always necessary to convey a message.... Members of high-context cultures are usually *implicit*; they will leave many things unsaid."[105] A "low context culture," on the other hand, will be "explicit and rich in detail."[106] The United States and Germany are examples of low context cultures, whereas the rest of Northwest Europe is "slightly more of a high context area."[107] Culturally different processes of conceptualization—disparate habits of thought in processing information—may therefore account for dramatic differences in the way different cultures formulate and apply customary international law norms, laden as those norms are with implicit assumptions regarding what is text and what is context.

The second problem with objectivist philosophies is the assumption of consistency—the belief that rationality requires all actors within a system to comport their conduct with moral precepts yielded by reason. But the categorical imperative is no response to the Nietzschean Superman—who acts solely for his own gratification and is altogether indifferent to any precedent that may flow from universalizing his behavior. For the Superman, there are no precedents—there is only power.

There is a final difficulty with objectivist philosophies, one sometimes referred to as the "problem of the normative source." The issue is, what is the source from which the philosophy's first principles derive? Any belief system rests upon some foundational premise or premises; where do these premises come from? Inevitably, *a priori,* objectivist philosophies are unable to answer this question satisfactorily, and in the effort to do so, they present us with principles that are either so vague or trivial that they can be used to support or oppose any conclusion that one might prefer.

The argument of Noam Chomsky against NATO's Kosovo intervention illustrates the futility of an objectivist approach—why

objectivism is illusory and why supposedly objective systems of validation are no substitute for law. Chomsky begins his argument with
three moral precepts (he calls them "truisms"[108]):

1. "[P]eople are primarily responsible for the likely consequences of
   their own action, or inaction."[109]
2. "[T]he concern for moral issues should vary in accordance with
   ability to have an effect (though that is of course not the only
   factor)."[110]
3. "[R]esponsibility mounts the greater the opportunities, and the
   more free one is to act without serious cost."[111]

Applying these principles to the facts of the Kosovo intervention,
Chomsky concludes not only that it was wrong, but that any one
who believes it was right is necessarily guilty of "intentional ignorance."*,[112]

   Like other objectivist arguments, his is easily turned on its head.
Each one of his precepts is, with no effort, capable of being flipped
to establish a conclusion opposite the one he reaches. That "people
are responsible for the likely consequences of their own action," for
example, does not necessarily mean that the leaders of the United
States and NATO are responsible for Serb ethnic cleansing in
Kosovo (which was, at least initially, accelerated by the NATO
bombing campaign). Precisely the opposite conclusion could be
reached pursuant to his truism: It was the Serbs who are responsible
for "Serb atrocities in Kosovo, which are quite real, and often
ghastly" (his words[113]) and not the leaders of NATO. To claim, as
he does, that it was NATO's "own action" that brought about
accelerated ethnic cleansing assumes the very point at issue: What
action is one's "own," and what is another's? How is responsibility
for action established? The issue has generated no little philosophical

---

*In using this phrase, repeated throughout his book, Chomsky refers to
words quoted in a 1985 report that I coauthored concerning human rights
abuses by the *contras* in Nicaragua. The words were used by a high-rank-
ing State Department official (who requested anonymity) to describe the
posture of the U.S. government toward reports of *contra* atrocities. Donald
T. Fox and Michael J. Glennon, *Report Concerning Abuses Against
Civilians by Counter-Revolutionaries Operating in Nicaragua* (published
and sponsored by the International Human Rights Law Group and the
Washington Office on Latin America, Apr. 1985).

controversy over the centuries; to Chomsky, possible ambiguities in the notion of "own" do not merit so much as a footnote.

Chomsky insists, similarly, that the United States' "responsibility mounts" with respect to its allies (as opposed to its adversaries) because its "ability to have an effect" on allies' human rights violations is greater. It might or might not be true that the United States controls its allies' human rights practices. What his "truisms" surely do not establish is that shirking supposed responsibility in one case justifies shirking responsibility in another. Chomsky criticizes the West for its failure to intervene in places like East Timor (his book was written before Western intercession occurred), seemingly thinking that those failures somehow render illegitimate NATO's intervention in Kosovo. But if NATO would have been "responsible for the consequences" of its own "inaction" in Kosovo, how could that responsibility conceivably be lessened by failing to act elsewhere? "It is a bizarre form of affirmative action," Michael Kinsley observes, "to suggest that we must let white people be slaughtered in Kosovo because we let black people be slaughtered in Rwanda."*

Second, what is the source of Chomsky's *a priori* precepts? To call them "truisms" hardly answers the question: that a lot of people may regard those or other precepts as true merely means that a lot of people regard them as true—not that the precepts have some overarching objective validity, as he implies. Chomsky criticizes my suggestion in *Foreign Affairs*[114] that the only morality on which NATO could act was what NATO itself "believe[d] to be just" and that the United States could act only on the basis of "what it thinks is right;"[115] on what *other* basis, one may ask, should they have acted? On the basis of what Slobodan Milocevic thought was right? Or Russia? China? Or does Chomsky believe that the community view of justice is always right—that civil disobedience is never justified?

The roulette wheel from which Chomsky and other closet objectivists select "controlling" moral precepts is the centerpiece of their methodology. There is no way to "prove," as Chomsky purports to do, that any human activity is objectively "moral" or "immoral."†

---

*Michael Kinsley, "Is There a Doctrine in the House?" *Slate*, Aug. 7, 2000.
†Compare the moral absolutism of Fernando Tesón, page above, which is deployed for precisely the opposite position—to support humanitarian intervention.

The contention that a particular act is moral or immoral is a value judgment and cannot possibly be proven true or false.[116] That it is "startlingly counter-intuitive to think that there is nothing wrong with genocide,"[117] for example, means only that individuals socialized in a given manner will regard it as counterintuitive—*not* that everyone, everywhere *must* regard it as immoral. What is counterintuitive to some is not necessarily immoral for all.* (Was the morality of genocide "startlingly counter-intuitive" to Adolph Eichmann?) Cost-benefit analysis—which, as I point out below, has by default filled the vacuum created by law's absence—surely offers no such "proof." Although cost-benefit analysis is hardly a "moral system"—it seems to be more an "approach" or "method"[118]—it surely rests upon implicit moral judgments, among them the consequentialist view there are no objective, *a priori* moral values of the sort upon which Chomsky relies.† One cannot escape arguments about moral philosophy through a linguistic sleight of hand, as Chomsky of all people should know. *Calling* a mode of analysis something other than a moral system does not make it one, any more than *calling* moral precepts "truisms" exempts them from the same scrutiny that is properly directed at any other first principles. All that cost-benefit analysis can do—all that *any* "moral system" does—is to offer people already predisposed to that approach a systematized methodology for working through problems in a way

---

* As Judge Posner points out, moralistic emotions such as this have no fixed object. "Members of a criminal gang are indignant about informers...." Richard A. Posner, *The Problematics of Moral and Legal Theory* 37–38 (1999).

† "Value skepticism" has no ideological implications, claims to the contrary notwithstanding. It is a frequent starting point of commentators of both the left and right. Stanley Fish, for example, often associated with the critical legal studies movement, writes that "there are no different or stronger reasons than policy reasons, and...the announcement of a formula (higher-order impartiality, mutual respect, or the judgment of all mankind) that supposedly out flanks politics, or limits its sphere by establishing a space free from its incursions, will be nothing more or less than politics—here understood not as a pejorative of, but as the name of the activity by which you publicly urge what you think to be good and true—by another name, the name but never the reality, of principle." Stanley Fish, "Mission Impossible: Settling the Just Bounds Between Church and State," 97 *Colum. L. Rev.* 2255, 2297 (1997).

that seems comfortable.* *If* one believes that human suffering should be minimized, cost-benefit analysis provides a way to assess whether a putative policy initiative will further that goal. But the major premises upon which it and other systems inevitably are based are too general—like Chomsky's—to lead to any nontrivial conclusion as to *whether* suffering should be minimized. To think otherwise is simply, as Robert Nozick has put it, "utopian":

> One persistent strand in utopian thinking is the feeling that there is some set of principles obvious enough to be accepted by all men of good will, precise enough to give unambiguous guidance in particular situations, clear enough so that all will realize its dictates, and complete enough to cover all problems which actually arise.[119]

There are no such principles. To the moral objectivist who finds this relativism discomfiting, I suggest only that—if the premises on which the objectivist relies are pushed back one by one with the simple question "Why?"—the objectivist comes, sooner rather than later, to a premise either too vague to require anything, or to no premise at all.

C. Conclusion

Law organizes and manages well when those who formulate its rules agree on what the public good is and how the public good is to be achieved and maintained. It neither organizes nor manages well when a fundamental rift exists as to what constitutes the public good or how the public good is to be pursued. A consensus is necessary as to both ends and means. While a consensus has emerged in recent years that, as an end, the public good rules out genocide, no consensus yet exists whether intervention is a permissible means of pursuing that end.

This issue of *means* implicates the most basic of community principles—the principle that assigns ultimate responsibility for the safety and well-being of a state's people. On this principle, the world is divided. One bloc of states answers that the responsibility

---

*For an extensive development of this idea, see Richard Rorty, *Achieving our Country: Leftist Thought in Twentieth-Century America* (1998).

lies with individual states. Another answers that the responsibility lies with the international community itself. Law cannot reasonably be expected to address that responsibility without a single, coherent, unified directive from the states that make the law.

Law is thus too demanding, too high-maintenance, to control use of force in the contentious international environment in which we still live. One might as well try operating a fine old grandfather clock in a Saharan sandstorm. Like democracy, the rule of law requires the right conditions in which to flourish. Absent those conditions, legal institutions wither and die—which is what happened to the use-of-force regime of both the League of Nations and the UN Charter.

Like it or not, all that remains in this lawless void is the relativity of consequentialism. But relativism hardly mandates inaction. Edmund Burke was no believer in objective, transcendent "rights of man," not, at least, in the sense that such rights have some independent, theoretical existence that predates and conditions civil society.* In Burke's conception, "rights" lay in "balances between differences of good, in compromises sometimes between good and evil, and sometimes between evil and evil."[120] Burke knew that the consequences of adherence to a given principle change from one set of circumstances to the next. "Circumstances," he wrote, "(which with some gentlemen pass for nothing) give in reality to every political principle its distinguishing color and discriminating effect."[121] Yet Burke vigorously opposed slavery. He argued insistently in Parliament that Britain's efforts to colonize India were evil—to the point that he was censured for alleged excesses in presenting the case.[122] And Burke's eloquent support for the American Revolution echoed across continents. Objectivism is not the only option for one who believes, as Burke did, that revolutionary reform may be called for by "grave and overruling necessity."[123]

---

*For an excellent discussion of Burke's philosophy, see Alexander M. Bickel, *The Morality of Consent* 20 (1975).

SIX

The International Parallel Universe: Is a Legalist Use-of-Force Regime Desirable?

In the face of the collapse of the legalist order governing the use of force, the international system has moved rapidly to a parallel universe of two systems, one *de facto*, the other *de jure*. The two exist side by side. In one universe a *de jure* regime continues the traditional pacific dispute settlement process established by the Charter. Its membership is universal. It consists of the unlike-minded states of the United Nations that share grievances, employ the "good offices" of the Secretary General, and engage in "preventive diplomacy" to avert conflict. The ordering principle of this system is sovereignty. Rules are made by the consent of states deemed to be sovereign equals. In the background is the "invisible college" of international lawyers, as they like to refer to themselves, who remind participant states of when they can and cannot use force under an elaborate body of inflexible rules that are honored more in the breach than in the observance. "This is the old regime in a nutshell," said de Toqueville (referring to France); "a rigid rule, lax implementation; this is its character. Anyone who judged the government of those times by the list of its laws would fall into the most foolish errors."[1]

In the other universe is a *de facto* system. It is a geopolitical regime over which the strong preside. It bears little resemblance to the formal regime of the Charter. Its ordering principle is not consent but power. Its rules are made not by students' international law journals but by NATO activation orders and the Pentagon's rules of engagement. Its membership is selective. Its participants are the like-minded states of NATO and other Western democracies.

Occasional rifts occur; these states, like others, are driven by forces described by Hobbes only three years after Westphalia[2] and unchanged since. But by and large they trust one another because they share the same values. They support the jaw-jawing of the *de facto* regime because they recognize that when pacific dispute settlement fails, it is they who will have to do the heavy lifting: When international order is threatened, whether by aggression or—as lately—by genocide, they are the ones to restore it. For them, international lawyers sojourning from the other universe may as well be invisible because nations do not act the way international lawyers think they act and would like them to act. Governmental officials know that[*] and have better ways to spend their time than arguing about whether a given use of force would violate a "peremptory norm" of customary international law or merely an outdated treaty prohibition. When British Foreign Secretary Robin Cook told U.S. Secretary of State Madeleine Albright that he had "problems with our lawyers" over using force without Security Council approval, she responded: "Get new lawyers."[†] The secret was out from the beginning of the legalist experiment. As Martin Wight put it, "[B]ehind the façade of the League" could be discerned "a continuation of the old system of the Concert of Europe, whereby the Great Powers settled matters by private bargains among themselves at the expense of small powers…. [T]he method throughout was the same—the Great Powers acting as a directorate. This is the system of power politics that the League of Nations was designed to supersede, but failed to do so."[3] Of course it is the same geopolitical system that the United Nations was also designed to supersede, but—as Kosovo demonstrated—also failed to do.

The incoherence of the current use-of-force regime recalls the schizophrenic state in which the law of war existed during the

---

[*]"[I]nternational legal description is patently out of step with elite expectations. The discrepancy is so painfully obvious that, outside the small circle of international lawyers, it brings discredit upon the very notion of international law. Small wonder that political advisors rarely use their international lawyers." W. Michael Reisman, "International Incidents: Introduction to a New Genre in the Study of International Law," in *International Incidents* 3, 15 (W. Michael Reisman and Andrew R. Willard eds., 1988).
[†]James P. Rubin, "Countdown to a Very Personal War," *The Financial Times*, Sept. 30/Oct. 1, 2000, at ix.

nineteenth century: While a body of concrete rules did exist, concerning, for example, the rights of neutrals and the permissibility of commerce and treaty relations with belligerents, those states powerful enough to use war as the ultimate diplomatic tool succeeded in maintaining the fiction that the existence of an actual "state of war" depended upon their subjective intent. The consequence was that such states could trigger the application of use-of-force rules during periods of tranquility, but during actual hostilities the rules were rendered inapplicable through rhetorical sleight-of-hand. Hauterive, writing anonymously for the French government in 1800, lamented that the "law of nations no longer existed except in appearance," so frequently had it been flouted by the governments of Europe since 1760.[4]

Some would say that, properly perceived, there is and has been only one system; that scholastic international lawyers have boxed themselves into a formalist view of law that can be escaped only through strained and disingenuous interpretation; and that the *real* regime that governs how states *should* behave is a function less of legal texts than of sociopolitical *con*texts—the elements of which are overlooked by scholastics and which are far more reliable in predicting decision makers' actions.[5] Indeed, adherents to this "policy-oriented" school—international law's legal realists—would wonder what all the fuss is about in trying to fit NATO's actions within the law; so fine is the line between law and policy preference that *anything* fits within the law, properly conceived.

But the so-called policy-oriented view of law mistakes what is for what ought to be, conflating policy preferences and legal commands.*[6] Some would say that the approach actually sees law as a subset of policy: "[B]y subordinating law to policy," Schachter wrote, "the McDougal approach virtually dissolves the restraints of rules and opens the way for partisan or subjective policies disguised as law."[7] The same policy-oriented approach can be employed with equal vigor to argue either side of a dispute.† That some indeterminacy

---

*As Ian Brownlie succinctly put it, the policy-oriented approach "tend[s] to confuse normative prescription with factual assumptions." Ian Brownlie, *The Rule of Law in International Affairs* 9 (1998).

†See, for example, W. Michael Reisman, "Coercion and Self-Determination: Construing Charter Article 2(4)," 78 *Am. J. Int'l L.* 642, 645 (1984): "The critical question in a decentralized system is not whether coercion has been applied, but whether it has been applied in support of or

is inevitable in rule-interpretation and fact-finding does not mean that it should be embraced; as legal systems evolve, indeterminacy is minimized. Arbitrariness in the law is hardly as great today as it was prior to the Magna Carta. That one finds a given policy compelling, by the same token, hardly provides ground for peddling that policy as the one and only correct answer for the rest of the community. It makes sense for law to seek to give effect to the expectations of a people, and it makes sense to look carefully for signs of those expectations. But it makes no sense for law to ignore the consciously selected signs of a peoples' expectations—agreed-upon texts, such as Article 2(7) and Article 39—and to think that one can "flee the straitened confines of the classical idiom and… romp…free…from the tyranny of words and majorities… ."[8] Words have meanings and majorities have expectations, and when majorities' expectations converge on specific meanings, we disregard those meanings at our peril.

If policy-oriented international law makes answers too easy, the scholastic school makes answers too hard. Indeed, one of the reasons for international lawyers' invisibility in policy-making circles is that they often can provide *no* answers, particularly in an area that is rapidly evolving. One of the analytic difficulties with customary international law, at least as it has been conceived by the scholastics in connection with the use of force, is that it is often impossible to know at what point a customary norm has actually changed. If there really exist customary use-of-force norms that do in fact evolve, then we must be able to say, at some specific point in time, that a norm that once *prohibited* now *permits,* or that a norm that once *permitted* now *prohibits.* But the received theory of customary international law is not helpful in pinpointing a specific date for the transition. There is a large hole in the spectrum between permission and prohibition in which no rule obtains. This possibility (*non liquet*) is one of the reasons, but hardly the only one, that I suggested earlier that international law provides no satisfactory answer to the question whether NATO acted legally in March 1999 when it commenced the bombing of Yugoslavia.* Clearly the *Charter* was

---

continued

against community order and basic policies, and whether it was applied in ways whose net consequences include increased congruence with community goals and minimum order."

*See pages 84–85.

breached, but *international law?* Using international law's traditional methods, no one can say.

For those who find legal answers where I do not, however, further issues arise. For those who see NATO's action as unlawful and believe that the law should have been honored, there is of course no difficulty; Kosovo is conceptualized as a straightforward instance of law violation, pure and simple.[9] But for those who believe that the law prohibited what NATO did but that the law *should* have been violated, there exist two different ways of thinking about NATO's action.

A. Dealing with the Kosovo Precedent

One could acknowledge that a violation occurred, but seek to limit the force of the resulting precedent. Alternatively, one could acknowledge that a violation occurred but seek to change the law rather than to limit the precedent, in effect institutionalizing the precedent. For the reasons I will discuss, I believe that—if, again, one posits that there indeed *was* applicable law—the second alternative is preferable. As a practical matter, however, the Charter's use-of-force rules cannot be changed, and for some time to come, those rules will continue to represent an inaccurate statement of the law.

There is, in political philosophy and tradition concerning domestic law observance, a long-held and time-honored belief that an unjust law may be—some have argued *must* be—disobeyed. In earlier times, the principle was stated in terms of a required correspondence between man-made law and higher law. Sir William Blackstone wrote that "[t]his law of nature being coeval with mankind and dictated by God himself, is of course superior in obligation to any other. It is binding all over the globe in all countries and at all times; *no human laws are of any validity, if contrary to this.*"[10] Two hundred years earlier, Jean Bodin's formulation of the theory of sovereignty posited that there are some laws—laws of reason, nature, and God—to which even the sovereign is subject and which the sovereign cannot abrogate.[11] From Thoreau to Gandhi to Martin Luther King, Jr., it has been argued that when law conflicts with some higher morality, that higher morality must prevail. Thoreau believed that there is a "higher and independent power" from which the state draws its authority.[12] "Under a government which imprisons any unjustly," he wrote, "the true place

for a just man is also a prison."[13] He spent a night in jail during the
U.S. war against Mexico for refusing to pay taxes to support the
war. Gandhi effectively led mass acts of civil disobedience to bring
about the independence of India. "An unjust law," he said, "is itself
a species of violence."[14] During the American civil rights movement
of the 1960s, Martin Luther King, Jr., espoused similar notions of
the primacy of justice over law. In his famous "Letter from
Birmingham Jail," King wrote: "[L]aw and order exist for the purpose of establishing justice and … when they fail in this purpose
they become the dangerously structured dams that block the flow of
social progress."[15] Whether the "higher" good to which the law
must correspond is called justice, morality, or merely politics, most
would today agree that mere legality cannot be the only test of civic
obligation. During the Third Reich, the law required acts that no
one should have considered obligatory. "It is not what a lawyer
tells me I *may* do," Edmund Burke said, "but what humanity,
reason, and justice tell me I ought to do."[16]

  Much the same principles apply with respect to the law of
nations. Like other law, international law seeks to approximate values external to the law itself. But there is no reason to believe that it
always succeeds. Achieving correspondence is a continuing struggle.
Constant readjustment is required. Some legal systems prove more
responsive than others. A principle of international law, like a principle of domestic law, can thus prohibit a state from doing, or
require a state not to do, something at odds with higher, or at least
prior, values that the law has not yet come to reflect. Political scien-
tists, perhaps because they are closer to the social ferment from
which law emerges, have long understood this. As Hans
Morgenthau famously wrote, "Law and political wisdom may or
may not be on the same side. If they are not, the insistence upon the
letter of the law will be inexpedient and may be immoral."[17]

  The cost-benefit approach that has filled the legalist void is a
form of "political wisdom" or, as J. L. Brierly puts it, "reasonableness" of the sort that has long been familiar to common law
lawyers:

  Even a slight acquaintance with the working of the English
  Common Law shows it perpetually appealing to reason as the
  justification of its decisions, asking what is a reasonable time, or
  what a reasonable price, or what a reasonable man would do in
  given circumstances. We do not suppose that our answers to

those questions will be scientific truths; it is enough if they are approximately just; but on the other hand we do not attempt to eliminate this test of reasonableness by substituting fixed rules, because it would be impossible to do so. But this appeal to reason is merely to appeal to a law of nature. Sometimes, indeed, English law still uses the term 'natural justice', and our courts have to do their best to decide what 'natural justice' requires in particular circumstances ... .[18]

So call it what you will—justice, natural law, reason, cost-benefit (or risk) analysis, or just plain "common sense"[19]—sometimes a rule of domestic or international law is so out of sync with *what it is intended to reflect* that the very principles that would otherwise lead to compliance with the law lead to its violation. "[W]e do as a legal order," Alexander Bickel wrote, "hold some values, some principles, by which we judge the process and even some of its outcomes."[20] When those values or principles are subverted by the legal order rather than advanced by it, those values or principles may counsel violation of that order.

International lawyers, however, are loathe to acknowledge that violation of international law could ever be appropriate. The view of Louis Henkin is not atypical. He wrote:

For my part, I cannot agree that there can be behavior that "has to be done" but which violates the law. No legal system accepts as law that which "has to be" violated. No view of international law, no interpretation of any norm or agreement, could concede that a nation may be legally required to do that which would lead to its destruction, or jeopardize its independence or security. Nations, surely, would not accept such law for themselves or impose it on others. If this issue has any reality, it may perhaps arise in a novel situation in which an act not contemplated when a norm was established appears to fall within its prohibition. In such circumstances, if there is a prevailing view in international society that the act in question should not be deemed a violation, governments, scholars, and courts would seize on any ambiguity in the law to conclude that it was in fact lawful. Even if there is no obvious ambiguity, exceptions might yet be carved out in order to avoid an absurd result. (This, I believe, can be said, for example, of the law as applied to Israel's raid at Entebbe.)[21]

Henkin goes on, in the footnote, to describe how any behavior can be forced into the law's pigeonholes:

> Jurisprudentially, the result might be justified in various ways. One might suggest that, as a matter of interpretation of relevant principles or provisions, those called upon to determine the law should adopt an interpretation that avoids an absurd result. One might suggest that an amendment in the law was being achieved by a new informal consensus of nations. Or one might say that the law, always dynamic, is, in fact, or has become other than had previously been thought, with the action in this instance and the reaction of the community both contributing to the process that achieved the change.

Much can be said in response to this extraordinary call for procrustean legal principles, beginning with the obvious question: *What's the point?* Why strain to find "absurdity" in a result that much of the world views finds wholly sensible? Why not acknowledge forthrightly that sometimes the law simply ought not be obeyed? Why dress up violation as compliance? Why not acknowledge, with the Charter, that the law and justice do not always coincide? When the law means anything, it means nothing—it means "Get new lawyers." States know that and act accordingly. Amendment of the Charter by "informal consensus," aside from the fact that no such consensus exists, would create a fundamental fairness problem, as pointed out by the delegate from Cuba, who spoke as follows in the General Assembly:

> It is self-evident that the concept of so-called humanitarian intervention is not enshrined in any of the Charter's provisions. Therefore, we wonder if it is contained in some proposed amendment to the Charter. If this is the case, the Organization has a procedure that must be observed. This procedure ... includes, among other basic requirements, discussion and decision-making with the participation of all Member States.[22]

Perhaps international lawyers are reluctant to counsel law violation because of concern about undermining the rule of law. Henkin conjures the specter of anarchy if law violation is undertaken without "common agreement":

> What should be clear is that we are talking about change in what was or had been thought to be the law when there is common

agreement that the law should be different. This is not to suggest that any nation can itself violate or reject law because it deems that existing law jeopardizes its security or other interests. That would destroy the very concept of law. No society could tolerate such self-judging exemptions from important principles.[23]

Yet, challenging *a* law is not synonymous with challenging the rule of law. In domestic as well as international jurisprudence, challenging a law that subverts "some values, some principles" is the highest respect that can be paid to the rule of law, and is often, indeed, the only avenue to law reform. "Common agreement," like law itself, can traduce those values and principles. The worse precedent is not law violation acknowledged as law violation, but law violation carried out under the pretense of compliance with the law, for the disingenuousness of disguised violation undermines the debate on which the evolution of the law depends.

Many of those who liked what NATO did but are concerned about the action's effect on the legal system simply assert that NATO's action created no precedent. The notion seems to be that *saying* that an act has no precedential effect causes any precedential effect to vanish. This was the mode of analysis of various German officials at the time of the Kosovo conflict.* But the import of NATO's act was not lost on the Russians and Chinese. "Would NATO be willing to bomb Chechnya, or Russia for that matter?" former Soviet president Mikhail Gorbachev asked. "Or bomb Tibet, and risk a full-scale response from China?"[24] (Gorbachev

---

* "European diplomats say NATO's threat to attack Yugoslavia without seeking authorization from the Security Council—where it faced a potential veto by Russia and China—does not constitute a precedent. 'We set great store by the principle that force—if it is needed as a last resort—requires a mandate from the United Nations and in international law,' said German Foreign Minister Joschka Fischer." William Drozdiak, "U.S., European Allies Divided Over NATO's Authority to Act," *Wash. Post*, Nov. 8, 1998, at A33. German Foreign Minister Klaus Kinkel, whom Fischer succeeded, had attempted the same approach in a speech before the Bundestag: "The decision of NATO [concerning use of force against Yugoslavia] must not become a precedent. As far as the Security Council monopoly on force is concerned, we must avoid getting on a slippery slope." Deutscher Bundestag, *Plenarprotokoll* 13/248, p. 23129 (Oct. 16, 1998).

was not being altogether facetious. A report issued October 2, 1998 by the President of NATO's North Atlantic Assembly, Senator William Roth, posited that "The NATO Allies should neither suggest that NATO missions will assume a 'global' character nor put artificial geographic limits on such missions."[25] Roth was not alone in pushing for an expanded NATO mission.*) Richard Holbrooke got it right: "This whole debate reminds of the pipe painting by the Belgian surrealist René Magritte, who scrawled the words 'This is not a pipe' over the image," he said. "People will continue to say that Kosovo was not a precedent for the alliance, but everybody realizes that it is really true."[26]

A more principled approach, one that does not abandon process for outcome, is that of Thomas Franck. He writes:

What does a nation like the United States—one with the power and the will to ameliorate a human catastrophe—do when, to act, it must violate general rules of the game? India faced that choice before invading East Pakistan to stop the slaughter of Bengalis in 1971. People stranded on mountains or in lifeboats face a comparable personal choice when, to save many, they contemplate cannibalizing one of their number. NATO's action in Kosovo is not the first time illegal steps have been taken to prevent something palpably worse.

Law gives those taking such illegal but necessary action several well-established defensive strategies. They may deny having been authors of the illegal act, or argue that the act is not actually illegal. They may call for a change in the law to make their action legal. Or they may argue mitigation, by showing that their illegal conduct was still the least-unacceptable possible outcome. Every law student knows that even cannibalism, if demonstrably the least-gruesome alternative in the circumstances, is treated leniently by the law.

---

*The N.Y. Times quoted a "senior official": "Of course, when America talks of the defense of interests, and not just territories, it leads to continued suspicions that the United States is seeking to globalize NATO. NATO is still Euro-Atlantic, but we should not artificially exclude what we might use NATO for." Roger Cohen, "A Policy Struggle Stirs Within NATO," N.Y. Times, Nov. 28, 1998.

But they also know that it would be no advance for civilized society if the legal impediments to cannibalism were dismantled. Laws, including the U.N. Charter, are written to govern the general conduct of states in light of historic experience and the requisites of good order. If, in a particular instance, a general law inhibits doing justice, then it is up to each member of the community to decide whether to disobey that law. If some so choose, however, their best strategy is not to ridicule, let alone change the law: It is to proffer the most expiating explanation of the special circumstances that ordained their moral choice.[27]

This, one might further argue, was the posture of President Abraham Lincoln who, during the Civil War, unconstitutionally suspended the writ of *habeas corpus*—while forthrightly acknowledged the illegality of doing so—on the theory that it was necessary to violate part of the Constitution to save the rest of it. Arthur Schlesinger has written that, while the Founding Fathers did not rule out the possibility that "crisis might require the executive to act outside the Constitution," neither did they intend to confer constitutional legitimacy on such acts, believing that the "legal order would be better preserved if departures from it were frankly identified as such than if they were anointed with a factitious legality and thereby enabled to serve as constitutional precedents for future action."[28] Much the same conclusion, one might argue, should obtain with respect to the UN Charter and international law in general.

While Franck's way of dealing with law violation is more respectful of the rule of law than is purposeful distortion, it too has its difficulties. First, it too proceeds from the illusory notion that *calling* a precedent a nonprecedent *makes* it a nonprecedent. It doesn't, of course. Nor is the rule of law better served if it is admitted that an act violates the law, which merely creates a precedent of a different sort: The precedent is no longer that this act *within* the system is permitted, but rather that this act, even though *not* within the system, is permitted. In a sense, this sort of extra-systemic precedent is all the worse, for *outside* the system there are no institutionalized restraints for dealing with transgressions. The danger is captured by the observation that the United States Constitution "is not a suicide pact,"[29] which could be said as well of the United Nations Charter (or any other constitutive instrument). At one level, the maxim counsels avoidance of the law's rigidities when those rigidities threaten survival. At another level, though, it provides an all-too-facile rationale for law avoidance when compliance is simply inconvenient, seemingly contemplating an extra-legal realm where no rules apply and where the test of right is only might. The problem with Lincoln's effort to narrow the precedent was not the intent, which was noble—to limit the damage of illegality; the problem was that admitting the illegality of an act has no effect in narrowing its precedent, and can actually broaden the precedent by providing historical evidence that it is appropriate to act unlawfully.

Second, none of Franck's "well-established defensive strategies" works in this context. NATO could hardly deny that it was "the author of" the act.* Franck himself does not believe that NATO's action was legal ("What does a nation ... do when, to act, it must violate general rules of the game?"[30]) and thus does not appear to believe that NATO should have argued that it was (its obligation being rather "to proffer the most expiating explanation"). The strategy of "call[ing] for a change in the law" is one about which, for some reason, he quickly has second thoughts ("their best strategy ... is not ... to change the law ... ."). The only alternative with which Franck is comfortable is to claim mitigating circumstances, in the manner of persons adrift in a lifeboat who argue that it is necessary to eat a companion to survive.

Arguing mitigation makes sense if one opposes changing the law; the objective then is to prevent the precedent, such as it is, from taking on life in justifying future violations. Thus Schlesinger saw wisdom in the insistence of the framers of the Constitution that violations of the domestic legal order be identified as such rather than disguised. But the premise, again, was the desirability of preserving *existing* rules intact. If the existing rules are deemed inadequate, different considerations obtain. Franck sees no problem with the "old rules," which "work as well, or as badly, as states want."[31] But he fails to ask the big question: Why did all 19 NATO democracies find it necessary to flout those rules? Franck himself suggested the answer in a 1970 article entitled "Who Killed Article 2(4)?"[32] "The prohibition against the use of force in relations between states has been eroded beyond all recognition," he wrote,

---

*The suggestion brings to mind the response of a person who was trying to rob an Iowa convenience store when the clerk, a former high school classmate, peered closely at the robber's skimpy mask and said "Joe Smith!" The robber reportedly responded, "It's not me!"

by "the wide disparity between" the prohibition and "the practical goals the nations are pursuing in defense of their own national interest."[33] (This is, of course, precisely the reason for the earlier failure of the League of Nations. "[T]he lesson to be learned…is not that the League could have avoided these weaknesses by being given more authority. It is that it could not have avoided them because it could not have been given more authority."[34]) My own view is that the cannibalism analogy is inapposite, because the Charter needs to be changed. Cannibalism for the purpose of survival is too rare to justify redefining murder, whereas intrastate genocide occurs all too often to remain legally protected. When the exigencies of justice repeatedly conflict with a given rule, the rule of law is better served by changing that law to make it just.

True, the International Law Commission (ILC) has proposed draft articles on state responsibility that would recognize a "state of necessity" under which certain actions not in conformity with international law would not be regarded as wrongful.* However, the

---

*The proposal is as follows:

Article 33. State of necessity
1. A state of necessity may not be invoked by a State as a ground for precluding the wrongfulness of an act of that State not in conformity with international obligation of the State unless:
   (a) the act was the only means of safeguarding an essential interest of the State against a grave and imminent peril; and
   (b) the act did not seriously impair an essential interest of the State towards which the obligation existed.
2. In any case, a state of necessity may not be invoked by a State as a ground for precluding wrongfulness:
   (a) if the international obligation with which the act of the State is not in conformity arises out of a peremptory norm of general international law; or
   (b) if the international obligation with which the act of the State is not in conformity is laid down by a treaty which, explicitly or implicitly, excludes the possibility of invoking the state of necessity with respect to that obligation; or
   (c) if the State in question has contributed to the occurrence of the state of necessity.

Report of the International Law Commission on the work of its 32d session (5 May–25 June 1980), Doc. A/35/10, A/CN.4/SER.A/1980/Add.1 (PT. 2) at 69.

proposal as formulated could not have been invoked by NATO as grounds for precluding the wrongfulness of its actions in Kosovo. The draft article on "state of necessity" would apply only if the otherwise wrongful act was the only means of safeguarding an essential interest "of the State" invoking it, not of some other state. NATO's intervention was undertaken to safeguard the interests of the people of Kosovo, not the interests of NATO states (occasional rhetoric to the contrary notwithstanding[35]). Moreover, the draft article would not apply if the violation "arises out of a peremptory norm of general international law," which, as noted earlier, are thought to include use-of-force violations. The ILC's circumspection in dealing with the necessity doctrine points up, again, the unavoidable deficiency in Franck's approach: its wide-open possibility for abuse. If the objective is to retain some semblance of the rule of law, a broad principle of necessity, as Helen Silving put it, "would constitute a real danger" and "has certainly no place in international law."[36]

The better approach, I therefore suggest, is to acknowledge that the Charter was violated by NATO's intervention in Kosovo; to acknowledge that the entirety of the law is not represented by the Charter alone; and to acknowledge that the law governing intervention is at best hopelessly confused and at worst illusory.

The question is whether it is worthwhile to seek to reestablish and to reformulate the law so as to approximate more closely the full range of values that it must reflect. Again, a legalist use-of-force regime is not feasible today; when the conditions do exist to establish such a system, would it be desirable? The issue, as Thomas Schelling has put it in a broader context, is whether "some collective and formally integrated attack on [global] issues can do a better job than coping piecemeal, ad hoc, unilaterally, opportunistically."[37] Would it be preferable to rethink collectively and comprehensively when intervention ought to be expected, rather than leave expectations to be formed in a cauldron of international violence?

There is of course ample precedent for the ad hoc, opportunistic approach. The Peace of Westphalia, concluding the Thirty Years' War in 1648, legitimated the notion of sovereignty and launched the modern state system. Following the Napoleonic Wars, the 1815 Congress of Vienna sought to balance one equal, independent state or group of states against another in the belief that the resulting equilibrium would secure a stable, lasting peace. It did[38]—for about 40 years, until percolating nationalism and liberalism proved uncontrollable. Proceeding ad hoc can create institutions and patterns of cooperation that expand and multiply, gradually moving the larger international culture closer to the point where a comprehensive legalist approach is possible. As Francis Fukuyama noted, "[a] Kantian liberal international order has come into being willy-nilly during the Cold War under the protective umbrellas of organizations like NATO, the European Community, the OECD, the Group of Seven, GATT, and others that make liberalism a precondition for membership."[39]

But the dream of mankind, since Pericles founded the Delian League 400 years before Christ, has been that humanity can do better than connecting the dots after the fact. Traversing more recent historic fault lines, mankind has attempted a formally integrative approach. Those who worked at formalization recognized that peace could not sustain itself, however delicately the scaffolding of state sovereignty might be balanced. The 1919 Treaty of Versailles represented the first effort at establishing an activist international peace-keeping mechanism, the League of Nations. And the 1945 UN Charter sought to perfect the collective enforcement model by establishing a supranational enforcement authority, the UN Security Council, to deal with miscreant states.

Both systems represented efforts to control the profusion of interstate violence. (Wilson declared that the League would be "99 per cent insurance against war."[40]) Both failed. Surprisingly, the legalist model failed more dramatically. As Eric Hobsbawm has pointed out, no world war was fought between 1815 and 1914; during that period, indeed, "no major power fought another outside its immediate region."[41] The greatest (post-Napoleonic) interstate conflict of the nineteenth century, the Franco-Prussian War of 1870–71, killed perhaps 150,000—about the same number killed during the Chaco War of 1932–35 between Paraguay and Bolivia. During the twentieth century, however, the number of war-related deaths that occurred—*after* the legalist model was put in place following World War I—has been put at over 140 million. Of course, the greater number of war deaths under the legalist approach to peace developed in the twentieth century does not necessarily signal the inferiority of that approach. Had weapons of mass destruction been available in earlier times, death counts surely would have been staggering. Still, mere numbers pose a sobering rebuttal to the instinct that a formalized, integrative approach is superior.

Neither the League nor the United Nations represented an effort to control intrastate violence, at least not through intervention.

Indeed, both effectively permitted intrastate violence to rage unabated in those instances where intervention constituted the only effective remedy. There is no reason, in principle, why this laissez-faire approach to intrastate violence was necessary. The ban on intervention flowed not from the nature of the "collective and formally integrated attack" on disorder that states had agreed upon; they could just as easily have agreed upon an interventionist regime. Rather, the ban flowed from their unwillingness join a collective and formally integrated system that would permit intervention. In this sense, an ad hoc, opportunistic approach is superior if the objective is to halt intrastate violence, since the willingness or unwillingness of a state to "join" is irrelevant: there is nothing in Schelling's piecemeal, unilateral alternative to "join." The ad hoc approach by definition produces no preagreed regime to which states can sign on. Its inherent unilateralism makes possible action that would be precluded by a regime grounded upon collective consent. By contrast, because it lacks the foundation of collective consent, the unilateral approach carries the risk of violent confrontation. Ad hoc intervention to halt intrastate violence can lead to violence on an interstate scale larger than that intended to be halted.

B. The Case for a Legalist Use-of-Force Regime

Functionally, therefore, the question remains open which approach better maintains world order. Neither can claim superiority in purely utilitarian terms. However, the two approaches yield different juridical products: the integrated approach produces treaties, whereas the ad hoc approach yields—if anything—customary norms, fraught with all the liabilities detailed earlier in this book.

Treaties are preferable. The history of international law in the twentieth century was largely a history of codification, a process in which one custom after another—diplomatic immunity, treaty law, use of force—was reduced to writing. Codification lessens the risk of error and promotes reliance. Enhanced predictability and more regularized behavior result. James Mill foresaw this: "It is perfectly evident," he wrote in 1828, "that nations will be much more likely to conform to the principles of intercourse which are best for all, if they have an accurate set of rules to go by …. There is less room for mistake … there is less room for plausible pretexts; and last of

all, the approbation and disapprobation of the world is sure to act
with a ten-fold concentration, where a precise rule is broken, familiar to all the civilised world, and venerated by it all."[42] The old
rules of the Charter were accorded the dignity of a solemnly negotiated text; anything less would produce new rules of lesser stature
and diminished probity.

It therefore does not do to continue indefinitely to "push the
envelope" (in Richard Holbrooke's phrase[43]) of use-of-force law in
the manner that NATO and the United States attempted in Kosovo.
The test is not whether humanitarian intervention can be contrived
to generate immediate popular support. Of course it can, at least in
influential Western publics, in ways known to all military planners
and their publicists: Cruise missiles and smart bombs can vanquish
a demon and vindicate national honor while producing few (CNN-
reported) civilian casualties and fewer still intervenor casualties.
(Kosovo of course produced none.) "The citizenry of the United
States," Ralph Peters observes, "will tolerate the killing of enormous numbers of foreigners, so long as that killing does not take
too long, victory is clear-cut, friendly casualties are comparatively
low, and the enemy dead do not have names, faces, and families."[44]
The script for successful military spinning is no state secret.

Neither, however, is that script a formula for giving a new interventionist regime long-term, sustained acceptance. The test is
whether succeeding generations throughout the community of
nations—not simply in centers of wealth and power—believe that
the decision to intervene has been made to pursue just objectives.
Case-by-case decisions to use force, made by the users alone, are
not likely to generate that support. Even if the purposes are widely
approved, sooner or later the exclusionary decision-making process
is likely to create resentment, particularly as foul-ups occur and
lives are prominently lost through error and oversight, as they
inevitably will be. Without widespread and sustained acceptance
that intervention is undertaken as a matter of right, the new interventionism will soon be seen as built on neither law nor justice, but
only on power. And if history is any guide, it will be only a matter
of time before the meddling of a lawless interventionist regime is
rejected just as roundly as the indifference of the one it replaced.
Bickel had it right: this alternative leads ultimately to "chaos, the
brutal domination of the strongest and cruelest; or revolution, a
Hobbesian war for a time, and then a legal order whose premises
may in fact be differently stated, and some of whose premises may

in fact be different, but which must finally acknowledge the same necessities at the present one."[45]

This is the reason why, in the long run, the legalist model holds more hope than an ad hoc, purely geopolitical approach. Case-by-case decisions leave too much room for abuse. It is tempting to think that a power so benevolent as turn-of-the-century America will remain benevolent forever. Perhaps it will, but history provides room for concern that, if it is not the United States that malevolently takes advantage of a lack of rules, another, emerging power will do so. Today, it is easy to think that the United States will always be there to stop international mischief-making; it is hard to imagine a world in which the United States is not militarily supreme. But no doubt it has *always* been hard to imagine a (future) world in which the (currently) reigning power was not supreme. Military hierarchies, it is worth remembering, can change very quickly. The Soviet Union—by at least one measure, more powerful than any nation in the history of the world, save the United States—vanished overnight. There is no reason as yet to fear for the demise of the United States or even for the diminution of its military power. The better part of prudence, though, is to recognize that—even if it is centuries in coming, as it may be—a legalist framework holds greater promise for safeguarding American interests *and* safeguarding human freedom and dignity in other nations.

Still, it makes little sense at this point to expend much effort in thinking about how the Charter (or some other treaty) *should* deal with interventionism. "Proposals such as the reform of the United Nations Charter," Natalino Ronzitti has accurately written, "are clearly impracticable and should be left aside."[46] Russia and China, by all accounts, are perfectly content with the old rule of *per se* illegality. Chinese President Jiang Zemin told *Le Figaro* in an interview on October 25, 1999 that "in every country human rights should be managed by its own government in full independence" and that the Chinese government opposed any foreign interference in its internal affairs.[47] As recently as July 8, 2000, Russian President Vladimir Putin contended that a "grim consequence" of the post–Cold War period was the doctrine of humanitarian intervention.

Thus, proponents of a rule permitting humanitarian intervention have a harsh reality to confront: A legalist regime that permits intervention will not command universal acceptance. Some states insist upon maintaining the old, absolute ban on intervention and simply will have no part of a new legalist order that permits it. Such

are the limits of a system grounded upon consent. Yet it is clear that
a regime that includes those states will not provide new guarantees
against intrastate violence. As Fukuyama has written, "If one
wanted to create a league of nations ... that did not suffer from the
fatal flaws of earlier international organizations, it is clear that it
would have to look much more like NATO than the United
Nations—that is, a league of truly free states brought together by
their common commitment to liberal principles."[48]

A fork in the road thus lies ahead for proponents of humanitarian interventionism: Are the benefits of an international system that
is *less than universal* outweighed by the benefits of an international
system that permits intervention? Is a qualified right to intervene
worth the cost of an international system that is no longer universal?

The choice requires a classic, consequentialist weighing of benefits against costs. "While the genocide in Rwanda will define for
our generation the consequences of inaction in the face of mass
murder," Kofi Annan observed, "the more recent conflict in
Kosovo has prompted important questions about the consequences
of action in the absence of complete unity on the part of the international community."[49] The "consequences of action in the absence
of complete unity" posed a question that generated considerable
debate at the founding of both the League and the United Nations.
Wilson originally envisioned League membership as less than universal. "Only the free peoples of the world can join the League of
Nations," he asserted. "No nation is admitted to the League of
Nations that cannot show that it has the institutions which we call
free."[50] Wilson's position was grounded on the Kantian notion
that, because democracies do not fight one another, "only a nation
whose government was its servant and not its master could be
trusted to preserve the peace of the world."[51] A heated debate
about universalism versus selectivity in the UN's membership
occurred in the United States in the 1950s. Some maintained, in the
face of the Security Council's deadlock, that the Soviet Union did
not share fundamental values with the West and that its presence in
the United Nations, armed with a veto, guaranteed that the dreams
of the organization's founders could never be realized. Much the
same was said of China, which was of course excluded for this reason until the late 1970s. A 1955 report of the Senate Foreign
Relations Committee counseled that the choice depended upon
which function one believed it most important for the United
Nations to fulfill.[52] The organization's two core functions, the

report suggested, are collective security and the pacific settlement of disputes. The report posed the possibility that a trade-off necessarily existed. If one views the UN's primary goal as maintaining collective security, and if one sees the conduct of enforcement actions as the principal means to that end, then one might settle for nonuniversal membership; enforcement operations are most effectively conducted, after all, by states that see eye-to-eye on basic values and are willing to do what it takes to vindicate those values. If, by contrast, one sees the UN's primary goal as the pacific settlement of disputes, the report suggested that one might prefer universal membership on the theory that an ongoing international gathering of unlike minds is best calculated to prevent the outbreak of hostilities.* (This tension between pacific dispute settlement and collective security, Hans Morgenthau pointed out, posed a source of considerable disagreement in the formation of the League of Nations. France "looked to the League as a kind of collective sheriff," whereas Great Britain considered it "primarily a kind of clearinghouse where the statesmen of the world would meet to discuss their common problems and seek agreement by way of compromise … . At the bottom of these [differences were] divergent standards of justice and … political principles … ."[53])

This is the juncture at which the world's leading states again find themselves as the new millennium dawns. They now confront,

---

*One is tempted, in considering this tension, to downplay the importance of pacific dispute settlement as implying the mere "debating society" that the United Nations is so often accused of representing. It is worth remembering, however, that the availability of a simple forum for the airing of grievances and exchange of conflicting views can prove invaluable. The onset of World War I has been blamed on the absence of just such a forum:

> The catastrophe began without a single conference. The nations were plunged into war by a handful of telegrams which in their portentous official phraseology are even today not fully understood. One false step led to another until the vicious circle was complete. No meeting ground was available, no obligation for discussion existent. The madmen who had worked for war could generate it without a pretence of discussion, without the simple human act of meeting their opponents face to face, without asking yea or nay of their peoples.

Arthur Sweetser, *The League of Nations at Work* 8–9 (1920).

again, much the same monumental choice that they did 50 years ago. With the Cold War over, is the pacific settlement of disputes less important than an effective regime to maintain international security and basic human rights?

Institutionalizing humanitarian intervention by amendment of the UN Charter would place precise limits on behavior and let all members of the international community know with some specificity what is acceptable and what is not. In providing limits agreed upon by the *full* community, adopted through preagreed processes, amendment of the Charter would remove the possibility of self-definition of those limits by states powerful enough to make their own rules.[54] "Is there not a danger," Kofi Anann has asked, "of such interventions undermining the imperfect, yet resilient, security system created after the second World War, and of setting dangerous precedents for future interventions without a clear criterion to decide who might invoke these precedents and in what circumstances?"

Yet a formal, legal right to intervene—even if it could be institutionalized—in and of itself would confer no benefit on anyone. The real issues are empirical, and they are two. First, how often are acts that justify intervention likely to occur? Second, when such acts do occur, will a state or coalition of states be able and willing to intervene effectively? If acts that justify intervention (such as genocide or crimes against humanity) are largely a thing of the past, or if no state is willing or able to do anything about them, there would be no point in further fracturing the legalist order; to do so might only make it impossible to resurrect it someday in the future when conditions are more propitious for its success. If, by contrast, such acts are likely to recur and if effective intervention is (at least sometimes) probable, a top-down revision of the system could be justified.

At this point one can only speculate, but the historical record provides little reason to believe that the scale and frequency of human barbarism is likely to diminish substantially. In this respect, the world has changed little since 1904, when Theodore Roosevelt proclaimed that "chronic wrongdoing, or an impotence which results in a general loosening of ties of civilized society, may ... ultimately require intervention by some civilized nation."[55] The difference, as NATO's intervention in Kosovo suggests, is that while peril surely remains, the community of nations can now absorb the cost of a qualified rule permitting limited humanitarian intervention. During the Cold War, an absolute ban on intervention excessively exalted stability at the price of basic human dignity. That ban was the product of a less safe and less humane world, a world of states whose human rights practices gave them good reason to oppose intervention for humanitarian reasons. But with the end of the Cold War, potential nuclear flashpoints between superpowers became dramatically fewer as one superpower faced into history.

C. A Humanitarian Strategy for the Age of Transition

What, then, is the transitional alternative for states concerned about the possibility of unchecked barbarism? Geopolitical probabilities would suggest the same solution had in Kosovo: Humanitarian intervention by preexisting regional coalitions of democracies. "Nothing prevents the like-minded from making law for themselves when less-than-universal agreements serve some purpose,"[56] Henkin has written. The same applies, for that matter, when preexisting alliances confront the centrifugal forces they inevitably face when crises arise. As David Yost put it, "If some of the [NATO] Allies—such as Canada or Germany—were unwilling to act without such a mandate [from the Security Council or the OSCE], other Allies might well form a coalition for action without its being an Alliance operation."[57] "[C]ivilization commonality," Huntington observed, "is replacing political ideology and traditional balance of power considerations as the principal basis for cooperations and coalitions."[58] During this age of transition, democracies likely will seek increasingly to strengthen those commonalities by joining together to cooperate on a regional basis in stopping human barbarism where and when they find it possible to do so.

Such cooperation will involve replication of the Kosovo dynamic in several key respects. First, the Kosovo intervention was *multilateral*. It is more difficult for a state to engage in subterfuge if it has partners.* As Michael Walzer puts it, "What one looks for in numbers is detachment from particularistic views and consensus on moral rules."[59] History is not without examples of exploitative alliances, but the greater abuses by far occur when states act unilaterally. The need to persuade allies to join in intervention makes it

---

*See Evan Luard, "Collective Intervention" in *Intervention in World Politics* 157 (Hedley Bull ed., 1984).

less likely that the intervention will be for ulterior motives;* hence, states desirous of precluding pretextual intervention will likely favor multilateral over unilateral intervention.

Second, the coalition of states that intervened in Kosovo existed *before* the intervention occurred. Preexistence of the intervening coalition furthers the likelihood of ingenuousness in its professed objective. A grouping of states formed around principle and predating a specific crisis (sometimes an international organization) enhances the probability that intervention will be calculated to carry out that principle.

Third, the NATO intervenors were *democracies*. Human rights are more highly respected in democracies than in nondemocracies. If the objective is furtherance of human rights, that goal is more likely achieved to the extent that the intervenors themselves uphold human rights. States that support humanitarian intervention will likely favor intervention by democracies rather than nondemocracies.

The fourth reason that the 19 NATO intervenors felt impelled to act was *proximity:* Ethnic cleansing in Kosovo was occurring in their own region. Except for the United States, Canada, and Iceland, the NATO states had real or potential economic and cultural contacts with the people of Kosovo that did not exist with others who were farther removed geographically. It is often noted that NATO felt a greater consanguinity of interests with Kosovo than it did with the people of Rwanda, East Timor, or Tibet, but the reverse might also be noted: No Asians or Africans participated in the effort to save ethnic Albanians in Kosovo from genocide. For better or worse, people tend to care more about the well-being of people whom they see as like themselves than they do about people whom they see as different from themselves.† The principle applies

---

*"My preference," Anthony D'Amato has written, "would clearly be in favor of multilateral intervention, such as that of France, Great Britain, and Russia in the Greco-Turkish conflict of 1827, one of the earliest cases of humanitarian intervention." Anthony D'Amato, "The Invasion of Panama Was a Lawful Response to Tyranny," 84 *Am. J. Int'l L.* 516, 519 (1990).
†Richard Posner offers a possible explanation:

Evolutionary biology hypothesizes that altruism derives from the evolutionary imperative of inclusive fitness—the drive to maximize the number of copies of one's genes by maximizing the number of creatures carrying them weighted by the closeness of the relation. The inclusive

equally to the Third World as to the First. To be sure, race is sometimes a factor, but the phenomenon is not synonymous with racism. Cultural, religious, linguistic, and even legal ties contribute to a propensity to altruism on the part of one people toward another, which includes a willingness to undertake humanitarian intervention. So states favoring a principled interventionism will recognize the tendency of neighbors to count on neighbors, and accordingly build incentives around a core concept of regional responsibility by regional organizations for regional crises. Kosovo, Liberia, East Timor, and Sierra Leone all foreshadow a greater emphasis on regional intervention as a solution more acceptable to neighboring states that remain insistent upon retaining protection under Article 2(7).[60]

The shift to regional coalitions will no doubt create new problems.[61] In the past, the United Nations has relied upon peace-keepers from states such as Canada, Fiji, and Sweden that were remote from hostilities and unlikely to have a geopolitical interest in the outcome. Disinterestedness is desirable on the part of intervenors.[62] Relying upon regional neighbors for help increases the risk of opportunistic intrusion. Careful selection of participants and support from equally disinterested Western financial sponsors will lessen the risk of unwanted meddling. Still, movement to regional mechanisms will require careful scrutiny to ensure that peace forces act for the benefit rather than the detriment of endangered populations.

Regionalization will not obviate the need for approval by the Security Council if nondefensive force is used;[63] a regional organization, as Judge Sofaer reminds us, can have "no greater authority to use force than its individual member states may exercise

---

continued

   fitness of a social animal like man is greatly increased by having a proclivity to help his relatives, so it is plausible that this proclivity evolved as an adaptive mechanism. In the prehistoric era in which our instinctual preferences were formed, people probably lived in small, isolated bands, so most of the people with whom they dealt were people with whom they had *continuous* dealings ... . The question of what duties we have to complete strangers may be baffling because it ... is remote from the questions that troubled our very distant ancestors.

Richard A. Posner, *The Problematics of Moral and Legal Theory* 33–35 (1999) (footnotes omitted) (emphasis in original).

collectively."[64] Thus all the issues discussed earlier in connection with intervention by individual states will also arise in connection with intervention by regional organizations that are forced to act in the face of Security Council paralysis.* (An adaptivist argument occasionally is made to the contrary,[65] but for the reasons given in Chapter 4, this argument is not persuasive.) Thus Javier Solana, the European Union's high representative for foreign and security affairs, emphasized that the EU's planned 60,000-man rapid reaction force could become a "backbone" of United Nations peace-keeping efforts.[66] Operations not approved beforehand by the United Nations Security Council apparently are not contemplated. And, as with peace enforcement undertaken by the Council itself, there are limits on the scope of the Council's authority—the matter must relate "to the maintenance of international peace and security."[67] Purely internal strife is therefore still off-limits to policing by regional organizations even with Security Council approval.

Reliance upon regional organizations of democracies may redound, in the end, to the formation of a genuine, worldwide legalist order to manage the use of force. The framers of the Charter's use-of-force system attempted to build from the top down. The top-down approach failed. Building from the bottom up may be more effective. Organizations like NATO and the European Union lay the groundwork for effective international organizations. Whether they gradually expand in membership or simply set an example for non-member states, they provide training grounds in diplomacy and laboratories for collaboration.[68] They provide a structure congenial to emulation on a larger scale. Sooner or later, the question will be asked why regional successes cannot be replicated internationally.

What standard will be employed to determine when to intervene? Because law currently provides no intelligible standard, little is available beyond simple cost-benefit analysis—which is precisely how NATO assessed the proposed intervention in Kosovo.

---

*UN Secretary General Kofi Annan has insisted that "it is imperative that regional security operations be mandated by the Security Council if the legal basis of the international security system is to be maintained." *Report of the Secretary-General on the work of the Organization*, U.N. GAOR Supp. (No. 1) at ¶ 113, U.N. Doc. A/54/1 (Aug. 31, 1999), http://www.un.org/Docs/SG/Report99/security.htm (last visited Feb. 9, 2001).

The principal benefit of humanitarian intervention is lessened long-term human suffering. The principal cost is increased short-term human suffering. If the benefit outweighs the cost, a putative intervention is seen as appropriate; otherwise, it is not. That, in a nutshell, is the calculus counseled by cost-benefit and by its cousin, risk assessment, which emphasizes sizing up the likelihood that given benefits will accrue or that given costs will be incurred. All impacts, favorable and unfavorable, are identified; values are assigned; the net benefit is calculated; and a choice is made.[69] The approach is thus similar to that proposed by the French philosopher Paul Ricoeur, who would have us focus on the amount of suffering caused by a given intervention set off by the amount of suffering alleviated.[70]

Unfortunately, the actual calculus is a bit more complicated.[71]

When applied to interventionism, cost-benefit analysis requires an assessment of impacts that often are difficult or impossible to quantify. In the case of Kosovo, those impacts included—had NATO not acted—risks not only of genocide but of a wider war and a weakening of human rights protections elsewhere if repressive regimes saw ethnic cleansing succeed in Europe itself; and—had NATO *acted*—risks also of a wider war and of weakening the United Nations, harming relations with Russia and China, and precipitating Serbian ethnic cleansing in response to mere threats of force by NATO. Often these assessments will be little more than informed guesses. Who possibly could know, for example, how long Milocevic would hold out? Milocevic *himself* probably could not have guessed—even after the bombs began to fall. Assessing the likelihood of his capitulating in, say, a week required assessing a variety of other related factors (the influence of his wife, of other aides, of the effectiveness of NATO bombing—or the likelihood of good weather) that simply did not lend themselves to reliable, quantifiable analysis, especially if long-term as well as short-term consequences are assessed. As General Wesley Clark said, "[W]e could never predict how long he would hold on because it wasn't a function of any specific set of losses. It was a function of variables that were beyond our predictions—ultimately, his state of mind."[72]

No analytic framework is without assumptions, and every analytic framework is therefore incomplete; a risk-based approach is no different.[73] Central among the assumptions that it must make—key among the elements that lie beyond it—is the propriety of the act in question. Is genocide acceptable? Is it acceptable to use force to stop genocide? Cost-benefit analysis leaves out a selection of ultimate ends. Cost-benefit analysis does not address, similarly, the issue whether there exists a moral obligation to intervene. Some have suggested that moral obligation is triggered when massive suffering can be curtailed with minimal hardship.[74] In a domestic context, as Judge Posner put it, "it is by no means obvious that the law should *not* impose a general duty to rescue strangers when the rescue can be effected without mortal peril to the rescuer. The laws of many European countries and now of many U.S. states do impose such duties... ."[75] If the lives of 10,000 innocent civilians can be saved by an intervention that would risk the lives of a dozen soldiers, should not such an action be seen as obligatory? Such considerations seemed pertinent when the United States intervened in Somalia. While surely not acting in response to any felt legal obligation to intervene, the United States intervention stopped a massive famine, saving, by some estimates, up to 20,000 Somali lives at the cost of the lives of 34 members of the American military and up to 10,000 Somalis who died in clashes with the United States.[76] But whether one "ought" or "ought not" step in to break up a fight will be answered differently by different individuals, in different cultures. Moral duty is a subset of moral right and wrong; it cannot be established objectively but is, rather, a function of socialized preference, deriving from personal, subjective answers. Cost-benefit analysis can inform the decision whether to intervene. It cannot provide an obligatory dimension to the decision.

Similarly, no cost-benefit framework can itself, in any objective sense, determine what factors should go into the analysis or how much weight they should be accorded. To take the example of Kosovo once again, how great was the risk that NATO's action would provoke the Russians to take military action against Chechnya? Risk assessment cannot tell a NATO decision maker whether that factor should be of concern; NATO may simply not have cared whether Russia moved again against Chechnya. Nor can risk assessment tell a decision maker how much that official should care if Russia *does* move against Chechnya. It can, however, assuming sufficient data, tell a decision maker whether Russia is *likely* to move against Chechnya. And that, obviously, can be useful information.

This is the final, important, assumption of cost-benefit analysis: sufficient data. Cost-benefit analysis is only as good as the data that goes into that assessment. If we do not know, once again, the inclinations of Milocevic's wife, but we do know that her influence could be determinative, we cannot accurately assess how long Milocevic is likely to hold out. Obviously, data often will be insufficient to permit any meaningful quantification of risk.

Thus whatever its practical difficulties, states have come to employ a cost-benefit approach, rather than seek guidance from the scholastic legalist alternative, for the simple reason that they see it as relying upon reality rather than myth.* For this reason, cost-benefit analysis lays the groundwork for the ultimate emergence of a legalist order that is based upon realistic values. Cost-benefit discourse quickly becomes normative: The discussion of why specific costs outweigh specific benefits, or *vice versa,* soon comes to involve judgments about why certain choices should be made and why some values are to be preferred over others. These evaluations are the grist of legal norms. In a world where the right conditions exist, these evaluations can *become* legal norms when embodied in a treaty, much as the patterns of cooperation embodied in the Concert of Europe did when reified in the legalist efforts of the twentieth century.

D. Conclusion

The scholastic international law rules purporting to govern intervention neither describe accurately what nations do, nor predict reliably what they will do, nor prescribe intelligently what they should do. Cost-benefit analysis is used by states because they see it as more realistic, as reflecting the full range of their interests. But the manifest shortcomings of the old legalist order create the risk that the benefit of a future but now-unattainable legalist order to govern the use of force will be undervalued. Undervaluation could lead states to act in ways that foreclose the possible emergence of a legalist order. Withdrawal from failed UN use-of-force institutions,

---

*For a concise examination of two key factors that go into risk analysis—budgetary costs and casualty estimates—see Michael O'Hanlon, *Saving Lives with Force: Military Criteria for Humanitarian Intervention* 62–81 (1997). See also Edward N. Luttwak, *Strategy: The Logic of War and Peace* 58 (1987) ("Under the impact of [war's] costs in blood, treasure, and agony, the worth of whatever was to be gained, or defended [by war], is reconsidered against its true price.").

for example, almost surely would prejudice the ultimate establishment of an authentic legalist order. The challenge for states committed to that goal is to make way for the new without remaining wedded to the old, while not doing damage to elements common to both. "We are at one of those rare points of leverage in history," the historian John Gaddis has written, "when familiar constraints have dropped away; what we do now could establish the framework within which events will play themselves out for decades to come."[77]

SEVEN

Conclusion

With the close of the twentieth century, the most ambitious of international experiments, the effort to subordinate the use of force to the rule of law, also came to an end—the victim of a breakdown in the consensus among member states concerning the most basic of issues: the scope of state sovereignty. Never a true legalist order, the use-of-force regime of the UN Charter finally succumbed to massive global disagreement pitting North against South and East against West over when armed intervention in states' internal affairs was permissible.

The old rules of the Charter had banned completely any use of force by individual states save force used in self-defense, as well as any use of force by the collectivity—the UN Security Council—save force used against a threat to international peace and security. But neither rule was honored. Individual states engaged in massive and frequent violation of the prohibition, culminating in its breach by 19 Western democracies in their 1999 air strikes against Yugoslavia. The Security Council, while initially faithful to the ban, came increasingly to breach it, intervening repeatedly in the domestic jurisdiction of a number of states. Hence, by century's end, the Charter's use-of-force regime had become all but imaginary.

International lawyers were loathe to acknowledge the legalist system's breakdown. Relying upon antiquated notions of causation and motive and stubbornly turning a blind eye to plain evidence, they looked only to states' words and ignored their deeds, insisting that the ban on state intervention had survived. They ignored the Security Council's unilateral expansion of its own power—notwithstanding words in the Charter that limited the power of the Council, words that had been relied upon by states that represented most of the world's population. It was of no consequence to legalism's defenders that the Security Council was a creature of state consent, and that it was empowered to exercise only the authority that states had actually delegated.

Fifty years after the drafting of the Charter, it is no longer possible to know when use of force by states violates international law. International law comprised than just the Charter; customary norms, its scholastic apologists reminded us, also count in limiting state behavior. But customary international law contained so many gaps and inconsistencies, and international lawyers had so often distorted it to reach preferred outcomes, that no one confidently could say when intervention was permitted or prohibited.

The legal vacuum encouraged reliance upon alternative systems of validation. Intervention increasingly was justified by resort to such notions as justice, legitimacy, natural law, and morality. Yet, unlike an authentic legalist order, none of these systems could command universal assent. And none could lay claim to objective validity. Thus, none could serve as a substitute for law, which alone remains capable of embodying a community's shared expectations.

But basic expectations were not shared within the international community. One group of states, comprised largely of states of the East and South, continued to defend the old rules, insisting that intrastate violence lay within the responsibility of the territorial sovereign and that intervention by individual states or by the Security Council remained impermissible. States of the West and North, by contrast—encouraged by the UN Secretary General—contended that intrastate violence could no longer be left outside the purview of international concern, and that, at least in extreme cases, intervention by individual states or by the Security Council was the appropriate remedy. The gap between the two groups of states precluded agreement on a matter essential to the proper working of the system. But the Charter never constituted a true legalist regime. A true legalist regime is characterized by universality and equality of obligation, a condition defeated by the Charter's exemption of veto-wielding members of the Security Council. The collapse of consent with respect to foundational principles concerning intervention merely underscored the weakness of the Charter's claim to the mantle of law.

There thus developed, at the century's end, an odd duality of interventionist regimes—one a *de jure* regime comprised of formal rules that states felt free to ignore, the other a *de facto* regime governed by geopolitical factors that states knew to be controlling. States continued to pay lip service to the former, but in fact comported their conduct with the latter. That conduct thus came to be governed by a weighing of the benefits of intervention against its costs—an imprecise calculus, to be sure, but one seen as more able to promote the political objectives of the state.

The process of weighing the costs of a possible intervention against its benefits can lay the groundwork for the emergence of a legalist regime in that it inevitably involves discussion and evaluation, which, repeated over time, could yield patterns of preferences and expectations that could form the foundation of a new treaty governing intervention. In this regard, movement towards regionalization has already begun and is likely to continue, with preexisting coalitions of neighboring democracies intervening to halt massive human rights violations. But global opinion is as yet far from agreement on the propriety of such intervention, whether embodied in the UN Charter or in some new treaty. In the meantime, states will continue to intervene, as NATO did in Kosovo, not where law tells them they may, but there wisdom tells them they should, where power tells them they can, and—perhaps—where justice, as they see it, tells them that they must.

Notes

Introduction

1. Zbigniew Brzezinski, *Out of Control: Global Turmoil on the Eve of the Twenty-First Century* 17 (1993).
2. Hans J. Morgenthau, *Politics Among Nations* 439 (4th ed. 1966).
3. Louis Henkin, *How Nations Behave* 47 (2d ed. 1979) (emphasis in original).
4. Henry A. Kissinger, *A World Restored* 4–5 (1964).
5. Press Release, The Pew Research Center for the People and the Press, Senate Test Ban Vote Little Noticed, Less Understood (Oct. 21, 1999).
6. Phillip R. Trimble, "International Law, World Order, and Critical Legal Studies," 42 *Stan. L. Rev.* 811, 833 (1990).
7. Václav Havel, Kosovo and the End of the Nation-State, Address Before the Canadian Senate and House of Commons, (Apr. 29, 1999), in *New York Review of Books,* June 10, 1999.

Chapter 1

1. See generally S. J. Hemleben, *Plans for World Peace through Six Centuries* (1943).
2. Elizabeth York, *Leagues of Nations* 179 (1919).
3. William Penn, *Towards the Present and Future Peace of Europe* 26–27 (American Peace Society 1912) (1694).
4. Charles Irénée Castel de Saint-Pierre, *Selections from the second edition of the Abrégé du Projet de Paix Perpétuelle* 36 (H. Hale Bellot trans., Sweet & Maxwell 1927) (1738).
5. *Id.*
6. See Giulio Alberoni, *Cardinal Alberoni's Scheme for Reducing the Turkish Empire to the Obedience of Christian Princes* (1736).
7. See generally Sylvester John Hemleben, *Plans for World Peace through Six Centuries* (1943).

8. *Letters of Voltaire and Frederick the Great* 160–161 (R. Aldington ed., 1927).

9. G. Lowes Dickenson, introduction to Jean-Jacques Rousseau, *Project of Perpetual Peace,* at xl (E. M. Nuttall trans., R. Cobden-Sanderson 1927).

10. Immanuel Kant, *Perpetual Peace* 257 (C. J. Friedrich ed., 1948) (1795).

11. Christopher Harvie, "The father of European federalism?" 47 *History Today* (July 1999).

12. A. C. F. Beales, *The History of Peace: A Short Account of the Organised Movements for International Peace* 127 (1931).

13. See generally Andreas Osiander, *The States System of Europe, 1640 – 1990: Peacemaking and the Conditions of International Stability* 248–315 (1994).

14. Jan Christiaan Smuts, *The League of Nations: A Practical Suggestion* 71 (1918).

15. Woodrow Wilson, Address to the Senate (Jan. 22, 1917), in *The Papers of Woodrow Wilson* 40: 536–37 (Arthur S. Link ed., Princeton University Press 1982).

16. See generally Geoff Simons, *The United Nations: A Chronology of Conflict* (1994); Michael Howard, "The Historical Development of the U.N.'s Role in International Security," in *United Nations, Divided World: The U.N.'s Roles in International Relations* 63 (Adam Roberts and Benedict Kingsbury eds., 1993).

17. Anthony Clark Arend and Robert J. Beck, *International Law and the Use of Force* 20–22 (1993).

18. F. H. Hinsley, *Power and the Pursuit of Peace: Theory and Practice in the History of Relations Between States* 338 (1963).

19. Ian Brownlie, *International Law and the Use of Force by States* 56 (1963).

20. Barton Gellman and Steven Mufson, "Balkans Conflict Tests NATO's Moral Mandate," *Wash. Post,* June 6, 1999, at A20.

21. Inis L. Claude, Jr., *Swords into Plowshares: The Problems and Progress of International Organization* 66 (4th ed. 1984) (emphasis in original).

22. J. L. Brierly, *The Law of Nations: An Introduction to the International Law of Peace* 105 (Humphrey Waldock ed., 6th ed. 1963).

23. See generally Leland M. Goodrich, "From League of Nations to United Nations," 1 *Int'l Org.* 3 (1947); Evan Luard, *A History of the United Nations* (1982); Frederic L. Kirgis, Jr., "The Security Council's First Fifty Years," 89 *Am. J. Int'l L.* 506 (1995).

24. Francisco de Vitoria, *Francisci de Victoria De Indis et De ivre belli relectiones* (John Pawley Bate trans., Ernest Nys ed., Carnegie Institution of Washington, 1917) (1557).

25. J. L. Brierly, *The Law of Nations: An Introduction to the International Law of Peace* 415 (Humphrey Waldock ed., 6th ed. 1963).

26. G. A. Res. 2131, U.N. GAOR, 20th Sess., 1408th plen. mtg., U.N. Doc. A/6220 (1965), reprinted in United Nations Resolutions 10:107 (Dusan J. Djnovich ed., 1964–65).

27. G. A. Res. 2734, U.N. GAOR, 25th Sess., 1932d plen. mtg., U.N. Doc. A/8028 (1970), reprinted in United Nations Resolutions 13: 337 (Dusan J. Djonovich ed., 1970–71).

28. G. A. Res. 2625, U.N. GAOR, 25th Sess., Supp. No. 28, at 123, U.N. Doc. A/8028 (1970).

29. 91st plen. mtg., Dec. 9, 1981, 33/103.

30. 81st plen. mtg., Dec. 16, 1993, 48/83.

31. For an analysis of the legal effect of General Assembly resolutions, see Oscar Schachter, "International Law in Theory and Practice: General Course in Public International Law," 178 *Recueil des Cours* 9, 111–121 (1982).

32. North Atlantic Treaty, Apr. 4, 1949, art. 1, 63 Stat. 2241, 34 U.N.T.S. 243.

33. Oscar Schachter, "International Law in Theory and Practice: General Course in Public International Law," 178 *Recueil des Cours* 9, 141 (1982).

34. See, for example, Julius Stone, *Aggression and World Order: A Critique of United Nations Theories of Aggression* (1958).

35. See, for example, Fernando R. Tesón, *Humanitarian Intervention* 151 (2nd ed. 1997). See also Anthony D'Amato, *International Law: Process and Prospect* 57–73 (1987).

36. The classic is perhaps Ian Brownlie, *International Law and the Use of Force by States* (1963).

37. Michael Akehurst, "Humanitarian Intervention," in *Intervention in World Politics* 95, 116 (Hedley Bull ed., 1984).

38. Ian Brownlie, "Humanitarian Intervention," in *Law and Civil War in the Modern World* 217, 219 (John Norton Moore ed., 1974).

39. Louis Henkin, *How Nations Behave* 137 (2d ed. 1979).

40. Oscar Schachter, *International Law in Theory and Practice* 128–29 (1991).

41. Tom J. Farer, "Human Rights in Law's Empire: The Jurisprudence War," 85 *Am. J. Int'l L.* 117, 121 (1991) (emphasis in original).

42. Military and Paramilitary Activities (Nicar. v. U.S.), 1984 I.C.J. Rep. 392, 426, para. 268 (Nov. 26).

43. Nigel S. Rodley, "Human Rights and Humanitarian Intervention: The Case Law of the World," 38 *Int'l & Com. L.Q.* 321, 332 (1989).

44. UK Foreign Office Policy Document No. 148, reprinted in 57 *Brit. Y.B. Int'l L.* 619 (1986).

45. House of Commons, Select Committee on Foreign Affairs, Fourth Report ¶ 124 (May 23, 2000), http://www.publications.parliament. uk/pa/cm199900/cmselect/cmfaff/28/2813.html (last visited Feb. 23, 2001).

46. Lord Robertson, NATO Secretary General, Law, Morality, and the Use of Force, Address Before the Institut de Relations Internationales et Stratégiques, Paris (May 16, 2000).

47. James P. Rubin, *U.S. Dept. of State Daily Press Briefing* 71 (June 15, 1998), http://secretary.state.gov/www.briefings/9806/980615db.html (last visited Aug. 3, 2000).

48. James P. Rubin, *U.S. Dept. of State Daily Press Briefing* 111 (Oct. 1, 1998), http://secretary.state.gov/www.briefings/9810/981001db.html (last visited Aug. 3, 2000).

49. Madeleine Albright, *U.S. Dept. of State Press Conference on "Kosovo"* (Mar. 25, 1999).

50. Madeleine Albright, U.S. Secretary of State, Interview with Middle East Broadcasting Corporation, in Washington, D.C., as released by the Office of the Spokesman, U.S. Department of State (Mar. 25, 1999), (last visited Feb. 23, 2001).

51. Neil A. Lewis, "A Word Bolsters Case for Allied Intervention," *N.Y. Times,* Apr. 4, 1999.

52. Statement of David R. Andrews, Legal Adviser, U.S. Dept. of State, "Legality of Use of Force (Yugoslavia v. United States of America)," May 11, 1999, http://www.icjcij.org/icjww/idocket/iyus/iyusframe. html (last visited July 19, 2000).

53. Statement from European Council to United Nations (S/1999/342), in *Transnat'l L. Exchange,* Special Supp., May 1999, at 1.

54. Statement by NATO Secretary General Javier Solena (S/1999/360), in *Transnat'l L. Exchange,* Special Supp., May 1999, at 1.

55. Statement by NATO Secretary General Javier Solena to permanent representatives of North Atlantic Council, Brunno Simma, "NATO, the U.N. and the Use of Force: Legal Aspects," Address to United Nations Association of the United States (Mar. 11–12, 1999), http://www.unausa.org/issues/sc/simma.html.

56. Statement by C.I.S. and P.R.C. (S/1999/343), in *Transnat'l L. Exchange,* Special Supp., May 1999, at 1.

57. Sergey Lavrov, "The Russian Approach: The Fight against Genocide, War Crimes, and Crimes against Humanity," 23 *Fordham Int'l L. J.* 415, 420 (2000) (quoting Igor Ivanov, *Nezavisimaya Gazeta,* June 25, 1999).

58. Viktor Chernomyrdin, "Comment: Impossible to Talk Peace with Bombs Falling," *Wash. Post,* May 27, 1999, at A39.

59. "China Urges NATO to cancel military action on Yugoslavia," *British Broadcasting Company, BBC Summary of World Broadcasts,* Mar. 25, 1999, available in LEXIS, News Library.

60. Statement of Sun Yuxi, Chinese Foreign Ministry Spokesman, Apr. 6 and 8, 1999, http://www.china.org.cn/BeijingReview/99Apr/ bjr99-17e–8.html (last visited July 19, 2000).

61. Statement of Sergey Lavrov, "Security Council fails to adopt draft on NATO military action against Yugoslavia," *Xinua News Agency,* Mar. 26, 1999, available in LEXIS, News Library.

62. Statement of Qin Huasun, *id.*

63. Oscar Schachter, "The Legality of Pro-Democratic Invasion," 78 *Am. J. Int'l L.* 645, 649 (1984).

64. S.C. Res. 1160, U.N. SCOR, 53d Sess., 3868th mtg., U.N. Doc. S/RES/1160 (1998).

65. S.C. Res. 1160, U.N. SCOR, 53d Sess., 3930th mtg., U.N. Doc. S/RES/1199 (1999).

66. S.C. Res. 1203, U.N. SCOR, 53d Sess., 3937th mtg., U.N. Doc. S/RES/1203 (1998).

67. S.C. Res. 83, U.N. SCOR, 5th Sess., 474th mtg., U.N. Doc. S/RES/83 (1950).

68. S.C. Res. 678, U.N. SCOR, 45th Sess., 2963d mtg., U.N. Doc. S/RES/678 (1990).

69. S.C. Res. 1031, U.N. SCOR, 50th Sess., 3607th mtg., U.N. Doc. S/RES/1031 (1995).

70. Roger Cohen, "NATO Shatters Old Limits in the Name of Preventing Evil," *N.Y. Times,* Oct. 18, 1999.

71. Youngstown Sheet & Tube Co. v. Sawyer, 343 U.S. 579 (1952).

72. See Louis Henkin, *How Nations Behave* 291 (2d ed. 1979).

73. Abram Chayes, "Law and the Quarantine of Cuba," 41 *Foreign Affairs* 550, 556 (1963).

74. See S.C. Res. 788, U.N. SCOR, 47th Sess., 3188th mtg., U.N. Doc. S/RES/988 (1992).

75. See generally Christopher J. Borgen, "The Theory and Practice of Regional Organization Intervention in Civil Wars," *N.Y.U. J. of Int'l L. & Pol.* 797, 818 (1994).

76. *Id.* at 820.

77. House of Commons, Select Committee on Foreign Affairs, Fourth Report ¶ 128 (May 23, 2000), http://www.publications. parliament. uk/pa/cm199900/cmselect/cmfaff/28/2813.html (last visited Feb. 23, 2001).

Chapter 2

1. *Restatement (Third) of the Foreign Relations Law of the United States* § 102 cmt.j (1987).

2. North Sea Continental Shelf (F.R.G. v. Den.), 1969 I.C.J. Rep. 3, 44 (Feb. 20).

3. Josef Kunz, "The Nature of Customary International Law," 47 *Am. J. Int'l L.* 662, 667 (1953).

4. This argument was actually advanced by the Legal Adviser of the U.S. Department of State. See Memorandum, R. B. Owen, quoted in Nash, "Contemporary Practice of the United States Relating to International Law," 74 *Am. J. Int'l L.* 418, 418–20 (1980). See also Yoram Dinstein, *War, Aggression, and Self-Defense* 98–103 (1988).

5. Oscar Schachter, "International Law in Theory and Practice: General Course in Public International Law," 178 *Recueil des Cours* 9 (1982).

6. U.N. Charter art. 103.

7. Hans Kelsen, "The Pure Theory of Law" (1934), reprinted in Louis Henkin et al., *International Law: Cases and Materials* 20 (1993).

8. *Restatement (Third) of the Foreign Relations Law of the United States* § 102 cmt. k (1987).

9. Egon Schwelb, "Some Aspects of International jus cogens as Formulated by the International Law Commission," 61 *Am. J. Int'l L.* 946 (1967).

10. Mark W. Janis, *An Introduction to International Law* 53 (1988).

11. North Sea Continental Shelf (F.R.G. v. Den.), 1969 I.C.J. Rep. 4, 42 (Feb. 20).

12. Edward McWhinney, *United Nations Law Making: Cultural and Ideological Relativism and International Law Making for an Era of Transition* 74 (1984).

13. Vienna Convention on the Law of Treaties, May 23, 1969, art. 53, 1155 U.N.T.S. 331, 344.

14. See generally Marjorie Whiteman, "Jus Cogens in International Law," *Ga. J. Int'l & Comp. L.* 609 (1977).

15. *Restatement (Third) of the Foreign Relations Law of the United States* § 102 reporters' note 6.

16. Military and Paramilitary Activities (Nicar. vs. U.S.), 1986 I.C.J. Rep. 14, 531 (June 27) (dissenting opinion of Judge Jennings).

17. Theodor Meron, *Human Rights and Humanitarian Norms as Customary Law* 51 n. 133 (1989).

18. See generally I. C. MacGibbon, "The Scope of Acquiescence in International Law," 31 *Brit. Y.B. Int'l L.* 143 (1954).

19. Louis Henkin, "Use of Force: Law and U.S. Policy," in Louis Henkin et al., *Right v. Might: International Law and the Use of Force* 53 (2d ed. 1991).

20. Military and Paramilitary Activities (Nicar. vs. U.S.), 1986 I.C.J. Rep. 14, 98 (June 27).

21. See Thomas M. Franck, "Sidelined in Kosovo? The United Nations' Demise Has Been Exaggerated; Break It, Don't Fake It," *Foreign Affairs* 116 (July/Aug. 1999).

22. Oscar Schachter, "The Right of States to Use Armed Force," 82 *Mich. L. Rev.* 1620, 1621 (1984).
23. J. L. Brierly, *The Law of Nations: An Introduction to the International Law of Peace* 69–70 (Humphrey Waldock ed., 6th ed. 1963).
24. Oscar Schachter, "In Defense of International Rules on the Use of Force," 53 *U. Chi. L. Rev.* 113, 119 (1986).
25. Arthur M. Weisburd, "Customary International Law: The Problem of Treaties," 21 *Vand. J. Transnat'l L.* 1, 33 (1988).
26. Interview with Tony Blair, U.K. Prime Minister, *The NewsHour with Jim Lehrer:* (PBS television broadcast, Apr. 23, 1999).
27. NATO Press Release NAC-S (99) 6524 (Apr. 1999), http://www. NATO.int/docu/pr/1999/p99–065e.html.
28. Abraham D. Sofaer, "International Law and Kosovo," 36 *Stan. J. Int'l L.* 1, 7 (2000).
29. A. Mark Weisburd, *Use of Force: The Practice of States Since World War II,* at 23 (1997).
30. Anthony D'Amato, *The Concept of Custom in International Law* 35 (1971).
31. Louis Henkin, *How Nations Behave* 2–3 (2d ed. 1979).
32. Anthony D'Amato, *The Concept of Custom in International Law* 73 (1971).
33. Oscar Schachter, "In Defense of International Rules on the Use of Force," 53 *U. Chi. L. Rev.* 113, 130 (1986).
34. *Id.* at 130–31.
35. Anthony D'Amato, "Trashing Customary International Law," 81 *Am. J. Int'l L.* 101, 105 (1987).
36. Louis Henkin, *How Nations Behave* 129 (1968).
37. See, for example, Abram Chayes and Antonia Handler Chayes, *The New Sovereignty: Compliance with International Regulatory Agreements* (1995); Thomas M. Franck, *Fairness in International Law and Institutions* (1995); Harold Hongju Koh, "Why Do Nations Obey International Law?" 106 *Yale L.J.* 2599 (1997).
38. Michael Howard, *The Lessons of History* 11 (1991).
39. J. L. Brierly, *The Law of Nations: An Introduction to the International Law of Peace* 72 (Humphrey Waldock ed., 6th ed. 1963).
40. Louis Henkin, "The Use of Force: Law and U.S. Policy" in Louis Henkin et al., *Right v. Might: International Law and the Use of Force* 53 (2d ed. 1991).
41. *Id.*
42. See generally Jack L. Goldsmith and Eric A. Posner, "A Theory of Customary International Law," 66 *U. Chi. L. Rev.* 1113 (1999); Jack L. Goldsmith and Eric A. Posner, "Understanding the Resemblance Between Modern and Traditional Customary International Law," 40 *Va. J. Int'l L.* 639 (2000) (arguing that behavioral regularities called

customary international law in fact reflect coincidence of interest or coercion, and thus lack normative import).

43. Jack A. Goldsmith and Eric A. Posner, "Understanding the Resemblance between Modern and Traditional Customary International Law," 40 *Va. J. Int'l L.* 639, 655 (2000).

44. Jack L. Goldsmith and Eric A. Posner, "A Theory of Customary International Law," 66 *U. Chi. L. Rev.* 1113, 1150 (1999).

45. *Trial of the Major War Criminals Before the International Military Tribunal, Nuremberg 14 Nov. 1945–1 Oct. 1946,* 1: 220–22 (1947).

46. Anthony D'Amato, "Trashing Customary International Law," 81 *Am. J. Int'l L.* 101, 102 (1987).

47. Thomas M. Franck, "Some Observations on the I.C.J.'s Procedural and Substantive Innovations," 81 *Am. J. Int'l L.* 116, 118–19 (1987).

48. Helvering v. Hallock, 309 U.S. 106, 121 (1940).

49. Anthony D'Amato, *The Concept of Custom in International Law* 81 (1971).

50. *Id.* at 84.

51. Quoted in Oscar Schachter, "Sovereignty and Threats to Peace," in *Collective Security in a Changing World* 29 (Thomas G. Weiss ed., 1993).

52. Oscar Schachter, "In Defense of International Rules on the Use of Force," 53 *U. Chi. L. Rev.* 113, 131 (1986).

53. Thalif Deen, "Politics: Humanitarian Intervention Remains a Divisive Issue," *Inter Press Service,* Mar. 9, 2000.

54. J. Patrick Kelly, "The Twilight of Customary International Law," 40 *Va. J. Int'l. L.* 470, 473 (2000).

55. Louis Henkin, *How Nations Behave* 334 (2d ed. 1979).

56. *Id.* at 146.

57. *Id.* at 320.

58. *Id.*

59. *Id.* at 148

60. *Id.* at 320.

61. *Id.* at 331.

62. Louis Henkin, "The Reports of the Death of Article 2(4) Are Greatly Exaggerated," 65 *Am. J. Int'l L.* 544, 547 (1971).

63. W. W. Buckland, *A Text-Book of Roman Law: From Augustus to Justinian* 52 (3d ed. 1966).

64. Hans Kelsen, *General Theory of Law and State* 119 (Anders Wedberg trans., 1949).

65. H. F. Jolowicz and Barry Nicholas, *Historical Introduction to the Study of Roman Law* 353–55 (3d ed. 1972).

66. Vienna Convention on the Law of Treaties, opened for signature May 23, 1969, 1155 U.N.T.S. 331.

67. See, for example, *Summary Records of the 37th Meeting of the Committee of the Whole,* [1968] U.N. Conference on the Law of

Treaties 209, U.N. Doc. A/Conf.39/11, U.N. Sales No. E.68.V.7 (remarks of Mr. Martinez Caro (Spain)).

68. *Report of the Commission to the General Assembly*, [1964] 2 Y.B. Int'l L. Comm'n 198, U.N. Doc. A/CN.4/SER.A/1964/ADD.1

69. *Id.*

70. *Report of the Commission to the General Assembly*, [1966] 2 Y.B. Int'l L. Comm'n 236, U.N. Doc. A/CN.4/SER.A/1966/ADD.1

71. *Id.*

72. See, for example, *Summary Records of the 37th Meeting of the Committee of the Whole*, [1968] U.N. Conference on the Law of Treaties 211, U.N. Doc. A/Conf.39/11, U.N. Sales No. E.68.V.7 (remarks of Mr. Maresca (Italy)).

73. *Id.* (remarks of Mr. Rosenne (Israel)).

74. *Id.* at 214 (remarks of Mr. Ruegger (Switzerland)).

75. *Id.* (remarks of Mr. de la Guardia (Argentina)).

76. *Restatement (Third) of the Foreign Relations Law of The United States* § 102 reporters' note 4 (1987).

77. Alexander M. Bickel, *The Morality of Consent* 107–08 (1975).

78. William Bishop, "General Course of Public International Law," 1965, 115 *Recueil des Cours* 151, 227 (1965).

79. 1 Y.B. Int'l Law Comm'n (1950).

80. *Id.*

81. Louis Henkin, *How Nations Behave* 306 (2d ed. 1979).

82. Daniel Bodansky, "Non Liquet and the Rule of Law," in *International Law at the Close of the 20th Century: The Nuclear Weapons Advisory Opinion* 154 (Philippe Sands and Laurence Boisson de Chazournes eds., 2000).

83. *Id.* at 164.

84. Hans Kelsen, *Principles of International Law* 440 (Robert W. Tucker ed., 2d ed. 1966).

85. Alexander M. Bickel, *The Least Dangerous Branch* 103 (2d ed. 1986).

86. A. Mark Weisburd, *Use of Force: The Practice of States Since World War II* 24 (1997).

87. See J. Patrick Kelly, "The Twilight of Customary International Law," 40 *Va. J. Int'l. L.* 449, 486 (2000); Daniel Bodansky, "Customary (and Not So Customary) International Environmental Law," 3 *Ind. J. Global Legal Stud.* 105, 111 (1995) (arguing that state practice and international environmental norms diverge).

88. Letter of Conrad K. Harper, Legal Adviser, U.S. Department of State, to Francisco Jose Aguilar-Urbina, Chairman, Human Rights Committee, quoted in Richard B. Lillich, "Introduction: The Growing Importance of Customary International Human Rights Law," 25 *Ga. J. Int'l & Comp. L.* 1, 20 n. 101 (1996).

Chapter 3

1. Burns H. Weston et al., *International Law and World Order* 259 (1980).
2. Anthony C. Arend and Robert J. Beck, *International Law and the Use of Force: Beyond the UN Charter Paradigm* 181 (1993).
3. Peter Wallensteen and Karin Axell, "Conflict Resolution and the End of the Cold War 1989 – 1993," 31 *J. Peace Research* 333 (Aug. 1994).
4. Louis Henkin, *How Nations Behave* 146 (2nd ed. 1979) (emphasis in original).
5. See generally Norimitsu Onishi, "War in Congo Rattles On Despite Accord," *N.Y. Times,* July 19, 1999, at A3.
6. Jennifer L. Balint, "Conflict, Conflict Victimization, and Legal Redress, 1945–1996," 59 *Law & Contemp. Probs.,* Autumn 1996, at 235.
7. Herbert K. Tillema, "Risks of Battle and the Deadliness of War: International Armed Conflicts 1945–1991" (paper presented to International Studies Association, San Diego, Apr. 16–29, 1996) quoted in *New Actors, New Issues, New Actions in International Intervention: New Norms in the Post–Cold War Era?* at 5, 6 (Peter Wallensteen ed., 1997).
8. The Carter Center, *Conflict Resolution Update: Update on World Conflicts,* Feb. 9, 1998.
9. See generally Edwin Borchard, "'Neutrality' and Civil Wars," 31 *Am. J. Int'l L.* 304 (1937).
10. Anthony D'Amato, "Trashing Customary International Law," 81 *Am. J. Int'l L.* 101, 102–03 (1987).
11. Thomas M. Franck, "Some Observations on the I.C.J.'s Procedural and Substantive Innovations," 81 *Am. J. Int'l L.* 116, 119 (1987).
12. See generally Edward Hallet Carr, *What is History?* (1967).
13. Fernando R. Tesón, *Humanitarian Intervention: An Inquiry into Law and Morality* 184 (2d ed. 1997).
14. *Id.*
15. *Id.*
16. *Id.* at 179.
17. *Id.* at 185.
18. R. W. Johnson, "Nyerere: A Flawed Hero," *The National Interest* 66, 75 (summer 2000).
19. *Id.* at 179.
20. *Id.*
21. *Id.* at 181.
22. *Id.* at 185.
23. *Id.*
24. *Id.* at n. 70.

25. *Id.* at 196.
26. *Id.* at 197.
27. *Id.* at 196. See also Keith Somerville, *Foreign Military Intervention in Africa* 171 (1990).
28. *Id.*
29. Anthony C. Arend and Robert J. Beck, *International Law and the Use of Force: Beyond the UN Charter Paradigm* 129 (1993).
30. *Id.* at 198.
31. *Id.*
32. Michael Akehurst, "Humanitarian Intervention," in *Intervention in World Politics* 95, 98 (Hedley Bull ed., 1984).
33. *Id.* at 202 (quoting International Commission of Jurists, *The Events in East Pakistan* 20–21 [1972]).
34. *Id.* at 204.
35. *Id.* at n. 166.
36. *Id.* at 203.
37. *Id.*
38. Sumit Ganguly, "Avoiding War in Kashmir," 69 *Foreign Aff.* 57, 62 (winter 1990).
39. *Id.* at 209–10.
40. *Id.* at 209.
41. *Id.* at 211.
42. *Id.*
43. *Id.* at 212.
44. *Id.*
45. *Id.* at 213.
46. *Id.*
47. *Id.* at 216.
48. *Id.* at 214–15.
49. Oscar Schachter, "The Right of States to Use Armed Force," 82 *Mich. L. Rev.* 1620, 1631 (1984).
50. Fernando R. Tesón, *Humanitarian Intervention: An Inquiry into Law and Morality* 216 (2d ed. 1997).
51. *Id.* at 220.
52. Tom J. Farer, "Human Rights in Law's Empire: The Jurisprudence War," 85 *Am. J. Int'l L.* 117, 121 (1991).
53. Michael Walzer, *Just and Unjust Wars: A Moral Argument with Historical Illustrations* 101 (2d ed. 1991).
54. Noam Chomsky, *The New Humanism: Lessons from Kosovo* 12–23 (1999).
55. Louis Henkin, *How Nations Behave* 52 (2d ed. 1979).
56. Edward Gibbon, *The Decline and Fall of the Roman Empire* 2: 1235 (1776–1788).
57. J. Patrick Kelly, "The Twilight of Customary International Law," 40 *Va. J. Int'l L.* 449, 474 (2000).

58. Michael Akehurst, "Humanitarian Intervention," in *Intervention in World Politics* 95, 97 (Hedley Bull ed., 1984).

59. Tom J. Farer, "Human Rights in Law's Empire: The Jurisprudence War," 85 *Am. J. Int'l L.* 117, 122 (1991).

60. U.N. GAOR, 54th Sess., 4th plen. mtg. at 4, 2 U.N. Doc. A/54/PV.4 (Sept. 20, 1999) (remarks of Kofi Annan, Secretary General).

61. *Report of the Secretary-General on the work of the Organization,* U.N. GAOR, 54th Sess., Supp. No. 1 ¶ 56, U.N. Doc. A/54/1 (Aug. 31, 1999), http://www.un.org/Docs/SG/Report99/security.html (last visited Feb. 23, 2001).

62. Fernando R. Tesón, *Humanitarian Intervention: An Inquiry into Law and Morality* 200 (2d ed. 1997).

63. *Id.* at 185.

64. *Id.* at 188.

65. *Id.* at 190.

66. *Id.*

67. *Id.* at 195.

68. *Id.* at XV.

69. See Richard Falk, *Revitalizing International Law* 96–97 (1989).

70. Quoted in *The Steel Seizure Case*, 343 U.S. 579, 637 (Jackson, J., concurring).

71. Adam Roberts, "Willing the End But Not the Means," *The World Today* 12 (1999).

72. Abraham D. Sofaer, "International Law and Kosovo," 36 *Stan. J. Int'l L.* 1, 20 (2000).

73. Anthony C. Arend and Robert J. Beck, *International Law and the Use of Force: Beyond the UN Charter Paradigm* 182 (1993).

74. Evan Luard, *The Balance of Power: The System of International Relations, 1648–1815,* at 345 (1992).

75. Louis Henkin, "Use of Force: Law and U.S. Policy," in *Right v. Might: International Law and the Use of Force* 52 (2d ed. 1991).

76. Adam Roberts and Benedict Kingsbury, "Introduction: The U.N.'s Roles in International Society since 1945," in *United Nations, Divided World: The U.N.'s Roles in International Relations* 1, 59 (Adam Roberts and Benedict Kingsbury eds., 1993).

77. William D. Rogers, "The Principles of Force, the Force of Principles," in *Right v. Might: International Law and the Use of Force* 95, 106 (2d ed. 1991).

78. Julius Stone, Aggression and World Order; A Critique of United Nations Theories of Aggression 96 (1958).

79. See generally James E. Rossman, "Article 43: Arming the United Nations Security Council," 27 *N.Y.U. J. Int'l L. & Pol.* 227 (1994).

80. "Agenda for Peace: Position Paper of the Secretary-General on the Fiftieth Anniversary of the United Nations," U.N. GAOR, 50th Sess., U.N. Doc. A/50/60 (1995).

81. See U.N. Charter art. 45.

82. Anthony C. Arend and Robert J. Beck, *International Law and the Use of Force: Beyond the UN Charter Paradigm* 178–79 (1993).

83. W. Michael Reisman, "Sanctions and Enforcement," in *The Future of the International Legal Order: Conflict Management* 3: 273 (Cyril E. Black and Richard A. Falk eds., 1971).

84. Djura Nincic, *The Problem of Sovereignty in the Charter and in the Practice of the United Nations* 76-77 (1970).

85. See *The Record of American Diplomacy* 461–70 (Ruhl J. Bartlett ed., 3d ed. 1954).

86. 58 Cong. Rec. 8777 (1919).

87. President Woodrow Wilson, Address at Coliseum, Indianapolis, Ind. (Sept. 4, 1919), reprinted in S. Doc. No. 66-120, at 22 (1919).

88. *Id.*

89. *Id.*

90. Alan Cranston, *The Killing of the Peace* 222 (1945) (remarks of Sen. G. Hitchcock).

91. *Id.* at 224.

92. *The Record of American Diplomacy* n. 19 (Ruhl J. Bartlett ed., 3d ed. 1954) (providing the "Statement of the 31," who were the 31 signatories to the statement).

93. David S. Yost, *NATO Transformed: The Alliance's New Roles in International Security* 16 (1998).

94. Cordell Hull, *The Memoirs of Cordell Hull* 1662 (1948).

95. H.R. Con. Res. 25, 78th Cong. (1943).

96. S. Res. 192, 78th Cong. (1943).

97. *The Private Papers of Senator Vandenberg* 95–96 (Arthur H. Vandenberg, Jr. ed., 1952).

98. Note, "Congress, the President, and the Power to Commit Forces to Combat," 81 *Harv. L. Rev.* 1771, 1800 (1968).

99. *Id. at* 1801.

100. *United Nations Participation Act,* Pub. L. No. 79-264, 59 Stat. 619 (1945) (codified as amended at 22 *U.S.C.* §§ 287–287e (1994 and Supp. IV 1998)) [hereinafter UNPA].

101. 91 Cong. Rec. 12, 267 (1945) (statement of Rep. S. Bloom).

102. Note, "Congress, the President, and the Power to Commit Forces to Combat," 81 *Harv. L. Rev.* 1771, 1800 (1968).

103. UNPA, § 287d.

104. *Id.*

105. *Id.* § 287d-1.

106. *Id.*

107. "Problems of World War II and its Aftermath," in House Comm. on International Relations, *Selected Executive Session Hearings of the Committee, 1943–1950,* pt. 1 at 142 (1976).

108. *Id.* at 143, 146.

109. H.R. Rep. No. 79-1383, at 8 (1945); S. Rep. No. 79-717, at 7 (1945) (emphasis added).
110. 91 *Cong. Rec.* 10, 966 (1945).
111. *Id.* at 10,967.
112. See *id.* (remarks of Sen. Vandenberg).
113. 91 *Cong. Rec.* 10, 967–68.
114. *Id.* at 12,267.
115. *Compare* Edwin Borchard, "The Charter and the Constitution," 39 *Am. J. Int'l L.* 767, 771 (1945) ("[T]he power to declare war, however perfunctory it may have become, is expressly reserved to Congress by the Constitution … ." Therefore, "Congress … must act before the President is warranted in executing its instruction by communicating with the delegate. The delay is unavoidable.").
116. Edward S. Corwin, *The President: Office and Powers* 251 (5th rev. ed. 1984).
117. Joint Committee Made Up of Senate Comm. on Foreign Relations and Senate Comm. on Armed Services, *Powers of the President to Send the Armed Forces Outside the United States,* 82d Cong., 1st Sess. 23 (Comm. Print 1951).
118. Leland M. Goodrich and Anne P. Simons, *The United Nations and the Maintenance of International Peace and Security* 398 (1955).
119. Walter Schiffer, *The Legal Community of Mankind* 199 (1954).
120. Thomas M. Franck, *Nation Against Nation: What Happened to the U.N. Dream and What the U.S. Can Do About It* 182–83 (1985). See also Stanley Hoffman, *World Disorders: Troubled Peace in the Post–Cold War Era* 182 (1998) ("An international or regional organization's impotence is always the result of its members' policies.").

Chapter 4

1. Louis Henkin, "Kosovo and the Law of Humanitarian Intervention," 93 *Am J. Int'l L.* (Oct. 1999).
2. Tom J. Farer, "A Paradigm of Legitimate Intervention," in *Enforcing Restraint: Collective Intervention in International Conflicts* 316, 330 (Lori Fisler Damrosch ed. 1993).
3. Richard B. Lillich, "Humanitarian Intervention Through the United Nations: Towards the Development of Criteria," 53 *Heidelberg J. Int'l L.* 557, 564 (1993).
4. Tom J. Farer, "Human Rights in Law's Empire: The Jurisprudence War," 85 *Am. J. Int'l L.* 117, 120 (1991).
5. *Id.*
6. *Id.*

7. Admission of a State to the United Nations (U.N. Charter art. 4), 1948 I.C.J. Rep. 57, 64 (Advisory Opinion of May 28).

8. Mohammed Bedjaoui, *The New World Order and the Security Council: Testing the Legality of its Acts* 28–29 (1994).

9. Tom J. Farer, "A Paradigm of Legitimate Intervention," in *Enforcing Restraint: Collective Intervention in Internal Conflicts* 242 (Lori Fisler Damrosch ed. 1993).

10. Secretary of State, 79th Cong., *The Charter of the United Nations: Report to the President on the Results of the San Francisco Conference* 88 (Comm. Print 1945).

11. D. W. Bowett, *United Nations Forces* 427 (1964).

12. *Id.* at 425–26 (emphasis in original).

13. Frederic L. Kirgis, Jr., "The United Nations at Fifty: The Security Council's First Fifty Years," 89 *Am. J. Int'l L.* 506, 512 (1995).

14. *Id.* at 515.

15. See J. Arntz, *Der Begriff der Friedensbedrohung in Satzung und Praxis der Vereinten Nationen* (1975).

16. See Inis L. Claude, Jr., *Swords into Plowshares: The Problems and Progress of International Organization* 185 (4th ed. 1984)

17. U.N. SCOR, 3d. Sess., 363d mtg. at 4 (Oct. 6, 1948).

18. *Id.*

19. Goronwy J. Jones, *The United Nations and the Domestic Jurisdiction of States: Interpretations and Applications of the Non-Intervention Principle* 62 (1979).

20. *The Charter of the UN: Hearings Before the Senate Comm. on Foreign Relations,* 79th Cong., 1st Sess. 51 (1945).

21. 79 *Cong. Rec.* 8014 (1945).

22. *Id.*

23. *Id.*

24. *Id.*

25. Sean D. Murphy, *Humanitarian Intervention: The United Nations in an Evolving World Order* 76–77 (1996).

26. Louis Henkin, *How Nations Behave* 174–75 (2d ed. 1979).

27. Ian Brownlie, *The Rule of Law in International Affairs: International Law at the Fiftieth Anniversary of the United Nations* 220 (1998).

28. *Id.* at 219.

29. *Id.* at 218.

30. *Id.* at 218–19.

31. J. S. Watson, "Autointerpretation, Competence, and the Continuing Validity of Article 2(7) of the UN Charter," 71 *Am. J. Int'l L.* 60, 73 (1977).

32. Innis L. Claude, Jr., *Swords into Plowshares: The Problems and Progress of International Organization* 169 (4th ed. 1984).

33. G.A. Res. 377, U.N. GAOR, 5th Sess., Supp. No. 20, at 10, U.N. Doc. A/1775 (1950).
34. UN Charter art. 10.
35. UN Charter art. 12.
36. S.C. Res. 217, U.N. SCOR, 20th Sess., 1265th mtg. at 8, UN Doc. S/INF/20/Rev.1 (1965).
37. S.C. Res. 221, U.N. SCOR, 21st Sess., 1277th mtg. at 5, UN Doc. S/INF/21/Rev.1 (1966).
38. S.C. Res. 232, U.N. SCOR, 21st Sess., 1340th mtg. at 7, UN Doc. S/INF/21/Rev.1 (1966).
39. See, for example, C. G. Fenwick, "When is there a Threat to the Peace?—Rhodesia," 61 *Am. J. Int'l L.* 753 (1967).
40. Editorial, "No Sanctions," *Wash. Post,* Dec. 14, 1966, at A24.
41. Editorial, "Sanctions?" *Wash. Post,* Dec. 9, 1966, at A20.
42. Dean Acheson, Letter, "Acheson on Rhodesia," *Wash. Post,* Dec. 11, 1966, at E6.
43. Myers S. McDougal and W. Michael Reisman, "Rhodesia and the United Nations: The Lawfulness of International Concern," 62 *Am. J. Int'l L.* 1, 16 (1968).
44. *Id.* at 18.
45. *Id.* at 15.
46. *Id.* at 19.
47. *Id.* at 9.
48. Sean D. Murphy, *Humanitarian Intervention: The United Nations in an Evolving World Order* 117–18 (1996).
49. S.C. Res. 418, U.N. SCOR, 32d Sess., 2046th mtg., U.N. Doc. S/RES/418 (1977).
50. See generally N. D. White, *Keeping the Peace: The United Nations and the Maintenance of International Peace and Security* 36 (1993).
51. S.C. Res. 688, U.N. SCOR, 46th Sess., 2982d mtg. at 31, U.N. Doc. S/PV.2982 (1991).
52. U.N. SCOR, 46th Sess., 2982d mtg. at 27, U.N. Doc. S/PV.2982 (1991).
53. U.N. SCOR, 46th Sess., 2982d mtg. at 28–30, U.N. Doc. S/PV.2982 (1991).
54. U.N. SCOR, 46th Sess., 2982d mtg. at 62, U.N. Doc. S/PV.2982 (1991).
55. Jane E. Stromseth, "Iraq's Repression of Its Civilian Population: Collective Responses and Continuing Challenges," in *Enforcing Restraint: Collective Intervention in Internal Conflicts* 77, 97 (Lori Fisler Damrosch ed., 1993) (footnotes omitted) (emphasis in original).
56. S.C. Res. 794, U.N. SCOR, 47th Sess., 3145th mtg., U.N. Doc. S/RES/794 (1992).

57. Frederic L. Kirgis, Jr., "The United Nations at Fifty: The Security Council's First Fifty Years," 89 *Am. J. Int'l L.* 506, 513 (1995).

58. Ruth Gordon, "United Nations Intervention in Internal Conflicts: Iraq, Somalia, and Beyond," 15 *Mich. J. Int'l L.* 519, 554 (1994).

59. Keith B. Richburg, "The World Ignored Genocide, Tutsis Say," *Wash. Post,* Aug. 8, 1994, at A1.

60. "France May Move in to End Rwanda Killing," *N.Y. Times,* June 16, 1994, at A12.

61. S.C. Res. 929, U.N. SCOR, 49th Sess., 3392d mtg., U.N. Doc. S/RES/929 (1994).

62. Raymond Bonner, "Rwandans Who Massacred Now Terrorize Camps," *N.Y. Times,* Oct. 31, 1994, at A1.

63. Sean D. Murphy, *Humanitarian Intervention: The United Nations in an Evolving World Order* 256–57 (1996).

64. S.C. Res. 940, U.N. SCOR, 49th Sess., 3413d mtg., U.N. Doc. S/RES/940 (1994).

65. S.C. Res. 794, U.N. SCOR, 47th Sess., 3145th mtg., U.N. Doc. S/RES/794 (1992).

66. S.C. Res. 929, U.N. SCOR, 49th Sess., 3392d mtg., U.N. Doc. S/RES/929 (1994).

67. D. Williams, "Powers Assert Influence in Peacekeeping Roles," *Wash. Post,* July 30, 1994, at A12. See also Edwin Mortimer, "Under What Circumstances Should the UN Intervene Militarily in a 'Domestic' Crisis?" in *Peacemaking and Peacekeeping for the New Century* 134 (Olara A. Otunnu and Michael W. Doyle eds., 1998).

68. Sean D. Murphy, *Humanitarian Intervention: The United Nations in an Evolving World Order* 392 (1996).

69. Vienna Convention on the Law of Treaties, opened for signature May 23, 1969, 1155 U.N.T.S. 331.

70. *Id.,* art. 4.

71. See, for example, I. M. Sinclair, "Vienna Conference on the Law of Treaties," 19 *Int'l & Comp. L. Q.* 47 (1970).

72. Jiménez de Aréchaga, "International Law in the Past Third of a Century," 159 *Recueil des Cours* 42 (1978-I).

73. See Tom Farer, "Conclusion: What Do International Lawyers Do When They Talk about Ethnic Violence and Why Does it Matter?" in *International Law and Ethnic Conflict* 326, 334 (David Wippman ed., 1998).

74. Mary Ellen O'Connell, "The UN, NATO, and International Law After Kosovo," 22 *Hum. Rts. Q.* 57, 69 (2000).

75. See generally Benedetto Conforti, *The Law and Practice of the United Nations* (1996).

76. See, for example, John Quigley, "The United Nations Security Council: Promethean Protector or Helpless Hostage?" *Texas Int'l L. J.* 129, 164–67 (2000).

77. Thomas M. Franck and Faiza Patel, "UN Police Action in lieu of War: 'The Old Order Changeth,'" 85 *Am. J. Int'l L.* 63, 66–67 (1991).
78. Oliver Wendell Holmes, *The Common Law* 1 (1881).
79. Eduard Schevardnadze, Address to the United Nations General Assembly (Sept. 25, 1999).
80. Letter from Thomas B. Macaulay to H. S. Randall (May 23, 1857) ("Your Constitution is all sail and no anchor."), in *The Selected Letters of Thomas Babington Macaulay* 286 (Thomas Pinney ed., 1982).
81. *Summary Records of the 37th Meeting of the Committee of the Whole,* [1968] U.N. Conference on the Law of Treaties 208, U.N. Doc. A/Conf.39/11, U.N. Sales No. E.68.V.7 (remarks of Mr. de Bresson (France)).
82. See generally Michael J. Glennon, "The Use of Custom in Resolving Separation of Powers Disputes," 64 *B.U. L. Rev.* 109 (1984).
83. 134 *Cong. Rec.* S6724 (daily ed., May 26, 1988). See generally Michael J. Glennon, *Constitutional Diplomacy* 137–41 (1990).
84. Strobe Talbott, Deputy Secretary of State, Address in Bonn, Germany (Feb. 4, 1999), quoted in Brunno Simma, NATO, the U.N. and the Use of Force: Legal Aspects, Address to United Nations Association of the United States in New York and Washington, D.C. (Mar. 11–12, 1999), http://www.unausa.org/issues/sc/simma.html.
85. Myers S. McDougal and W. Michael Reisman, "Rhodesia and the United Nations: The Lawfulness of International Concern," 62 *Am. J. Int'l L.* 1, 14 (1968).
86. U.S. Const. art. II, § 2, cl. 2.
87. Louis Henkin, "Kosovo and the law of 'Humanitarian Intervention,'" 93 *Am J. Int'l L.* 824, 828 (Oct. 1999).
88. *Summary Records of the 37th Meeting of the Committee of the Whole,* [1968] U.N. Conference on the Law of Treaties 208, U.N. Doc. A/Conf.39/11, U.N. Sales No. E.68.V.7 (remarks of Mr. de Bresson (France)).
89. *Summary Records of the 37th Meeting of the Committee of the Whole,* [1968] U.N. Conference on the Law of Treaties 211, U.N. Doc. A/Conf.39/11, U.N. Sales No. E.68.V.7 (remarks of Mr. Martinez Caro (Spain)).
90. *Summary Records of the 37th Meeting of the Committee of the Whole,* [1968] U.N. Conference on the Law of Treaties 211, U.N. Doc. A/Conf.39/11, U.N. Sales No. E.68.V.7 (remarks of Mr. Carmona (Venezuela)).
91. Committee on Foreign Relations, U.S. Senate, "Review of the United Nations Charter," S. Doc. No. 164, at 40 (1955).
92. Committee on Foreign Relations, U.S. Senate, "Review of the United Nations Charter," S. Doc. No. 164, at 54 (1955).

93. Certain Expenses of the United Nations, 1962 I.C.J. Pleadings 133 (July 20).

94. Certain Expenses of the United Nations, 1962 I.C.J. Rep. 151, 196–97 (July 20) (separate opinion of Judge Spender).

95. Thomas M. Franck and Faiza Patel, "UN Police Action in Lieu of War: 'The Old Order Changeth,'" 85 *Am. J. Int'l L.* 63, 67 (1991).

96. F. H. Hinsley, *Power and the Pursuit of Peace: Theory and Practice in the History of Relations Between States* 316 (1963).

97. *Summary Records of the 37th Meeting of the Committee of the Whole,* [1968] U.N. Conference on the Law of Treaties 211, U.N. Doc. A/Conf.39/11, U.N. Sales No. E.68.V.7 (remarks of Mr. Alvarez (Uruguay)).

98. U.N. GAOR, 54th Sess., 4th plen. mtg. at 4, 2, U.N. Doc. A/54/PV.4 (Sept. 20, 1999).

99. U.N. GAOR, 54th Sess., 8th plen. mtg. at 16, U.N. Doc. A/54/PV.4 (Sept. 22, 1999) (remarks of Tang Jiaxuan).

100. U.N. GAOR, 54th Sess., 11th plen. mtg. at 37, U.N. Doc. A/54/PV.4 (Sept. 23, 1999) (remarks of Ali Alatas).

101. U.N. GAOR, 54th Sess., 12th plen. mtg. at 15, U.N. Doc. A/54/PV.4 (Sept. 24, 1999) (remarks of Pérez Roque).

102. U.N. GAOR, 54th Sess., 12th plen. mtg. at 4, U.N. Doc. A/54/PV.4 (Sept. 24, 1999) (remarks of Mohammed Said Al-Sahaf).

103. U.N. GAOR, 54th Sess., 29th plen. mtg. at 22, U.N. Doc. A/54/PV.4 (Oct. 7, 1999) (remarks of Mr. Amer).

104. U.N. GAOR, 54th Sess., 32nd plen. mtg. at 18, U.N. Doc. A/54/PV.4 (Oct. 8, 1999) (remarks of Mr. Kanju).

105. U.N. GAOR, 54th Sess., 35th plen. mtg. at 23, U.N. Doc. A/54/PV.4 (Oct. 20, 1999) (remarks of Mr. Aboul Gheit).

106. U.N. GAOR, 54th Sess., 36th plen. mtg. at 9, U.N. Doc. A/54/PV.4 (Oct. 20, 1999) (remarks of Mr. Li Hyong Choi).

107. *United Nations Review,* Dec. 1956, at 95.

108. Hedley Bull, "Conclusion" in *Intervention in World Politics* 181, at 195 (Hedley Bull ed., 1984).

109. Stanley Hoffman, "What Is To Be Done?" *New York Review of Books,* May 20, 1999, at 17.

110. Julius Stone, *Aggression and World Order* 43, 95 (1958).

111. George F. Kennan, *American Diplomacy, 1900–1950,* at 84 (1951).

112. William V. O'Brien, *The Conduct of Just and Limited War* 23 (1981).

113. Myres S. McDougal and Florentino P. Feliciano, *Law and Minimum World Public Order: The Legal Regulation of International Coercion* 18–19 (1961).

114. Anthony C. Arend and Robert J. Beck, *International Law and the Use of Force: Beyond the UN Charter Paradigm* 34 (1993).

115. Note from Foreign Minister Rodriguez Larreta, reprinted in M. Whiteman, 5 *Digest of Int'l Law* 417 (1965).
116. See, for example, Edward C. Luck, *Mixed messages: American Politics and International Organization, 1919–1999* (1999).
117. 91 *Cong. Rec.* 7964 (1945).
118. See, for example, Edward C. Luck, "A Road to Nowhere," 78 *Foreign. Aff.* 118–19 (July–Aug. 1999).
119. 108 *Cong. Rec.* 5673 (1962).
120. Edmund Burke, *Tracts Relating to Popery Laws,* ch. 3, pt. 1 (1765) quoted in *The Writings and Speeches of Edmund Burke* (Paul Langford ed., 1991).
121. See generally Inis L. Claude, Jr., *Swords into Plowshares: The Problems and Progress of International Organization* 77 (4th ed. 1984).
122. Lord Robertson, NATO Secretary General, Law, Morality, and the Use of Force, Address Before the Institut de Relations Internationales et Stratégiques, Paris (May 16, 2000).
123. Martin van Creveld, *The Transformation of War* (1991).
124. "20th Century Survey, A League of Evil," *The Economist,* Sept. 11, 1999, at 7.
125. Olmstead v. United States, 277 U.S. 438, 485 (1928) (dissenting opinion).

Chapter 5

1. John Austin, *Lectures on Jurisprudence* (5th ed. 1885).
2. Glanville L. Williams, "International Law and the Controversy Concerning the Word '*Law*,'" 22 *Brit. Y.B. Int'l L.* 146 (1945).
3. See H. L. A. Hart, *The Concept of Law* 77–96 (1961).
4. Oscar Schachter, "General Course in Public International Law," 178 *Recueil des Cours,* 1982–V at 59.
5. John Sadler, *The Rights of the Kingdom* (1649).
6. Ian Brownlie, *The Rule of Law in International Affairs: International Law at the Fiftieth Anniversary of the United Nations* 214 (1998).
7. See Andreas Osiander, *The States System of Europe, 1640–1990: Peacemaking and the Conditions of International Stability* 16–89 (1994).
8. Samuel Pufendorf, *De jure naturae et gentium libri octo,* bk. 3, ch. 2, § 1 (C. H. and W. A. Oldfather trans., Carnegie ed., 1934) (1688).
9. Emmerich de Vattel, *The Law of Nations or the Principles of Natural Law,* bk. 2, lxiii (Charles Fenwick trans., Oceana Publications 1964) (1758).

10. 10 Wheat. 66, 122 (1825).

11. U.N. Charter art. 2, para. 1.

12. Evan Luard, *The Balance of Power: The System of International Relations, 1648–1815,* at 126–27 (1992).

13. Barton Gellman and Steven Mufson, "Humanitarian War: Conflict Tests a Paradigm of Values-Based International Action," *Wash. Post,* June 6, 1999, at A20.

14. George F. Kennan, *American Diplomacy, 1900–1950,* at 84 (1951).

15. Michael Howard, *The Lessons of History* 39, 41 (1991).

16. George F. Kennan, *Around the Cragged Hill: A Personal and Political Philosophy* 89 (1993).

17. *Id.*

18. Hans J. Morgenthau, *Politics Among Nations* 461 (4th ed. 1966).

19. U.N. Charter art. 27, para. 3.

20. See generally N. D. White, *Keeping the Peace: The United Nations and the Maintenance of International Peace and Security* 12 (1993).

21. Martin Wight, "The Balance of Power and International Order," in *The Bases of International Order: Essays in Honour of C. A. W. Manning* 85, 113 (Alan James ed., 1973).

22. U.N. Charter art. 2 para 6.

23. Luzius Wildhaber, *Wechselspiel zwischen Innen und Aussen: Schweizer Landesrecht, Rechtsvergleichung, Völkerrecht* 27 (1996).

24. *Id.*

25. David S. Yost, *NATO Transformed: The Alliance's New Roles in International Security* 283–4 (1998).

26. Michael Wines, "Two Views of Inhumanity Split the World, Even in Victory," *N.Y. Times,* June 13, 1999, § 1, at 1.

27. Steven Erlanger, "NATO was Closer to Ground War in Kosovo than is Widely Realized," *N.Y. Times,* Nov. 7, 1999, § 1, at 6.

28. Paul Beaver and David Montgomery, "Belgrade got NATO Attack Plans From Russian Spy," *The Scotsman,* Aug. 27, 1999, at 1.

29. Henry Kissinger, Editorial, "U.S. Intervention in Kosovo is a Mistake," *Boston Globe,* Mar. 1, 1999, at A15.

30. Michael Wines, "Two Views of Inhumanity Split the World, Even in Victory," *N.Y. Times,* June 13, 1999, § 1, at 1.

31. P. Renouvin, *L'Idée de Fédération Européene dans la Pensée Politique du XIXe Siècle* 15–16 (1949).

32. Immanuel Kant, *Perpetual Peace* 921–93 (M. Campbell Smith trans., Macmillan 1903) (1795).

33. Michael Wines, "Two Views of Inhumanity Split the World, Even in Victory," *N.Y. Times,* June 13, 1999, § 1, at 1.

34. "International Papers," *Slate News,* Oct. 21, 1999.

35. Erik Eckholm, "Russian Leader Complains of Lack of Respect from U.S.," *N.Y. Times,* Dec. 10, 1999, at A14.

36. *Face the Nation* (CBS television broadcast, May 9, 1999) (transcript available from Burrelle's Information Services) ("Well, no question that we're hostages here. In other words, we—we've not been able to get out of here for over two days now, and I don't know how long this will continue. That's not an overstatement to say that we're hostages here in this embassy . . . .").

37. Katherine Seelye, "Jiang, Clinton Discuss Relations," *N.Y. Times*, May 15, 1999, at A9.

38. Philip Shenon, "Besieged but Unbowed, Ambassador is Optimistic on China," *N.Y. Times*, Aug. 30, 1999, at A12.

39. Serge Schmemann, "Now, Onward to the Next Kosovo—if there is one," *N.Y. Times*, June 6, 1999, § 4, at 1.

40. Barbara Crossette, "U.N. Chief Wants Faster Action to Halt Civil Wars and Killings," *N.Y. Times*, Sept. 21, 1999, at A1.

41. Thalif Deen, "Politics: Non-Aligned Movement Slams 'Humanitarian Intervention,'" *Inter Press Service*, Apr. 6, 2000.

42. *Id.*

43. "Russia Welcomes Non-Aligned Meeting," *Interfax News Agency*, Apr. 13, 2000.

44. Tadeo Martnez, "Development: Non-Aligned Movement Concerned Over Unipolar World," *Inter Press Service*, Apr. 8, 2000.

45. "UN chief, Russian envoy give views on 'humanitarian intervention,'" *BBC Summary of World Broadcasts*, Jan. 31, 2000.

46. Louis Henkin, *How Nations Behave* 333, n. 20 (2d ed. 1979).

47. U.N. GAOR, 54th Sess., 6th plen. mtg. at 14, U.N. Doc. A/54/PV.4 (Sept. 21, 1999) (remarks of Igor S. Ivanov).

48. U.N. GAOR, 54th Sess., 11th plen. mtg. at 32, U.N. Doc. A/54/PV.4 (Sept. 23, 1999) (remarks of Rosario Green).

49. U.N. GAOR, 54th Sess., 15th plen. mtg. at 17, U.N. Doc. A/54/PV.4 (Sept. 25, 1999) (remarks of Nguyen Manh Cam).

50. U.N. GAOR, 54th Sess., 15th plen. mtg. at 22, U.N. Doc. A/54/PV.4 (Sept. 25, 1999) (remarks of Adhi Godana).

51. U.N. GAOR, 54th Sess., 17th plen. mtg. at 3, U.N. Doc. A/54/PV.4 (Sept. 29, 1999) (remarks of Seymour Mullings).

52. U.N. GAOR, 54th Sess., 29th plen. mtg. at 12, U.N. Doc. A/54/PV.4 (Oct. 7, 1999) (remarks of Nejad Hosseinian).

53. U.N. GAOR, 54th Sess., 32d plen. mtg. at 11, U.N. Doc. A/54/PV.4 (Oct. 8, 1999) (remarks of Mr. Hasmy).

54. U.N. GAOR, 54th Sess., 32d plen. mtg. at 22, U.N. Doc. A/54/PV.4 (Oct. 8, 1999) (remarks of Mr. Picasso).

55. U.N. GAOR, 54th Sess., 33d plen. mtg. at 6, U.N. Doc. A/54/PV.4 (Oct. 11, 1999) (remarks of Mr. Ibrahim).

56. U.N. GAOR, 54th Sess., 33d plen. mtg. at 11, U.N. Doc. A/54/PV.4 (Oct. 11, 1999) (remarks of Mr. Moushoutas).

57. U.N. GAOR, 54th Sess., 35th plen. mtg. at 11, U.N. Doc. A/54/PV.4 (Oct. 20, 1999) (remarks of Valdivieso).

58. U.N. GAOR, 54th Sess., 35th plen. mtg. at 22, U.N. Doc. A/54/PV.4 (Oct. 20, 1999) (remarks of Mr. Bouah-Kamon).

59. Barton Gellman and Steven Mufson, "Humanitarian War: Conflict Tests a Paradigm of Values-Based International Action," *Wash. Post,* June 6, 1999, at A20.

60. "Kosovo and the End of the Nation-State," *New York Review of Books,* June 10, 1999.

61. Prime Minister Tony Blair, Address to the Economic Club of Chicago, Apr. 22, 1999.

62. Barton Gellman and Steven Mufson, "Humanitarian War: Conflict Tests a Paradigm of Values-Based International Action," *Wash. Post,* June 6, 1999, at A20.

63. See William Shawcross, *Deliver us from Evil: Peacekeepers, Warlords, and a World of Endless Conflict* (2000).

64. Javier Pérez de Cuéllar, *Report of the Secretary-General on the Work of the Organization* 12 (1991).

65. OSCE, CSCE Helinski Document 1992, "The Challenges of Change," para. 8 (1992 Summit).

66. See Jane Perlez, "Chechnya Challenge: War Threatens U.S. Strategic Goals," *N.Y Times,* Nov. 15, 1999, at A14.

67. Abraham D. Sofaer, "International Law and Kosovo," 36 *Stan. J. Int'l L.* 1, 8 (2000).

68. F. H. Hinsley, *Power and the Pursuit of Peace: Theory and Practice in the History of Relations Between States* 312 (1963).

69. Francis A. Boyle, *Foundations of world order: the legalist approach to international relations (1898–1921),* at 24 (1999).

70. George Bernard Shaw, *Caesar and Cleopatra,* act 2.

71. Adamantia Pollis and Peter Schwab, "Human Rights: A Western Construct with Limited Applicability," in *Human Rights— Cultural And Ideological Perspectives* 9 (A. Pollis and P. Schwab eds., 1979).

72. R. J. Vincent, *Human Rights and International Relations* 40 (1986).

73. *Id.*

74. *Id.* See also Mojekwu, "International Human Rights: The African Perspective," in *International Human Rights: Contemporary Issues* 93 (J. Nelson and V. Green eds., 1980).

75. Bilhari Kausikan, "Asia's Different Standard," 92 *Foreign Pol.* 24 (1993).

76. Marasinghe, "Traditional Conceptions of Human Rights in Africa," in *Human Rights and Development in Africa* 32, 36 (C. Welch and R. Malzner eds., 1984).

77. Said, "Human Rights in Islamic Perspective," in *Human Rights—Cultural and Ideological Perspectives* 91 (A. Pollis and P. Schwab eds., 1979).

78. Adamantia Pollis and Peter Schwab, "Human Rights," in *Human Rights* 9 (A. Pollis and P. Schwab eds., 1979).

79. Samuel P. Huntington, "The Clash of Civilizations," 72 *Foreign Aff.* 29 (summer 1993).

80. Erica Goode, "How Cultures Molds Habits of Thoughts," *N.Y. Times,* Aug. 8, 2000, at D1.

81. *Id.* at D4.

82. *Id.*

83. Immanuel Kant, *Perpetual Peace* 259 (M. Campbell Smith trans., Macmillan 1903) (1795).

84. John Micklethwait and Adrian Wooldridge, *A Future Perfect: The Challenge and Hidden Promise of Globalization* (2000).

85. A. J. P. Taylor, *The First World War: An Illustrated History* 286 (1963).

86. John Stuart Mill, *Considerations on Representative Government* 21 (1862).

87. *The Federalist No. 2* (John Jay).

88. See generally Hans J. Morgenthau, *Politics Among Nations* 484–88 (4th ed. 1966).

89. Quoted in Inis L. Claude, Jr., *Swords into Plowshares: The Problems and Progress of International Organization* 74 (4th ed. 1984)

90. *Id.* at 75.

91. Hans J. Morgenthau, *Politics Among Nations* 422 (4th ed. 1966).

92. Stanley Hoffman, *World Disorders: Troubled Peace in the Post–Cold War Era* 182 (1998).

93. George F. Kennan, *American Diplomacy, 1900–1950,* at 85 (1951).

94. U.N. GAOR, 54th Sess., 4th plen. mtg. at 4, 2 U.N. Doc. A/54/PV.4 (Sept. 20, 1999) (remarks of Kofi Annan, Secretary General).

95. Paul Kahn, "Speaking Law to Power: Popular Sovereignty, Human Rights, and the New International Order," 1 *Chi. J. Int'l L.* 1, 18 (2000).

96. Hans Kelsen, *The Law of the United Nations* 17–18 (1950).

97. Emerich de Vattel, *The Law of Nations or the Principles of Natural Law,* bk. 2, ch. 4, § 56 (Charles G. Fenwick trans., Oceana Publications 1964) (1758).

98. Hugo Grotius, *De jure belli ac pacis libri tres,* bk. 2, ch. 22, § 11 (Francis W. Kelsey trans., Oceana Publications 1964) (1646).

99. The Declaration of Independence (U.S. 1776).

100. Immanuel Kant, *Critique of Practical Reason* 63 (L. Beck trans., 1945).

101. See *id.* at 346–50.
102. See generally John Rawls, *A Theory of Justice* (1971).
103. Jacques Barzun, *A Stroll with William James* 59, 65 n. * (1983).
104. Edward T. Hall, *The Silent Language* (1959).
105. Torbjørn Sirevåg, *Westerners: Six Reasons why Americans are Different: A View from Northwest Europe* 144 (1999).
106. *Id.* at 145.
107. *Id.*
108. Noam Chomsky, *The New Military Humanism: Lessons from Kosovo* 39 (1999).
109. *Id.*
110. *Id.*
111. *Id.*
112. *Id.* at 78, 154.
113. *Id.* at 16.
114. See Michael J. Glennon, "The New Interventionism: The Search for a Just International Law," 78 *Foreign Aff.* 2 (May/June 1999).
115. Noam Chomsky: *The New Military Humanism: Lessons from Kosovo* 79 (1999).
116. See generally Richard A. Posner, *The Problematics of Moral and Legal Theory* (1999).
117. Ronald Dworkin, "Objectivity and Truth: You'd Better Believe It," 25 *Philosophy & Public Affairs* 87, 118 (1996)
118. Compare Richard A. Posner, *The Problematics of Moral and Legal Theory* xii (1999) (describing pragmatism).
119. Edward Rothstein, "Paradise Lost: Can Mankind Live Without Its Utopias?" *N.Y. Times*, Feb. 5, 2000.
120. Edmund Burke, *Reflections on the Revolution in France* 22 (T. Mahoney ed., 1982) (1990).
121. *Id.* at 8.
122. James G. Wilson, "Justice Diffused: A Comparison of Edmund Burke's Conservatism with the Views of Five Conservative, Academic Judges," 40 *U. Miami L. Rev.* 913, 936 (1996).
123. Quoted in Alexander M. Bickel, *The Morality of Consent* 23 (1975).

Chapter 6

1. Alexis de Toqueville, *The Old Regime and the Revolution* 1; 142 (Alan S. Kahan trans., François Furet and Françoise Mélonio eds., 1998).
2. Thomas Hobbes, *Leviathan, or the Matter, Forme and Power of a Commonwealth, Ecclesiasticall and Civil* (M. Oakshot ed., New York, Macmillan 1962) (1651).

3. Martin Wight, *Power Politics* 214–215 (1978).
4. See F. H. Hinsley, *Power and the Pursuit of Peace: Theory and Practice in the History of Relations Between States* 186 (1963).
5. W. Michael Reisman, "International Incidents: Introduction to a New Genre in the Study of International Law," in *International Incidents* 3, 12–13 (W. Michael Reisman and Andrew R. Willard eds., 1988).
6. See, for example, Harold Lasswell and Myres S. McDougal, *Jurisprudence for a Free Society: Studies in Law, Science, and Policy* (1992); Myres S. McDougal and Florentino P. Feliciano, *Law and Minimum World Public Order: The Legal Regulation of International Coercion* (1961).
7. Symposium, "McDougal's Jurisprudence: Utility, Influence and Controversy," 79 *Am. Soc'y Int'l L. Proc.* 266, 267 (1985).
8. Tom J. Farer, "UN Police Action in lieu of War: The Old Order Changeth," 85 *Am. J. Int'l L.* 63, 123 (1991).
9. See, for example, Jules Lobel, "Benign Hegemony? Kosovo and Article 2(4) of the U.N. Charter," 1 *Chi. J. Int'l L.* 19 (2000); Bruno Simma, "NATO, the UN and the Use of Force: Legal Aspects: Kosovo: A Thin Red Line," http://www.ejil.org/journal/Vol 10/No 1/ab1–2.html, visited Jan. 12, 1999; Richard B. Bilder, "Kosovo and the 'New Interventionism,'" 9 *J. Transnat'l L. & Policy* 153 (fall 1999).
10. William Blackstone, *Commentaries on the Laws of England*, Introduction.
11. Jean Bodin, *Six Livres de la République* (1576).
12. Henry David Thoreau, *Civil Disobedience* (1849).
13. *Id.*
14. Mohandas K. Gandhi, *Non-Violence in Peace and War* 1949, bk. 2, ch. 150 (Garland Pub. 1972).
15. Martin Luther King, Jr., *Why We Can't Wait* 85 (1963).
16. Quoted in Alexander M. Bickel, *The Morality of Consent* 103 (1975).
17. Hans J. Morgenthau, "Diplomacy," 55 *Yale L.J.* 1067, 1080 (1946).
18. J. L. Brierly, *The Law of Nations: An Introduction to the International Law of Peace* 24 (Humphrey Waldock ed., 6th ed. 1963).
19. Richard A. Posner, "The Jurisprudence of Skepticism," 86 *Mich. L. Rev.* 827, 838 (1988); see also Richard A. Posner, *The Problematics of Moral and Legal Theory* 227–310 (1999) (discussing legal pragmatism).
20. Alexander M. Bickel, *The Morality of Consent* 116–17 (1975).
21. Louis Henkin, *How Nations Behave* 333 (2d ed. 1979).
22. U.N. GAOR, 54th Sess., 32d plen. mtg. at 3, U.N. Doc. A/54/PV.4 (Oct. 8, 1999) (remarks of Rodríguez Parrilla).
23. Louis Henkin, *How Nations Behave* 333–34, 387 (2d ed. 1979).

24. William Drozdiak, "U.S., European Allies Divided Over NATO's Authority to Act," *Wash. Post,* Nov. 8, 1998, at A33.

25. William V. Roth, Jr., *NATO in the 21st Century* ¶ 122 (1998).

26. William Drozdiak, "U.S., European Allies Divided Over NATO's Authority to Act," *Wash. Post,* Nov. 8, 1998, at A33.

27. Thomas M. Franck, "Sidelined in Kosovo?; The United Nations' Demise Has Been Exaggerated; Break It, Don't Fake It," 78 *Foreign Aff.* 116 (July/Aug. 1999).

28. Arthur M. Schlesinger, Jr., *The Imperial Presidency* 9 (1973).

29. Kennedy v. Mendoza–Martinez, 372 U.S. 144, 160 (1963) (Goldberg, J.) (paraphrasing Terminiello v. Chicago, 337 U.S. 1, 37 (1949) (Jackson, J., dissenting)).

30. Thomas M. Franck, "Sidelined in Kosovo? The United Nations' Demise Has Been Exaggerated; Break It, Don't Fake It," 78 *Foreign Aff.* 116 (July/Aug. 1999).

31. *Id.*

32. Thomas M. Franck, "Who Killed Article 2(4)?" 64 *Am. J. Int'l L.* 809 (1970).

33. *Id.* at 835–37.

34. F. H. Hinsley, *Power and the Pursuit of Peace: Theory and Practice in the History of Relations Between States* 315 (1963).

35. See, for example, "Clinton on Kosovo: We Can Make a Difference" (weekly radio address delivered Dec. 13, 1998), *N.Y. Times,* Feb. 14, 1999.

36. Helen Silving, "In Re Eichman: A Dilemma of Law and Morality," 55 *Am J. Int'l L.* 307, 321 (1961).

37. T. C. Schelling, "The Global Dimension," in *Rethinking America's Security: Beyond Cold War to New World Order* 196, 199 (Graham Allison and Gregory F. Treverton eds., 1992).

38. See Andreas Osiander, *The States System of Europe, 1640–1990: Peacemaking and the Conditions of International Stability* 166–247 (1994).

39. Francis Fukuyama, *The End of History and the Last Man* 283 (1992).

40. Woodrow Wilson, Address at the Armory, Tacoma, Washington (Sept. 13, 1919), in *The Public Papers of Woodrow Wilson: War and Peace* 2:169 (Ray Stannard Baker and William E. Dodd eds., 1970).

41. Eric Hobsbawm, *The Age of Extremes* 23 (1994).

42. James Mill, *Essays on Government, Jurisprudence, Liberty of the Press, and Law of Nations* 4–5 (August M. Kelley Publishers 1967) (1825).

43. William Drozdiak, "U.S., European Allies Divided Over NATO's Authority to Act," *Wash. Post,* Nov. 8, 1998, at A33 ("We realize we are pushing the envelope and making up history as we go along.").

44. Ralph Peters, *Fighting for the Future: Will America Triumph?* 104–105 (1999).
45. Alexander M. Bickel, *The Morality of Consent* 117 (1975).
46. Natalino Ronzitti, "Lessons of International Law from NATO's Armed Intervention Against the Federal Republic of Yugoslavia," 34 *The International Spectator* 45, 53 (July–Sept. 1999).
47. "International Papers," *Slate News,* Oct. 27, 1999.
48. Francis Fukuyama, *The End of History and the Last Man* 282–83 (1992).
49. Barbara Crossette, "U.N. Chief Wants Faster Action to Halt Civil Wars and Killings," *N.Y. Times,* Sept. 21, 1999, at A1.
50. Hamilton Foley, *Woodrow Wilson's Case for the League of Nations* 64 (1923).
51. *Id.*
52. Committee on Foreign Relations, U.S. Senate, *Review of the United Nations Charter,* S. Doc. 83–164, at 80 (2d Sess. 1955).
53. Hans J. Morgenthau, *Politics Among Nations* 450 (4th ed. 1966).
54. Barbara Crossette, "U.N. Chief Wants Faster Action to Halt Civil Wars and Killings," *N.Y. Times,* Sept. 21, 1999, at A1.
55. Quoted in William Safire, "Tall Man Falls Short," *N.Y. Times,* Dec. 2, 1999, at A35.
56. Louis Henkin, *How Nations Behave* 38 (2d ed. 1979).
57. David S. Yost, *NATO Transformed: The Alliance's New Roles in International Security* 254 (1998).
58. Samuel P. Huntington, "The Clash of Civilizations," 72 *Foreign Aff.* 35 (summer 1993).
59. Michael Walzer, *Just and Unjust Wars: A Moral Argument with Historical Illustrations* 107 (2d ed. 1991).
60. See Michael Hirsh, "The Rise of 'Rego-Cops,'" *Newsweek,* May 22, 2000, at 38.
61. See generally Tom J. Farer, "The Role of Regional Collective Security Arrangements," in *Collective Security in a Changing World* 153 (Thomas G. Weiss ed., 1993).
62. See A. Rougier, "La théorie de l'intervention d'humanité," 17 *Rev. Gén. D. Int'l Pub.* 468 (1910).
63. U.N. Charter art. 2, para. 4.
64. Abraham D. Sofaer, "International Law and Kosovo," 36 *Stan. J. Int'l L.* 1, 2 n. 2 (2000).
65. See, for example, Mary Ellen O'Connell, "The UN, NATO, and International Law After Kosovo," 22 *Hum. Rts.* Q. 57, 64 (2000).
66. David Buchan, "United States Diplomat warns Europe over defence," *Financial Times,* May 19, 2000, at 2.
67. U.N. Charter art. 52(j), para. 1. Compare Article 2(7) on page and Article 39 on page.

68. See generally Inis L. Claude, Jr., *Swords into Plowshares: The Problems and Progress of International Organization* 107 (4th ed. 1984).

69. Edith Stokey and Richard Zeckhauser, *A Primer for Policy Analysis* 136 (1978).

70. See Paul Ricoeur, *Intervenir? Droits de la Personne et Raisons d'Etat* (1994).

71. See generally E. J. Mishan, *Cost-Benefit Analysis: An Informal Introduction* (1976).

72. Dana Priest, "The Battle Inside Headquarters; Tension Grew with Divide Over Strategy," *Wash. Post*, Sept. 21, 1999, at A1.

73. See Robert Schlaifer, *Analysis of Decisions Under Uncertainty* (1969).

74. See, for example, Larry Minear and Thomas G. Weiss, *Mercy Under Fire: War and the Global Humanitarian Community* 63 (1995).

75. Richard A. Posner, *The Problematics of Moral and Legal Theory* 54 (1999) (footnotes omitted) (emphasis in original).

76. Noam Chomsky, *The New Military Humanism: Lessons from Kosovo* 69–70 (1999).

77. John L. Gaddis, "Coping with Victory," *Atlantic Monthly*, May 1990, at 49.

INDEX

custom: "non-acts" considered acts, 50,
52–56; approval, inference of,
43–44; assumptions underlying, 3;
categorization, futility of, 70–84;
different contexts, 8, 171; elasticity
of state "action," 50–52;
governmental vs. non-governmental
actors, 124; "instant" customary
law, 38, 62, 84; vs. practice, 56, 208;
particularized vs. generalized, 51–52,
63, 170–171; silence, effect of, 53,
56–57; source of international law,
38–65, 208; vs. treaties, 192–193; vs.
inconsistent treaties, 60–61, 99;
traditional conception, 38. *See also*
international law; law; United
Nations Charter.
Cyprus, 160
Czechoslovakia, 67

D'Amato, Anthony, 46, 48, 49, 54, 55,
69, 199
Declaration of Independence, 151
Declaration on Principles of
International Law concerning
Friendly Relations and Co-operation
among States (1970), 20
Declaration on the Inadmissibility of
Intervention (1965), 20
Declaration on the Inadmissibility of
Intervention and Interference in the
Internal Affairs of States (1981), 20
Declaration on the Strengthening of
International Security (1970), 20, 21
decolonization, 69
Delian League, 191
democracy, 23, 30, 134, 176
deontological approaches to justice,
169–170
DePaul University, International
Human Rights Law Institute, study
on armed conflict, 68
desuetude, 9, 60–64, 84
Djibouti, 139
domestic jurisdiction of states,
106–108, 115, 118, 134. *See also*
civil war; internal strife; Article 2(7);
Article 39.
Dominican Republic, 67

Douglas, Paul, 96
Dulles, John Foster, 45, 136
Dupuy, René-Jean, 140

East Pakistan (Bangladesh), 73–74, 78,
80
East Timor, 64, 139, 173, 199, 200
ECOWAS, 34
Egypt, 67, 135
Eichmann, Adolph, 174
El Salvador, 139
Entebbe, 183
equality of states, 10, 135, 147–148,
150–151, 208
Equatorial Guinea, 139
Eritrea, 68, 139
Ethiopia, 68, 139
European Union, 27, 191, 201
evolutionary biology, 199–200

Falk, Richard, 68, 84
Falkland Islands, 67
"fallacy of the last move," 142
Farer, Tom J., 23, 50, 76, 80, 102, 103,
129
Fiji, 200
Fish, Stanley, 174
Fischer, Joschka, 185
Flanders, 14
Fleury, André Hercule de (Cardinal), 14
force, use of: rules governing, 3;
commitments concerning, 9; per se
prohibition, 21; since 1945, 67–70,
86, 140; among UN member states,
68; status of governing law, 84. *See
also* domestic jurisdiction of states;
internal strife; self-defense; Article
2(4); Article 2(7); Article 39; Article
43; Article 51;
Foreign Affairs, 173
Fox, Donald T., 172
France, 15, 39, 67, 73, 80, 117, 129,
149, 162, 169, 177, 199
Franck, Thomas M., 43, 52, 54, 56, 60,
69, 87, 99, 168, 186–189
Frankfurter, Felix, 32
Frederick the Great, 14
freedom principle (of international
law), 9, 63–64, 84. *See also* custom.

Solana, Javier, 27–28, 29–30, 201
Somalia, 110, 118, 120, 137, 141
South Africa, 116–117
sovereignty, 3, 100, 105, 118, 133,
    134, 181, 207; myth and reality,
    147–151; as ordering principle, 8,
    147, 149, 166. *See also* Article 2(4);
    Article 2(7); consent of states;
    international law.
Soviet Union, 2, 15, 33, 39, 59, 67, 71,
    109, 113, 194, 195
Spain, 129
Spanish Civil War, 62, 113
Spender, Percy, 121, 130, 131–132
Sri Lanka, 139, 158
St. Pierre, Abbé de, 14
stability vs. justice, 99, 135–139
state behavior: approval, inference of,
    43–44, 48–49; causes of, 3, 42,
    53–54, 58–60, 70–72; desire to avoid
    confrontation, 27, 42–43, 57–58;
    desire to avoid specific explanation,
    27; political will, 164–165. *See also*
    consent of states; international law;
    motive; sovereignty.
stealth fighter shoot-down, 155
Steel Seizure Case (Youngstown Sheet
    & Tube v. Sawyer [1952]), 32
Stettinius, Edward, 106
Stimson, Henry L., 93
Stone, Julius, 89, 136
Strategic Defense Initiative ("Star
    Wars"), 131
Stromseth, Jane, 117
Sudan, 139
Sully, Duc de, 12
Sweden, 148, 200
Sweetser, Arthur, 196
Switzerland, 61

Taiwan, 83
Talbot, Strobe, 127
Tallyrand-Périgord, Charles Maurice
    de, 55
Tanzania, 67, 72–73, 77
Taylor, A.J.P., 164
Tesón, Fernando, 72–75, 82–84, 173
The Economist, 141
Third Reich, 182

Third World, 134, 158, 200
Thirty Years' War, 4
Thoreau, Henry David, 181–182
threat to the peace, defined, 107, 108
Thucydides, 51
Tibet, 83, 139, 185, 199
Tienanmen Square, 110, 113
Tillema, Herbert K., 69
Tocqueville, Alexis de, 177
Togo, 139
treaties: amendment, 130, 197;
    bilateral vs. multilateral, 132; vs.
    customary law, 192–93;
    interpretation, 121–126. *See also*
    custom; consent of states.
Trimble, Phillip, 4
Truman, Harry S, 32, 98
Tshombe, Moise, 115
Tunisia, 158
Turkey, 117

Uganda, 67, 68, 72, 76
United Arab Emirates, 158
United Kingdom, 15, 24, 39, 67, 93,
    105, 115, 117, 148, 176, 199
United Nations Charter: 1, 93, 99;
    amendment of, 11, 124, 194, 197;
    civil war, 69; constitutive treaty,
    122–123; delegation of power to
    Security Council, 99, 104, 125, 208;
    equality principle, 148, 208;
    Preamble, 125, 168; prohibition
    against nondefensive force, 2, 8, 136;
    humanitarian intervention, 2, 134;
    intrastate genocide, 4, 76, 150; as
    "living" document, 101–102, 122,
    127, 133; limits on power, 41–42,
    57, 88–89, 99, 101; internal affairs,
    102–108, 133; relationship to
    international law, 85, 180; *travaux
    préparatoires*, 22, 102; as world
    constitution, 38; organs vs. member
    states, 100, 125–126, 133; purposes,
    17, 89, 99, 102, 111–112, 128, 132,
    136, 140, 142, 195; universal vs.
    selective membership, 194–197; and
    Covenant of the League of Nations,
    93–95, 195–196; vs. subsequent
    practice of Security Council, 99,